ZERO POINT TEACHINGS

Selected Writings of Mystical Psychologist &
Scientist Christopher P. Holmes

ZERO POINT

Institute for Mystical and Spiritual Science
Box 700, 108 Clothier Street East, Kemptville,
Ontario, Canada K0G 1J0

zeropoint@bell.net / (613) 258-6258
www.zeropoint.ca

ZERO POINT Publications 2011

Copyright - Christopher P. Holmes, Ph.D. 2009
All rights reserved.

Current Edition — 2011
First Printing — January 2007

Portions of this book may be reproduced without permission from the author, although not in complete form or for profit. However, the reader is free to quote passages in criticism, reviews or other writings, or as portions might be used in educational settings. Inquiries are welcome.

Graphic Design and Prepress: Željka Županić
Cover Illustration: Jeff Meloche

Zero Point Teachings:
Selected Articles and Writings of Mystical Psychologist & Scientist Christopher P. Holmes

ISBN 978-0-9689435-7-1

TABLE OF CONTENTS

PREFACE 8

YOU ARE A STAR - K.T.H. 11

ZERO POINT TEACHINGS 14

Zero point teachings: *www.zeropoint.ca* 15

Zero Point Institute for Mystical and Spiritual Science 17

Quotations and Illustrations of Zero Point Dynamics 20

Within-Without from Zero Points: A quantum approach
to Consciousness and the Physics and Metaphysics
of Being and Nothingness 24

Zero Points & Heart Spaces: *Tone* Magazine 27

The Kabbalist Universe & Self 30

Zero Point Fields 39

2011 & the Countdown to 2012 45

CRITIQUES OF 'NEW THINK' 50

What the Bleep do we know!? Not too much according to Dr. Holmes' radical critique of this popular new age movie nightmare. 51

THE SECRET of the Cult of Narcissism: Quantum magic for sheep 54

How to Know *Mr. God* with your Mind and Brain: A critical account of *How to Know God* by Deepak Chopra 58

ENTANGLED MINDS: Extrasensory perception in a quantum reality by Dean Radin: A review 71

LETTERS TO *ContactMusic.com* on Guy Ritchie, Madonna & Kabbalah 82

On Nuts and Oak Trees: Gurdjieff's Tale 87

A Tribute to the Music of Jeff Martin and *Tea Party* 89

MARK COMINGS, physicist, mathematician, and space science researcher 85

HIGHER EDUCATION & SPIRITUAL SCIENCE: On the Failure of Post Secondary Education and the New Inquisition

INTRODUCTION: 'A CERTAIN HOPELESSNESS' 102

THE PUBLIC'S BELIEFS AND INTERESTS 105

AN INTERNET SURVEY RESULTS CANADIAN UNIVERSITY PSYCHOLOGY DEPARTMENTS 107

THE STRANGE CASE OF PROFESSOR Z: ON THE IDEALS OF MURRAY ROSS, ACADEMIC FREEDOM & THE RIGHTS OF STUDENTS 113

PUBLIC ACCOUNTABILITY AND THE FAILURE OF MODERN EDUCATION & MODERN PSYCHOLOGY 119

Intelligent Design 122

GOD AND THE SCIENTISTS:
BOOK REVIEW OF THE GRAND DESIGN 122

DEITY IN EVERY POINT 139

THE ORIGIN AND NATURE OF HUMAN CONSCIOUSNESS 152

I
The Heart Doctrine 154

ABSTRACT 155
THE MYSTERIES OF CONSCIOUSNESS 155
THE HEAD DOCTRINE 157
THE HEART DOCTRINE 161
    Eastern sources 161
    Western sources 169
    Concluding remarks 173

II
Zero Point Hypothesis 174

ABSTRACT 175
THE ZERO POINT HYPOTHESIS 176
YOGIC SCIENCE OF THE SOUL 182
DIVINE SPARKS OF KABBALAH 185
FROM GNOSTICISM TO ADI DA 194
SUFI SECRETS 198
RELATIONSHIPS TO SCIENCE 199
CONCLUDING REMARKS 202

III
Towards a Holographic Metaphysics of the Human Heart 203

ABSTRACT 204
ESOTERIC DIMENSIONS OF SELF 205
YOGANANDA'S EXPERIENCE OF COSMIC CONSCIOUSNESS 207
THE EMERGENCE OF THE HOLOGRAPHIC PARADIGM 211
DAVID BOHM ON WHOLENESS AND THE IMPLICATE ORDERS 221
BLAVATSKY'S HOLOGRAPHIC SPACE AND ZERO POINT DYNAMICS .. 227
CONCLUDING REMARKS 231

IV
An Alternate Model of the Higher Dimensional
Structure of Human Existence 232

ABSTRACT 233
COSMIC EVOLUTION 234
ZERO POINT FOUNDATIONS & THE ROLE OF FOHAT 236
THE UNIVERSE AS A HOLOGRAM 242
BLACK HOLES & ALTERNATE SPACE DIMENSIONS 247
THE ILLUSION OF GRAVITY 250
COMPARATIVE COMMENTS 254
CONCLUDING REMARKS 259

Zero point publications 262

Preface

The *Fool at the Zero Point* represents myself--as a mystic, psychologist, scientist and individual-- interested in the nature of reality, love and truth, attaining Self and knowing God. I represent myself as a fool partially to capture the sense of the Biblical verses: *"We speak the wisdom of God in a mystery.... If any man among you seemth to be wise in this world, let him become a fool, that he may be wise."* Corinthians I, 7/18 This work explores a wide range of mysteries, including those of life and death, the mind and heart, being and non-being, science and religion, human consciousness and cosmic creation. Through such studies, I attempt to assume the role of a fool in assuming nothing and dismissing no possibility in the search for truth and learning through life experiences. By admitting how little I ultimately know about life and creation, I have become wise beyond what I might have imagined as a person asleep.

The Fool card in the Tarot deck is numbered 0 and stands between the 21 cards of the Major Arcana above—representing the spiritual and archetypal world and the 56 cards of the Minor Arcana below—detailing the material worlds (with four suits representing the elements of nature--fire, air, water and earth). The Fool card thus represents a point of transition between the higher and lower worlds, or a portal from the lower into the higher dimensions. Similarly, I hope that these writings can be useful in helping you to penetrate some of the *"veils"* which obscure the true nature of Self and to arrive at an alternative understanding of your own higher dimensional nature.

The zero point teachings are a portal of some sort and I invite you to consider an alternative view of the nature and structure of reality--to view the world in a magical and mystical way. The basic concept is that all living beings, including you, have a zero point centre within connected to the higher dimensional physics of the heart. This is the means by which *"the*

Gods and other invisible powers clothe themselves in bodies" — as explained by mystic scholar Madame Blavatsky in *The Secret Doctrine* (1888). Just as the scientists now conceive that our huge universe grew from an infinitesimal singularity out of the quantum vacuum, so also, I am suggesting that you also have such a hidden zero point or singularity source condition- -a singular I within the Heart. Further, we ourselves emerge *"out of nothingness"* in some mysterious way unknown to modern science and contemporary understanding, but consistent with modern views of the physics of the quantum vacuum, as void and plenum, filled with light and zero point fields.

Mystic Aivanhov (1976) elaborates upon the significance of the zero point concept: *"I ... engraved the symbol of the knowledge of the Initiates: a circle with a point in the center. ... Understand me once and for all: I am speaking from experience, for me it is not mere theory, all my life has been based on this symbol of the circle with its central point. This center which is in us, we must find ... ."* (*Love and Sexuality*, I, pp. 25-6) Imagine that, Aivanhov states that much of his life had been based on this symbol and striving to find his own centre! However, this symbol has also been used for dark purposes, according to Henry Makow in his book *Illuminati*, who notes: "... *the Illuminati symbol, the dot in a circle ....*`` Personally, I was somewhat shocked to recently read this in Makow, as I had no knowledge of his claim that this is an Illuminati symbol. I had at arrived at the zero point concept through my studies of Blavatsky's *Secret Doctrine* and through personal experiences, and have used the zero point symbol for the past ten years as the 'home button' on my website — a point within a circle or sphere. This simple and basic symbol has many deep levels of significance.

Human beings are not simply material biological beings which live and die with their bodies, but multi-dimensional beings who are embodied in different vehicles or bodies and dimensions. Scientific evidences for all kinds of psychical phenomena document the existence of such afterlife or alternate realms and possibilities, although modern science has little understanding of this because of the routine materialist perspective on life.

Zero Point Teachings includes writings drawn from my *www.zeropoint. ca* web site and an article series published within a online journal *www. esotericstudies.net*.

On May 6 of 2011, Karen T. Hale passed away unexpectedly and suddenly at the age of 55. Karen had been the love of my life over the past 12 years and we had shared varied adventures together during that time. Karen was a remarkable woman who somehow did not fit into the madness of things about us and was deeply affected by all that we learnt through the years after waking up to the fraud of 9-11 and then the additional crimes being committed against citizens around the world. The horror of it all, led Karen and I into months and years of experiences ranging from bliss, rapture and illumination, to dread and fearfulness, confusions and difficulties. By the time of her death, Karen had in a magical way attained something within herself through her conscious labours and intentional suffering, and her bravery in the face of it all. Karen has been with me during the whole time of the development of this *ZPT* book, although not to see this work in print. Of course, one cannot know for certain when she might or might not be around *in spirit*.

Sometimes, I consider that I am a fool to explore such wondrous and alternative studies as I pursue and to take such risks in my life, as both Karen and I have done through the past years. Yet, I would not change my life adventures in consciousness studies, in psychical investigations and mystical-scientific inquiry, forensic analysis of the life of modern man and truth activism, for another story. It certainly has been a grand Tale and it is not over yet, with dramatic things yet to unfold over time in stages.

This book is dedicated to you sweetheart Karen, for your bravery, love and struggle to live in truth. To me, Karen you were and are a Star.   May I *live to tell* of our adventures together.

Christopher P. Holmes
July 2011

You are a Star

You are a star birthed from within without the night
you are a star reflecting some light
you are a star, that's what you are
you are a star

You are a star that cries out *I am* before flight
you are a star that's been pushed out into the light
you are a star that's what you are
you are a star.

You are a star filled with luminous light
you are a star blissful and bright
you are a star that's what you are
you are a star.

You are a star a pearl of great price
you are a star stuck in a jar
you are a star
that's what you are
you are a star.

You are a star turned topsy-turvy from the flight
you are a star filled with limit-less light
you are a star that's what you are
you are a star.

You are a star playing hide & seek in God's place
you are a star within a heart space
you are a star that's what you are
you are a star.

You are a star that heals with a smile
you are a star
that's who you are
you are a star.

You are a star reflecting sunlight
you are a star
no matter where you are,
you are a star
stuck in a jar.

You are a star in a jar!

K. T. H.

ZERO POINT TEACHINGS

> "... 'material points without extension' (zero-points) are ... the materials out of which the 'Gods' and other invisible powers clothe themselves in bodies ..."
>
> **H. P. Blavatsky**,
> *The Secret Doctrine*, 1888

Zero Point Teaching

Dedicated to the investigation of the origin and nature of human consciousness; psychology as a science of the heart and soul; the magic of life, love and creation; studies of modern physics, ancient metaphysics and the multi-dimensional nature of reality; the awakening of humankind before the completion of the nightmare parable of the new world psychiatric order.

THE ZERO POINT HYPOTHESIS

The Zero Point hypothesis is that living beings have zero point centres rooted into the grounds of being and these are associated with the higher dimensional physics and metaphysics of the human heart. Such ideas are found within *The Secret Doctrine* of H. P. Blavatsky, mystic scholar and founder of Theosophy, within esoteric Judaism and Kabbalah, mystical and Gnostic Christianity, Islam and Sufism, the teachings of the Dalai Lama and other sources. The significance of this idea has completely escaped the attention of the modern *'scientists of new formation.'* Christopher explores such concepts in the terms of an individual's experience of Self and the science of human consciousness, as well as in the terms of modern quantum and holographic physics.

In this view, each individual is a Star - having a divine source emanation established within the higher seven dimensional hyperspace of the human heart. This is the Monad of H. P. Blavatsky, the God Spark described by Shirley McLaine, the 'divine spark' referred to by Sufi masters and Kabbalists, the jiva-atma described in Vedic teachings of Hinduism. Christopher explores the higher dimensional science of such possibilities and the mysteries of human consciousness and the heart. This is a wholly alternative conceptualization of the nature of human consciousness, existence and reality than otherwise offered in the mainstream of modern thought and science, or in new age wiseacring. It suggests that we must understand the higher dimensional physics and metaphysics of consciousness and the heart in order to attain to a knowledge, understanding and wisdom of Self.

Christopher P. Holmes is a clinical and forensic psychologist, and mystic scientist. His work explores the enigmas of human consciousness, the mysteries of the Heart, psychology as a science of the soul, the physics/metaphysics of creation and Zero Point dynamics. He is most concerned with the psychopathological state of humanity, the mass hypnosis of western society and the importance of the awakening of human consciousness and the heart in this time of epic lunacy and madness, fascist, Satanic and alien influences.

The *Zero Point Teachings* present a novel way of relating ancient metaphysics and the wisdom teachings to modern physics and cosmology in order to explore consciousness and creation, and the nature of a multidimensional holographic universe. Christopher is studied in the teachings of H. P. Blavatsky, G. I. Gurdjieff, Kabbalah, yoga and Vedic science, and esoteric Christianity, has investigated psychic and paranormal phenomena for over forty years. His work draws from ancient esoteric teachings, modern science and personal experience to provide an inspiring perspective on the mysteries of life, death & everything in between.

Zero Point Institute for Mystical & Spiritual Science

Zero Point as an institute is dedicated to the research and investigation of the esoteric mystical and spiritual teachings of humanity. The aim is to examine the basis of such teachings by relating them to modern science, philosophy and psychology. Our hope is that this work will help to make the profound wisdom teachings more accessible to people, bringing them into the public forum, into science and into the educational system. From a mystical perspective, the so-called "institutes of higher learning," particularly universities, completely neglect these most important areas of study, the science of consciousness and the soul. In modern science and psychology, the deep insights and realizations of the mystics, saints and Sacred Messengers, are ignored, despite their profound implications for every area of human knowledge. Science lacks a spiritual and metaphysical perspective and psychologists for the most part completely neglect the ancient idea of "psychology" as a "science of the soul." However, the many enigmas faced within modern psychology and science point to fundamental misunderstandings in common knowledge, even in knowledge supposedly *scientific*. The nature of human consciousness remains the central fundamental enigma in psychology, science and life.

It is over forty years since Christopher began his studies of these traditions while a graduate student in clinical psychology interested in the development of consciousness within psychotherapy. The study of western views of consciousness led to the realization that the western science has failed to make any significant progress in resolving the most profound issues of consciousness. In fact, modern thought is seriously misguided in their presumptions about this subject. The central issue can be expressed in terms of the difference between the *head doctrine* of modern science, the *belief* that consciousness is produced by material, neurological processes centered in the mind assumed to be in the head; and the *heart doctrine* of the esoteric traditions, which identifies the deepest levels of Self, mind and the origins of consciousness with the heart. By *heart* is meant not only the physical heart, but also psychical and spiritual levels to the heart, and ultimately a divine element and Space which underlie it.

Christopher's book series *Within-Without from Zero Points* explores not only the mysteries of consciousness and the heart, but further, the idea of the *point source* origins of Self. A true understanding of these ideas can help to bring about a profound transformation within an individual, as his or her experienced center-of-gravity-of-being can pass from the mind within the head to the deeper levels of Self within the Heart. This involves the dissolution of false mind into the lotus of the Heart, which is how a yogi defines the process of Self realization. This is so easy to express but so difficult to comprehend in its deep implications. There is a whole higher dimensional physics and metaphysics to the human heart and this is what the mind scientists do not know and to which the masses of humankind are asleep.

A second major emphasis in these studies concerns the comparative analysis of modern physics and cosmology with esoteric metaphysics and cosmology. Christopher has throughout his life been amazed by the correspondences between these perspectives, which are almost completely overlooked within the mainstream of science. Mystical teachings provide a profound alternative perspective by which we can examine the concepts and theories of modern physics.

A third major emphasis in these studies and teachings concerns the general unconscious, sleepwalking state of humankind and the horrors of the current situation of humanity. People live in a state of forgetfulness about their true nature and do not "remember themselves." As a psychologist, Christopher draws from his mystical and spiritual studies and has developed innovative group and individual approaches to psycho-spiritual change. He developed a program of "the awakening of consciousness and the heart in criminal offenders," as an alternative to the traditional cognitive-behavioural approaches to offender rehabilitation, which ignore the life of the heart and soul, and the awakening of consciousness.

Christopher has given public lectures on the Zero Point Teachings and held smaller groups within his home and the larger community. From 2006 to the present, Christopher has hosted his own Zero Point Radio show through www.bbsradio.com. The show airs every second Saturday live from 4-6 pm Eastern time.

In his life's work, Christopher has shared, grown, discovered and explored with particularly dear friends and fellow adventurers: Anita J. Mitra, James A. Moffatt. and Karen T. Hale. Anita, Jim and I originally formulated a charter for the *Institute for Mystical and Spiritual Science* in the summer of 1984 in Maple Ontario. Anita and I then founded I.M.S.S. in Maple Ontario (1984), the Rainbow Center in downtown Toronto (1986) and the Zero Point Center in Kemptville (1998). Anita is a talent artist and a number of her prints are incorporated into Christopher's books. Anita and I also had four talented and gifted children now established in their own right and life adventures. Jim has been a friend since high school and shared with me through our adult lives concerning studies of mysticism and science. Jim is a co-host on the Zero Point radio show and has played a major role in editing and commenting upon my writings. From 1999 to 2011, Karen helped me to further the aims of *Zero Point* as an Institute, accompanying me to talks and lectures, all while exploring the mysteries of our own Hearts and Selves. Karen was a fearless soul and brave heart, researcher and street warrior, in service for love and truth. Karen died unexpectedly at the age of 55, on May 6th, 2011.

Speaking on behalf of these individuals, I can state that we are grateful to the enlightened masters and mystics of the ages who have served to promote the light and love within the Hearts of humankind and we feel privileged to engage in the investigation of such revealed teachings about the higher dimensional origins of life and human consciousness. I pray that this work contributes also to the awakening of humankind to the nightmare scenario being concocted for them by the so-called new world order elites. There is a hope and possibility that justice and righteousness might be attained on this planet, to truly bring about a new age, not of chaos and cruelty, but of world peace, international justice and the healing of humanity—all through the awakening of consciousness and the human heart.

Quotations and Illustrations of Zero Point Dynamics

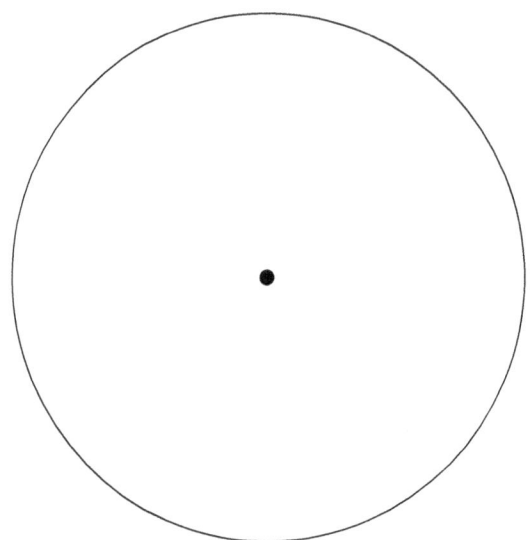

An Archaic Manuscript ... is before the writer's eye. On the first page is an immaculate white disk within a dull black ground. On the following page, the same disk, but with a central point. The first ... Kosmos in Eternity, before the re-awakening of still slumbering Energy, the emanation of the Word ... The point in the hitherto immaculate Disk, Space and Eternity in Pralaya, denotes the dawn of differentiation. It is the Point in the Mundane Egg, the germ within the latter which will become the Universe, the ALL, the boundless, periodical Kosmos, this germ being latent and active, periodically by turns. The one circle is divine Unity, from which all proceeds, whither all returns.

H. P. Blavatsky, *The Secret Doctrine*, 1888 (I., p.1)

THE SONS EXPAND AND CONTRACT THROUGH
THEIR OWN SELVES AND HEARTS; THEY EMBRACE
INFINITUDE. . . .
EACH IN TURN A PART OF THE WEB. REFLECTING THE
"SELF-EXISTENT LORD" LIKE A MIRROR, EACH BECOMES
IN TURN A WORLD.

(*Stanza of Dzyan,* III, 11-12, *The Secret Doctrine*)

"... the Universe is contained in ovo in the first
natural point ...."

(*S.D. I,* p. 118)

"... such a point of transition must certainly possess special and
not readily discoverable properties."

(*S.D. I,* p. 628)

"... space-time came into existence by being squeezed out of a
point.... a space-time structure (is created) out of a single point!
With this interpretation of space-time, certain paradoxes of
nonlocality which require super-luminal speeds are no longer
paradoxes. The reason is that everything is always connected
because everything is really part of the same point."

(physicist J. Dea writing about *The Secret Doctrine,* 1984, p.91)

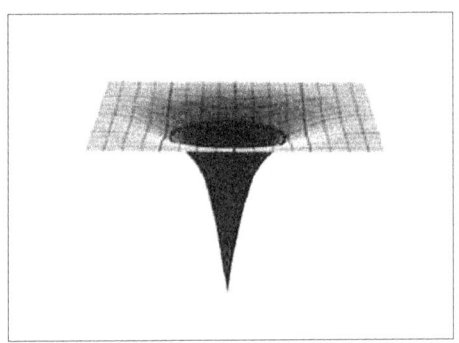
"The zero-dimension or the point is a limit. This means that we see something as a point, but we do not know what is concealed behind this point. It may actually be a point, that is, a body having no dimensions and it may also be a whole world, but a world so far removed from us or so small that it appears to us a point. ... seven cosmoses related to one another in the ratio of zero to infinity." P. D. Ouspensky *In Search of the Miraculous*, 1949

"In this Process of Translation, we pass as if through a point in space, at the root center of the heart. All awareness converges on that point in a kind of spiral or vortex. And that point is so small it is without dimensions, or any conceptions, or any objects. The independent self seems to dissolve in this *narrow* Passage .... The Divine Translation is a matter of Transcendence of separate bodily, emotional, mental, astral, supermental, and egoic states of experience. It is a Transition through the infinitesimal space of the Heart." Heart Master Adi Da, 1978

"The secret of secrets is the divine spark within each of us. Remembrance is remembering that which we already know. It is to get in touch with that divine spark that God has placed within each human being. ... And that divine spark is the secret of secrets. ... And it is within every one of us. Who we are is far more than who we think we are. Robert Frager/Sheikh Ragip, psychologist and Sufi (Cott, 2005)

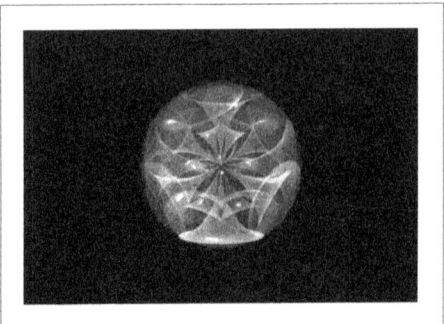
"In Jesus, the Christ or Central Spark which is God in us all, living in everybody today, was drawn forth to show itself perfectly ruling the material body or flesh man. It is in this way that He did all His mighty works, not because He was in some way different from you. ... He did these works because this same

Divine Spark, which the father has implanted in every child, was fanned into a brighter flame by His own efforts in holding Himself in conscious communion with God Himself, the source of all Life, Love and Power."
Baird T. Spalding, *Life & Teaching of the Masters of the Far East*. (V1, p.122)

"I cognized the center of the empyrean as a point of intuitive perception in my heart. Irradiating splendour issued from my nucleus to every part of the universal structure. ... "

Yogananda, *Autobiography of a Yogi*. (1998, p.168)

... the divine spark [is] buried deep in every soul. ... we must leave the physical world of matter far behind and rise to the luminous world above to attain the divine principle of our superior soul. ... I ... engraved the symbol of the knowledge of the Initiates: a circle with a point in the center. ... Understand me once and for all: I am speaking from experience, for me it is not mere theory, all my life has been based on this symbol of the circle with its central point. This center which is in us, we must find ... .

Michael Aivanhov (1976, pp. 25-6)

When God created the world, He had to limit Himself. From being Infinity ... He decided to limit Himself, to become concentrated, and He gathered Himself into a single Point from which He now projects Himself into the whole universe.

M. Aivanhov (1977)

Within-Without from Zero Points: A Quantum approach to Consciousness and the Physics and Metaphysics of Being and Nothingness

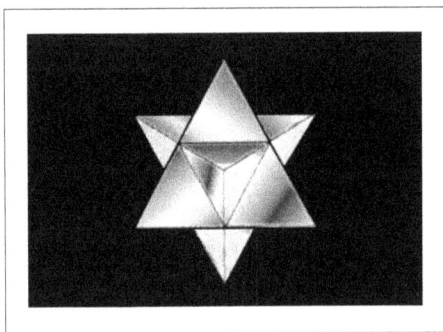

"The Universe is worked and guided from within outwards. As above so it is below, as in heaven so on earth; and man-the microcosm and miniature copy of the macrocosm- is the living witness to this Universal Law and to the mode of its action."

(H. Blavatsky, 1888, p. 274)

Esoteric mystical and spiritual teachings provide a profoundly alternative view of the origin and nature of the universe, and of the origin and nature of consciousness. Generally, these perspectives are unknown within modern psychology and science, in consciousness studies, and in quantum approaches to the mind. However, the ancient mystery teachings are profoundly relevant to the current issues of consciousness, physics and cosmology. These perspectives allow a wholly different understanding of the possible quantum or zero point origin of human consciousness, and a way of approaching the deep physics and meta-physics of being.

In 1888, Blavatsky described the universe as originating within-without from a zero point source, "an unextended point" rooted within the aether of higher space dimensions. She described the "Gods and other invisible powers" as "clothing themselves in bodies" through zero point dynamics by which the influences and forces of higher realms are brought down and made manifest into material nature. Thus all cosmoses are guided and worked from within/without and all things are rooted into the "seeming void" and yet "divine plenum" of the Absolute. Any Son, or created universe, originates from a point source within the plenum, expands from within/without and eventually contracts from without/within, resolving back into the underlying realm. The fundamental dogma of the ancient wisdom, according to Blavatsky's Secret Doctrine, is that there is *"one indivisible and absolute Omniscience and Intelligence in the Universe, and this thrills throughout every ... infinitesimal point of the whole finite Kosmos."* Zero points are the means by which individual lives are focused out of this underlying unified Omniscience and Intelligence.

Remarkably, the creation dynamics elaborated by Blavatsky in 1888 have anticipated the newest views of modern physics. Scientists now trace the creation of the universe to a first instant of time, 10^{-43} seconds, at a particular level of material differentiation, at 10^{-33} centimetres. This is the point at which physical differentiation began out of the seeming void and plenum of the quantum vacuum. In the vacuum genesis account, creation proceeds as the singularity expands from within/without and symmetry breaking occurs in higher dimensional space, to precipitate dimensions of being out of nothingness.

However, although science accepts the idea of the universe originating from a singularity, the same model is never considered in relationship to consciousness studies, This paper proposes that the physics and metaphysics derived from the study of the macrocosm, be applied directly to understand the microcosm: Human consciousness originates from a zero point source established in higher space dimensions, within the seeming void and plenum. Further, mystics identify this zero point center most immediately with the mystical dimensions of the heart. Whereas, the last century of modern science has focused on the brain as a physical mechanism, which somehow produces consciousness, the ancient wisdoms depict the Heart as the true center of the inner cosmos of consciousness. Blavatsky quotes an ancient Stanza: *"The Sons expand and contract from their own Selves and Hearts."* Thus, at the "heart" of a living being is a zero point center-the quantum Self, or I, a point source of supernal light established within higher dimensional Space. The Dali Lama describes this conjunction of the light of pure mind and infinitesimal space particles as the basis for individual consciousness. In the Vedas, the supersoul (or paramatma) is infinite, while the individual spirit soul is infinitesimal, and described as an inherently self-illuminating quantum of consciousness established within the "cave of Brahman" or the "lotus of the heart." Ramana Maharshi (1995) describes "self realization" as involving the "dissolution of the mind in the

Heart lotus." Consciousness is further rooted into the void/plenum and the deep substratum of existence. A Sufis sage comments: "Not since God brought man out of nothingness, has he ceased to be a traveler."

From a mystical perspective, modern theorists make a series of mistakes about the nature and origin of consciousness. Firstly, it is associated with the mind and brain, instead of the heart (and the circulation of blood). As a quantum system, the heart, not the head, is the center of a human being, as the electromagnetic volume of the heart is estimated at five thousand times that of the brain. (Pearsall, 1999) Mystics describe the heart as the Sun of the body, while the mind is associated with the moon, which has no light of its own but reflects the light of the Self within the heart Space. In this view, consciousness is not dependent upon neurological processes at all, as these simply provide varied "contents" of experience. The vast evidence for near-death and out of body experiences, states of awakening and enlightenment, clearly suggests that consciousness is not produced by material processes within the brain. A further mistake within the modern holographic paradigm is the assumption that experiences only occurs in the brain, and that as Karl Pribram comments, "there are no laser beams in the brain." Mystical teachings suggest that a zero point source of coherent light within the Heart Space establishes the holographic basis of human consciousness.

Mystical approaches to creation involve the study of numbers and metaphysical principles embodied within the creation process. God is said firstly to be One, then Three and Seven; as a ray of pure white light divided by a three-sided prism yields a spectrum of seven colors.. The Laws of Three and Seven permeate all cosmic phenomena on all planes of being. In fact, these principles are latent within the nothingness of pre-existence. Similarly, there are three modes of nature representing intelligence, energy and matter, which manifest on successively dense planes of material existence. This creates a seven dimensional universe all out of a seven dimensional hyperspace that existed before the beginning. When God sculpts the void, and order arises out of disorder or chaos, it does so according to an inner geometry of being involving these divine principles. These principles can be applied to the study of physics and cosmology, and to the study of the circulation of light within the inner cosmos of consciousness.

Zero Points & Heart Spaces:
Tone Magazine

Article published May 2002 in *Tone* magazine, Ottawa, Ontario

The term 'zero point' is taken from the mystic Madame Helena Blavatsky, author of *The Secret Doctrine* (1888). Blavatsky explains: "... material points without extension (zero-points) ... are the materials out of which the "Gods" and other invisible powers clothe themselves in bodies." Any Son, any created cosmos, whether a universe or an individual human being has a zero point center. Another *Stanza of Dzyan* from *The Secret Doctrine* reads: "The Sons *expand and contract through their own selves and hearts; they embrace infinitude. ... Each is a part of the web. Reflecting the "Self-existing Lord" like a mirror, each become in turn a world.*" The Sons expand and contract through the dimensions of the heart space. Ramana Maharshi explains that in samadhi or enlightened consciousness, it is the Self within the Heart that supports him in that state. The mystical conjunction of zero point divine sparks within the hyperspace dimensions of the Heart gives rise to human consciousness. The zero point divine spark is the quantum self, a point source of divine light and life, of spiritual and divine consciousness within the human being, the I that I AM, the hidden Self pointed to by mystics and sages throughout the ages.

In order to understand the nature of zero points, we have to consider the nature of space, both the four dimensional space we are familiar with, and the subtle, higher dimensional Space which sustains it. The mysteries of consciousness are intimately interrelated to the mysteries of space and the inner dimensions of being. Consciousness arises from the conjunction of divine sparks within the Divine Mother, the aether of space. The zero point reflects the qualities of the Divine Father, the Self Existing Lord, the zero point source of supernal light; while the sacred aether of Space embodies the mysteries of the Divine Mother, the Akasha or Aether. Understanding the conjunction of the zero point within the heart space is a key to unlocking the mystical origins of consciousness and self, and transforms our experience of life and the world.

The sevenfold nature of creation and of Space is another basic teaching of the divine wisdom, which helps us to understand the world orders, and the Space within which we exist, as I. Blavatsky states: *"Everything in the metaphysical as in the physical Universe is septenary."* Divine sparks descend through various higher space dimensions within the seven depths of the Divine Mother. This is depicted by the mystic poet Kabir, who writes: *""Inside this jar there are seven oceans and innumerable stars.""*

The mystics suggest awesome possibilities for human consciousness and experience in a profoundly deep universe. Humans live in forgetfulness of their true nature, of self, and of the higher dimensional nature of Space within which we live, move and have our being. The mysteries of consciousness are intimately tied to the mysteries of heart space. Unfortunately, people asleep think that this is all romanticism or metaphor, which it both is and is not. There is also a science of consciousness and the Heart.

Aleister Crowley, in *The Law is for All*, elaborates these mysteries in explanations of Hadit and Nuit. Hadit is an infinitely small and atomic point, while Nuit is infinite space, the root principle of creation which allows for the manifestation of Hadit. The conjunction of Hadit, the supernal point within cosmic space, Nuit, is the root for all manifestation. Hadit and Nuit are identified with various dualities; the masculine and feminine principles, yang and yin, motion and matter, the star or point of light within the darkness and emptiness of space. The term Nuit is French for night and suggests the darkness of a night sky, populated by stars, all manifestations of Hadit.

"Every man and every woman is a star." The Book of the Law states that each individual is comprised in their magical nature as a point of divine light within cosmic space. The Body of Nuit is the macrocosm and is symbolized by 0, zero. In contrast, Hadit is: the sun, one point concentrating space, the core of every star, and the unit of the macrocosm, an infinitely small zero point source represented by the number 1, which stands like I. Thus, Crowley writes: *"... in the Temple called Man is the God, his Soul, or Star, individual and eternal, ... inherent in the Body of Our Lady Nuit. I am the flame that burns in very heart of man, and in the core of every star."*

Various veils obscure the relationship between Hadit and Nuit. The "secret light" within is identified with consciousness - "our light is the inmost point of illuminated consciousness." Just as the sun illuminates the outer cosmos, so Hadit is an innermost point of consciousness illuminating the experiences and dimensions of the inner cosmos. There can be no regular temples of Nuit or of Hadit and Crowley describes the religion of the era as the cult of the Sun, as this is our particular star in the outer world within the Body of Nuit. The aim within *magick* is for the individual to consummate the marriage of Nuit and Hadit within themselves." All of life, especially love and love making, should be devoted to Nuit and her infinite possibilities for being known. Hadit knows Nuit most deeply through love. The individual is to be Hadit and to worship Her, and offer ourselves unto Nuit, *"pilgrims to all her temples."* The key to the worship of Nuit is: *"The uniting of consciousness with infinite space by the exercise of love ... Let love be "under" or "unto" the Body of Nuit."* These concepts depict the mystical dimensions of love and the deepest origin of Self, the point interval Star within.

The *Book of the Law* is spoken by Nuit, the Divine Goddess, and states that the uniting of Hadit and Nuit shall "bring the glory of the stars into the hearts of men." The aim of magick is to consummate this mystical marriage. The *Book of the Law* depicts ecstasy as a key to reality: *"Religious ecstasy is necessary to man's soul."* As a star, each individual must come to attain to Divine Will and to manifest Love under Will, in order to re-unite with Nuit.

This brings us to Crowley's most simple magical formula of the Universe: $1 + (-1) = 0$. Crowley notes: "Ultimate Reality is best described by Numbers and their interplay" and his magical formula is a profound illustration of this. The $+1$ represents the male yang principle; and the -1, the female yin principle or alternatively, heaven and earth, spirit and matter, the sun and moon, or Hadit and Nuit. When these forces are in perfect balance, the equation is solved, the complex of differentiation resolves back into the primary nothingness. It all adds up to Zero, O. On a psychological and metaphysical level, Crowley relates this magical formula to the uniting of consciousness with infinite space by the exercise of love.

The essence of love and of life is that it must be a sacrament unto Nuit. This will bring the glory of the stars into the hearts of a human being. The resolution of consciousness back into its zero point source within infinite space; merging into the Nothingness and plenum, the root principles of creation. Ultimately, perfect symmetry involves the mystical marriage of Hadit and Nuit, in which only Nothingness remains: $+1 + (-1) = 0$. This simple equation expresses the most profound ideas about the inner cosmos of consciousness and the mysteries of Space. Crowley describes his own experiences of enlightenment:

> "I lost consciousness of everything but a universal space in which were innumerable bright points, and I realized this as a physical representation of the universe, in what I may call its essential structure. I exclaimed: Nothingness, with twinkles!" ... "But what Twinkles!

What exactly does all of this mean and what are the implications and applications of such deceptively simple concepts? These are the deep mysteries explored by the fool at the zero point.

The Kabbalist Universe & Self

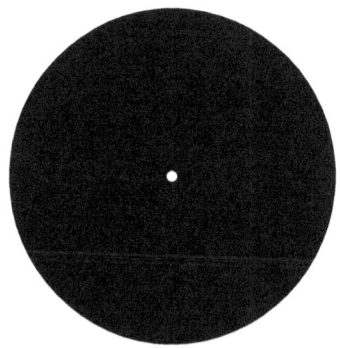

"… the void of Unmanifest Existence … was … the size of a dimensionless dot in the midst of the Absolute."

Halevi, Kabbalist, 1977

"… the heart is truly a wonder, for its creative action mirrors the original act of Creation."

Anatomy of The Soul, **Chaim Kramer, 1998**

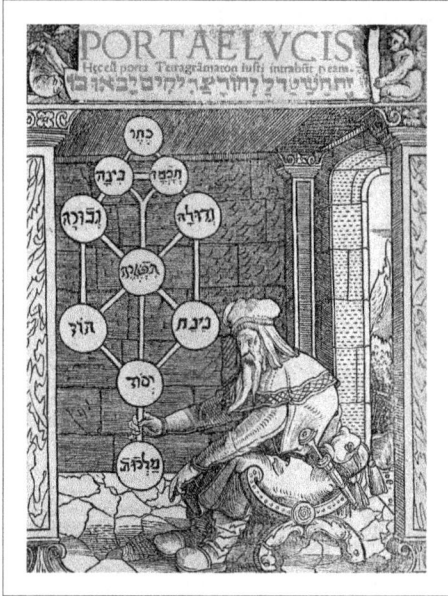

In ancient Kabbalah as in modern physics, creation emerge from within-without from Zero Point sources, out of a seeming void which is paradoxically, a plenum, through a hierarchy of broken symmetries in higher dimensional Space, which precipitate dimensions of being out of apparent non-being.

An ancient mystical axiom states: *As above, so below*. According to this formula, we might consider a human being as a microcosm of the macrocosm and embodying the same principles of creation and design as evident within the larger universe. The teachings of Kabbalah offer a complex mathematical and metaphysical model of the inner geometry of being and non-being, and the higher dimensional origins of consciousness within the heart Space. Key Kabbalist ideas concerning the creation of the universe provide then a valuable model for the emergence of human consciousness.

Kabbalists describe *three Realms of Negative Existence* as underlying and sustaining the worlds. These three realms are *Ayin,* or Nothingness, *En Soph,* the Plenum or All, and *En Soph Aur,* the limitless light. These dimensions or realms are associated with the numbers of 0, 00 and 000. To illustrate the three realms of NEGATIVE EXISTENCE, Ayin 0 is not depicted as it designates Nothingness and is therefore Unspeakable; En Soph OO is completely black, containing all things within the pleroma or plenum; and En Soph Aur OOO is white, the limitless Light.

Ayin

En Soph ■ ☐ *En Soph Aur*

Rabbi Yehuda Ashlag describes the "plenum" of the En Soph:

> The matter is as follows: all the worlds, and all that is in this world, all the creatures of the universe, in whatever age they were to exist, before they ever entered into this world, with all the souls now on earth, and those that are destined still to be created, together with their complete curve of development until the final goal of completion and perfection-all these were previously included in the world which is called "Endless," "En Soph," along with their beauty and all their fulfillments. (1984, p. 57)

The En Soph as the plenum is the root principle for the material side of nature. The En Soph includes all the varied kinds of beings and their qualities and beauties, and all the laws and forces and particles of the universe. It contains all of these things in all of their possibilities for involution and evolution, growth, change and perfection. The whole structure of the world orders on different dimensions and on different scales of existence over all times are all pre-existent in non-existence— latent within the Endlessness of the En Soph. Kabbalist, Halevi states: *"the mystic knows that everything has its origin in Absolute Nothing and Absolute All..."*

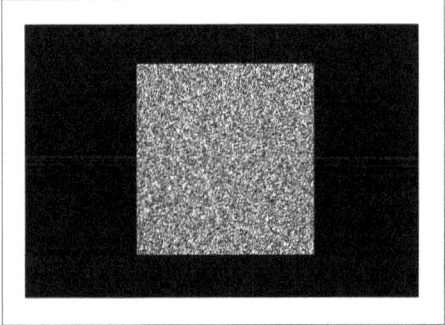

If these two illustrations (and one non-illustration) are superimposed on one another to represent the three realm of NEGATIVE EXISTENCE, they can be depicted by an infinite number of dots distributed throughout infinity but latent in Non-Being.

Next, take two enlargements of NEGATIVE EXISTENCE. On the left, the dots begin to emerge as discrete elements or I's, stepping out of the background of Negative Existence into Positive Existence. These dots represent infinitely small points beyond material measurement, zero points of no dimension. On the right, one dot is taken as an "I" of the Creator.

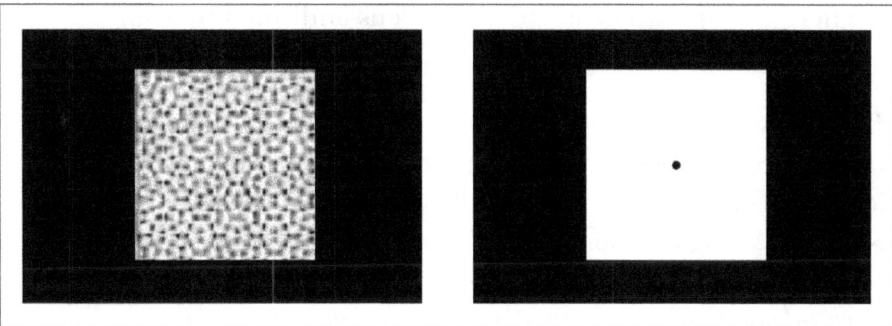

The point represents the Creator in the state called EHEIEH (ee-eye-ah), which means, *"I shall be."* Creation emerges out of NEGATIVE EXISTENCE into Positive Existence from a zero point source of unfoldment. A Macrocosm or Universe and a Microcosm, an individual human being, are described in Kabbalah as having such interior zero point origins.

Kabbalists portray the creation of the universe as emerging from a supernal point of no-dimension out of a background in NEGATIVE EXISTENCE. It is quite astonishing that this creation scenario is so similar to modern scientific accounts. In quantum physics, the quantum vacuum is regarded as a seeming void, which is paradoxically 'full' — the quantum plenum. The scientific theory of "vacuum genesis" is in fact quite consistent with the Kabbalist description of creation as emerging from within the three realms of Negative Existence — the *creation ex nihilo* of the mystics. Mystics and scientists both regard creation as emerging from point sources out of the seeming Nothingness, which is paradoxically the Plenum. A modern physicist declares, *"All of physics is in the vacuum"* and this is supportive of the Kabbalist ideas concerning the three realms of negative existence.

Kabbalists described the zero point origin of the universe well ahead of the modern scientists who imagine that they originated such a concept. In *Visions & Voices,* Jonathan Cott (1987) interviewed Rabbi Lawrence Kushner, whose writings explore the parallels between modern science and Jewish mysticism:

> *Jonathan Cott*: Cosmologists have speculated that at the first explosive moment of the birth of the universe, everything that exists -or ever will exist -was contained within a single spark

of energy, smaller than an atom's nucleus and ruled by a single primordial law.

Rabbi Lawrence Kushner: One dot - a point of light. Perhaps the fact that contemporary cosmologists talk about a dimensionless point of light from which all being sprang and that the Kabbalists long ago came up with precisely the same image (in the fourteenth century, Moses de Leon spoke of *"a hidden supernal point"* whose *"primal centre is the innermost light, of a translucence, subtlety, and purity beyond comprehension"*) means that this awareness comes from something we all carry within us. We're walking Torahs ... if we could just shut up and listen to it. As Rabbi Dov Baer of Mezritch said: "I shall teach you the best way to say Torah. You must cease to be aware of yourselves. You must be nothing but an ear, which hears what the universe of the word is constantly saying within you." (p.209)

Kabbalists and Rabbis, as well as modern scientists, suggest the zero point origins of the universe—depicting it as originating from *"a dimensionless dot in the midst of the Absolute"* (Halveri, 1977); a 'supernal point' or '*primal centre.*' However, the Kabbalist extends this notion to apply to ourselves—as we are living Torahs with the Word and the laws of God written into our very being—in fact into the Heart. So also, we might imagine a human being as having such zero point origins in a type of ultra-physics of consciousness and the heart. This figure from mystic Jacob Boehme depicts the name of God inscribed within the heart—although a spiritual heart of flames turned upwards relative to the material heart.

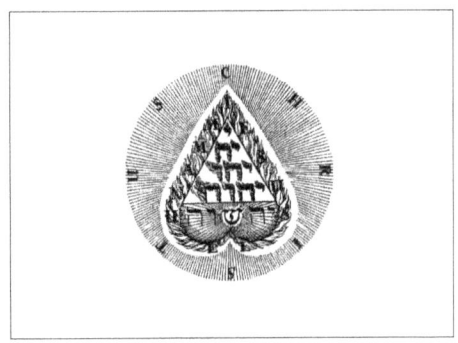

Kabbalists maintain that there are such Divine source Emanations or Divine Sparks, as stars in space, points of supernal light within the higher dimensional vacated Space of the heart! Kramer describes such 'sparks of holiness' and their emergence from the primordial realm of *Adam Kadmon*:

The consequences of Adam's fall can be compared to a beautiful and expensive piece of crystal that is dropped from a

> great height and shatters into thousands of tiny pieces which become scattered over a large area. Adam had contained within himself the souls of all mankind in a state of perfect unity. His fall shattered that holy unity into countless *"sparks of holiness"* which subsequently became dispersed throughout the entire world. It has since been man's mission, utilizing the spiritual inclinations incorporated within his system, to search for, find, purify and elevate these sparks, that they may return to their source. This will ... even improve upon, the vessel from which they originated—Adam. ... (p. 56)

Human beings have a remarkable nature according to Kabbalist teaching— as 'sparks of holiness.' "I" originates from within the deepest realms as an infinitesimal point source of Divine Will and Light Consciousness— "I" stands out and declares *"I AM."*

> *"... every created being cries out the name I AM as it emerges from Kether, before plunging into the Cosmic Sea below."*
> - Halevi, 1977 -

Kabbalist teachings certainly support the zero point hypotheses and the notion that human beings have such a 'primal centre.'

Another creation process described by the Kabbalists involves the withdrawal of the Infinite Light (the En Soph Aur) from around a central point—which creates an empty space or vacuum. This concept has application to understanding the mysteries of the vacated heart Space and the psychology of human beings. Luria describes the *Zimzum* or Self-constriction:

> BEHOLD HE THEN RESTRICTED HIMSELF, IN THE MIDDLE POINT WHICH IS IN HIM, PRECISELY IN THE MIDDLE, HE RESTRICTED THE LIGHT. AND THE LIGHT WAS WITHDRAWN TO THE SIDES AROUND THE MIDDLE POINT. AND THERE HAVE REMAINED AN EMPTY SPACE, ATMOSPHERE, AND A VACUUM SURROUNDING THE EXACT MIDDLE POINT.

God as the Creator withdrew the Limitless Light from that Space surrounding an exact middle point. This created a vacuum and empty space surrounding a middle point—a form of *'nothingness at the heart of Being.'* It is of course quite logical that the Infinite Being would have to withdraw from a space in order to allow a finite being or Universe to come into existence. Without this self-contraction, everything is swallowed up in the Infinite. Kramer explains the *"Torah of the Vacated Space,"* known in Hebrew as the *Challal HaPanuy*:

> Prior to the Creation, there was only God. ... Since God is everywhere, there was no "room" for the Creation to come into being, no *place* which could accommodate His Infinite Light. God thus restricted His Light away from a "center point," as it were, to create the Vacated Space. In this space would be created all the supernal Universes, and also the material world ... God contracted His Light, as it were, concealing Himself from man, making it seem to man's limited vision as if there is a vacuum, a place devoid of Godliness. This is the mystery of the Tzimtzum (Self-constriction). (1998, p. 207)

Kramer explains that the action of the Heart *"mirrors the original act of Creation"* and the Heart is such a hollow Space within us. In this sense, there is a form of *"nothingness at the heart of being."* Kramer explains: *"the passion of the heart is really an infinite desire for the Ein Sof."* (p. 211)

The concept of the vacated Heart Space (of Binah) is of a profound nature and has applications to understanding creation physics and both normal and supernormal psychology. If we take the idea literally, as we should, it suggests a model of how human beings are rooted within into zero point fields with a vacated space at the heart of being, which can be illumined by the light of consciousness. All things exist within such higher dimensions, which underlie, sustain and unify them. The Heart is further the place wherein Godliness can be revealed in stages:

> "The heart must make of itself a hollow space wherein Godliness can be revealed in stages. The verse thus states (Psalms 109:22), "My heart is hollow within me." Thus the heart (binah) corresponds to the hollow of Creation, the Vacated Space. Within the Vacated Space is placed Godliness,

but gradually, in stages. This is the meaning of (Exodus 31:6), "In the hearts of the wise, I have placed wisdom." For Godly Chokhmah is concealed within Binah, which corresponds to the heart. Thus, even in the Vacated Space, Godliness exists in concealed form. Binah, then, is conceptually the Vacated Space wherein the formation of all the Universe takes place." (C. Kramer, 1998, pp. 211-212)

The heart is an empty space, embodying Binah, the Divine Mother; wherein the light of the Divine Father is concealed--all as a zero point centre within a human being. If we consider such Kabbalist concepts from the perspective of modern physics, with an understanding of the quantum vacuum, singularities, and higher dimensions, then we can arrive at a profound model of the multidimensional origins and nature of human consciousness.

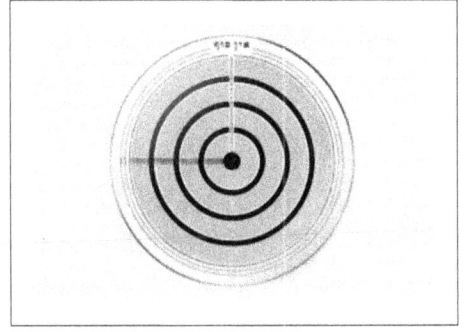

Source: Manly Hall, *Secret Teachings of All Ages*

'I' emerges from a zero point source rooted into higher dimensional space, crosses the abyss and declares 'I Am.' From a divine source emanation, to a spiritual spark, to a world of formation or ensoulment, and finally into the physical world made, a human being expands and contracts from within without the Spaces of the Heart and clothed in different bodies within a multidimensional universe. An individual has such a deep inward physics and metaphysics to Self, a nature far beyond the simplistic materialist views dominant in modern science and psychology, and beyond anything which people ordinarily image.

Kabbalist views of creation have anticipated a series of the newest ideas in modern physics and cosmology. Kabbalah essentially provides a mathematical model of the inherent structure of the quantum vacuum! People do not realize that this is what the *Tree of Life*, the *Ladder of Jacob*, or *the Star of David*, represent, Christopher offers a modern interpretation of Kabbalist metaphysics and symbols--in the light of modern physics and science. Dr. Holmes illustrates the relationship of the "matrix of creation" established around the divine source emanation, illustrated by a Kabbalist on the left below, to the newest concept of a seven dimensional Calabi Yau Space, underlying every point within the four dimensional space-time complex, described by physicists Green and Atkins in recent science writings.

On the left we have a Kabbalist depiction of the 'matrix of creation' (or intelligence) surrounding a zero point centre, with the Star of David within the inner geometry. On the right, we have the 7 dimensional Calabi-Yau Spaces depicted in the newest models of physics.

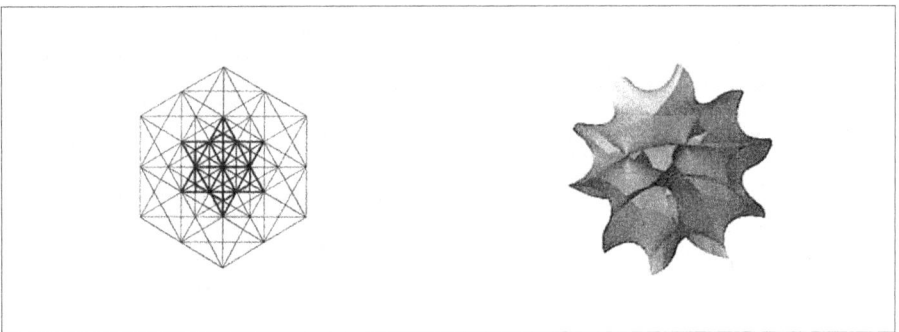

Imagine that, perhaps every man, every woman and every child is such a little Star, and has such a higher dimensional metaphysics within the heart. This would be such a principle of magic, for a world of magic. All little pixels on a screen of higher dimensions!

Zero Point Fields

> Quantum physics predicts the existence of an underlying sea of zero-point energy at every point in the universe ... referred to as the electromagnetic quantum vacuum since it is the lowest state of otherwise empty space. This energy is so enormous that most physicists believe that even though zero-point energy seems to be an inescapable consequence of elementary quantum theory, it cannot be physically real, and so is subtracted away in calculations. From this perspective, the ordinary world of matter and energy is like a foam atop the quantum vacuum sea. (www.calphysics.org)

The emerging *new physics* offers profound revisions of the basic concepts in science concerning the nature of space, the quantum vacuum, zero point fields, and the nature of mass and gravity. Of course, most scientists researching such possibilities would dismiss the idea that there is anything mystical about any such subjects or that their studies of the *new physics* have anything to do with the study of consciousness, life and the nature of Self. However, the newest concepts in physics concerning the zero point fields illustrate and substantiate the ancient wisdom teachings about the nature of the underlying realms of Space.

The zero point field is a ground state field of energy, which constantly interacts with all subatomic matters. It is called the zero point field because fluctuations in the field are evident even at a temperature of absolute zero, when all matter has been removed. Fluctuations of the zero point field drive the motion of subatomic particles. It may be likened to the Ceaseless Eternal Breath within the Eternal Parent Space (of Blavatsky or as an underlying *holomovement* within the ether of the quantum vacuum, in Dr. David Bohm's theory of wholeness and the implicate order.)

Particles continually interact with the underlying zero point field and these interactions are mediated by "virtual particles." Virtual particles appear out of quantum vacuum, combining and annihilating each other in the briefest instances of time (approximately 10^{-23} seconds, depending upon the mass of the particles). All matter is supported and sustained by activity from within the underlying zero point field. The zero point field is a repository of numerous fields and ground energy states for the different forces in nature and all the virtual particles which mediate these forces. Thus, the zero point field is a *plenum* -defined by McTaggart (2002) as *"a background substructure filled with things."* (p. 22)

The dynamics of the zero point fields are now regarded as providing answers to many of the most intriguing enigmas of modern physics -such as the uncertainty principle, the wave/particle duality and the manner in which infinities continually pop up in the mathematics of quantum theory. All of the fluctuations and motions of particles involve dynamics within the zero point field, itself composed of diverse subfields.

The idea of the zero point field is derived from one of quantum physics' central tenets: Heisenberg's "uncertainty principle." The uncertainty principle states that certain pairs of measurement, such as the position and momentum of a particle, cannot both be known exactly at the same instant of time. There is instead, an *"intrinsic quantum fuzziness in the very nature of energy and matter."* If we attempt to precisely define the position of the particle, then uncertainty about its momentum becomes infinite; and if we attempt to exactly define its energy, then uncertainty about its position becomes infinite. *"Even at absolute zero temperature, a particle must still be jittering about: if it were at a complete standstill, its momentum and positions would both be known precisely and simultaneously, violating the uncertainty principle."* (1997, p. 83)

Electromagnetic radiation may be pictured as waves flowing through space at the speed of light. These waves carry energy and have specific directions, frequencies and polarizations. These states are referred to as the various 'propagating modes of the electromagnetic field.' Since each of these modes is subject to the uncertainty principle, it must have a certain minimum energy (given by the formula $hf/2$). Although the modes carry minuscule amounts of energy, the number of modes is enormous. The product of the energy per mode and the huge number of modes yields a very high theoretical level of energy latent within every cubic centimeter of space. From this line of reasoning, quantum physics predicts that all of space must be filled with electromagnetic zero-point fluctuations (also called the zero-point field) creating a universal sea of zero-point energy (www.calphysics.org).

The Cal Tech group suggests that since space breaks down into a quantum foam at the tiny distance specified by the Planck scale (of 10^{-33} centimeters), the zero point fluctuations might cease at the related Planck frequency of 10^{43} Hertz. In this case, *"the zero-point energy density would be 110 orders of magnitude greater than the radiant energy at the center of the Sun." www.calphysics.org.*

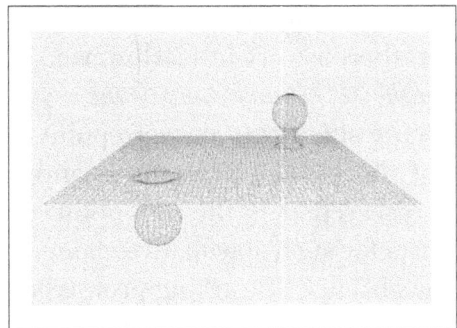

The existence of the zero-point field has long lurked in the background of modern science and quantum theory in particular. Historically, scientists have dealt with the enigmas posed by the mathematics of quantum theory by a process of the "re-normalization" of quantum field equations. Thus, when the mathematics of quantum theory leads to infinite values, theorists eliminate the infinities through the "re-normalization" of quantum field theories. In this way, positive infinities are used to cancel out negative infinities yielding a sum of zero and other mathematical practices are used to leave a finite residue. In a *Scientific American* article, the infinities were described as being *"exorcized"* from nature through the tricks of re-normalization.

Nevertheless, to think of a vacuum as being simply empty space is no longer valid. If all matter and radiation were extracted from a volume of space, this space is still permeated by the zero-point field with its ceaseless electromagnetic fluctuations. B. Haisch explains: *"if you add up all these ceaseless fluctuations, what you get is a background sea of light whose total energy is enormous: the zero-point field. The "zero-point" refers to the fact that even though this energy is huge, it is the lowest possible energy state. All other energy is over and above the zero-point state."* (www.science-spirit.org)

The universe exists within this vast sea of underlying light and electromagnetic activity—what Blavatsky described as the electric ocean of life. However, because this zero point energy permeates everything and is the lowest possible energy state, it is invisible and unobservable to us. It is completely uniform and pervades us from every direction. The world of light which we do see is over and above the zero-point field. Just how deep is this underlying quantum sea of light? McTaggart reports: *"It has been* *calculated that the total energy of the Zero Point Field exceeds all energy in matter by a factor of 10^{40}, or 1 followed by 40 zeros."* (2002)

In a *Scientific American* article (1997), P. Yam explores the controversial idea of extracting energy from the underlying zero-point field. The article *Exploiting the zero-point energy* has the caption: *"Energy fills empty space, but is there a lot to be tapped, as some propound? Probably not?"* The article notes that exactly how much zero point energy is within the vacuum is "unknown" and that the conventional view has been that there is very little. However, there is a core of researchers who *"think that the 21st century could be the zero-point energy age."* The implications of being able to tap the zero point fields would be utterly profound -in terms of alternate energy sources and possible means for space travel.[1] Of course, researchers in the zero point camp are criticized by more orthodox theorists for such speculative claims— pointing to the lack of scientific data and the absence of working prototypes or devices which tap this zero point energy. Of course, conspiracy theorists have realized that many such inventions have been intentionally suppressed in order to maintain the monopolies of the psychopathic elites, but that's another story.

The zero-point theory is also used to explain the concepts of mass and inertia in a novel way and to question the traditional understanding of the nature of gravity. In reference to inertia, which refers to a material object's resistance to acceleration, the novel idea is that inertia is due to the *"drag effects of moving through the zero-point field."* Matter resists acceleration as it interacts with surrounding fields of virtual particles. In this case, a zero point "wake" is left behind as an object moves through space, with virtual particles continuously popping in and out of existence, and moving in relation to the material particles. Both inertia and gravity could be due then to the interaction between the electromagnetic quantum vacuum and the fundamental charged particles (quarks and electrons) that compose matter.

In the case of gravity, an object fixed above the earth would experience the *"electromagnetic momentum flux"* created by the earth within the zero point field and this gives rise to its weight and acceleration towards the earth. Gravitational effects are thus produced by "asymmetry" within

---

[1] One suggestion is that the zero point energy might act as a "negative mass" system for the propulsion of spacecraft; or that the Casimir effect might be used to create pressure differentials within the zero point field.

the electromagnetic zero point fields within the quantum vacuum. One futuristic idea is that the advanced forms of propulsion for space travel could involve modifying the electromagnetic quantum vacuum and/or its interaction with matter to nullify inertial and gravitational forces (www.calphysics.org). The search for such mysteries of zero point energies and fields has long been explored as explanations for UFO propulsion, anti-gravity devices and spacecraft.[2]

McTaggart (2002) points out that since all subatomic matter is continually interacting with the zero point fields, this creates a record of everything that happens. She describes the Zero Point Field as *"a kind of shadow of the universe for all time, a mirror image and record of everything that ever was. In a sense, the vacuum is the beginning and the end of everything in the universe."* (p. 26) The zero point fields embody information about the whole.

Certainly, the newest concepts of the zero point fields are quite startling. Space itself has a depth and is a plenum. The vast energies and information latent within the zero point fields permeate all of matter, sustaining the phenomena of the created world. Contemporary physics, far from arriving at "the end of science" -as some writers have speculated (c.f., John Horgan) – is encountering even stranger and more fantastic possibilities. B. Haisch and A. Rueda of the CalTech physics group comment: *"... we dare to predict that physics and astrophysics of the 21st century are going to love the quantum vacuum."* (2003)

The zero-point field is a new approach to the traditional idea of the "ether," although most scientists shy away from using the term ether because this idea was supposedly discredited when nineteenth century researchers were unable to demonstrate an "ether drift." However, space itself, at the level of the quantum vacuum is a pleroma of energies, virtual particles and information, which provides a medium for physical manifestation. Electromagnetic fluxes within the underlying electromagnetic ocean indeed constitute such 'ether drifts,' and may even be responsible for gravitational effects. Physicist P. Davies comments: *"So clearly the quantum vacuum resembles the ether,"* which he refers to as the *"quantum ether."* (2001, p.33)

---

[2] Nick Cook, a journalist, explores the classified world of the aerospace industry, and documents the secretive work carried out over the past fifty years in his book, *The Hunt for Zero Point* (2001).

Scientist Ervin Laszlo, in the highly acclaimed *Science and the Reenchantment of the Cosmos* (2006), comes closest to the ideas of the aether as propounded by Blavatsky. Laszlo's refers to Blavatsky in reference to the term *Akasha*, in a chapter entitled *The Rediscovery of the Akashic Field*. Laszlo explains that in the "disenchanted world … *inert matter moves impersonally against a backdrop of passive space*"—the familiar mechanist and materialist science. In contrast, in the "enchanted world" revealed by modern physics, biological science, paranormal and consciousness studies, "*the universe, with all things in it, is a quasi-living, coherent whole. All things in it are connected.*" (p. 1) The medium for this interconnectedness is of course the Akashic field—the zero point information fields within the quantum vacuum which interpenetrate and sustain all physical manifestation.

Laszlo provides this summary description of the Akasha:

> … the unified vacuum fills all of space, … it is superdense and superfluid, … it brings forth the particles that furnish local universes and receives them back at the end of their evolutionary cycle, and .. it generates the force-fields of gravitation, electromagnetism, and the strong and weak nuclear interactions, as well as the holographic field that instantly and enduringly interconnects particles and atoms, and all things built of them, in space and time. Science's emerging vision of reality is the vision of a reality that is interconnected and whole—it is an integral view of reality. (p. 86)

In the enchanted world, 'information' is a third force in relation to matter and energy and this information is holographically encoded within space itself.

Laszlo explains that particles have 'spin' properties associated with a specific 'magnetic momentum' and that this is registered in the vacuum through "particle-triggered secondary vortices" which carry 'information'—just as do magnetic impulses on a computer disk. The interactions of particles create interference patterns which holographically carry information on the entire set of the particles that create them. Thus, "interfering vacuum-vortices are nature's holograms." Since the vacuum is superfluid, these interactions do not produce friction and information can propagate at speeds many multiples of c, the speed of light. This is why the enchanted world is essential 'non-local' and the Akashic Field is a "cosmic holofield" wherein even vast areas of the universe can be interconnected. Laszlo remarks: "... the A-field of the vacuum records all things that happen in the universe." In this view, the evolution of advanced forms of life is due to *"vacuum-based information."* Further, Laszlo maintains that "life on Earth was not biologically, but *informationally seeded."* (pp. 48-9) Edgar Mitchell, astronaut and consciousness researcher, and commentator in Laszlo's book, similarly refers to "the holographically information embedded *in the quantum zero-point energy field."*

H. P. Blavatsky describes exactly such an idea, that Space itself—not the created space-time complex but the underlying "Eternal Parent Space" with its "Ceaseless Breath" or movement—is the foundation for all physical manifestation. Space is the Aether wherein there is a correlation of all forces and an Omniscience which thrills throughout every finite point of the universe. The zero point fields are latent within the Aether -the invisible foundation for physical manifestation.

2011 & the Countdown to 2012

"The individual is handicapped by coming face to face with a conspiracy so monstrous he cannot believe it exists."

J. E. Hoover, former head of the FBI

"Humanity is the victim of a monstrous conspiracy of unspeakable proportions."

(**H. Makow**, *Illuminati*, p. 76)

Humankind is at a critical period in modern history. A grand epic tale of psychopaths, cruelty and criminality, is unfolding on the world stage. Forces of evil are having their days of cruelty, deceit, perversion and power, and bringing about new stages of international terrorism, violence and the poisoning of populations. The banking and corporate elites continue the intentional looting of the wealth of nations, poisoning the populace and environment, secretly dissolving democratic institutions and sovereignties, and carrying out state-sponsored terrorist acts around the world. Their lethal arsenals include new biological weapons and inoculations, mind control technologies and police state weapons, weather modification and earth upheavals played on a nightmare HAARP. Their upcoming plans include massive genocide, internments, famines, starvation and impoverishment. Mass genocides can be effected through the release of biological weapons and/or enforced inoculations, and even a World War III – all in service of the eugenic plans of the psychopaths, perverts and Satanists who came to rule to world--who consider themselves 'the elites' and 'illuminated.'

Wow, what a wild story and it is true, however beyond the capacity of most pea-brains to grasp. The attempt to enlighten the masses of humankind is like trying to fill a sieve and the slaves to do not have the courage, or *'new heart,'* required to face the real Beast in modern times. The enemies were domestic all the time and not foreign--within our own nations instead of half way around the world in some invaded and desecrated countries, like Afghanistan and Iraq, rich in oil, drugs and human suffering. There were no Muslims attacking the US in high jacked airplanes on 9-11, as the public was led to believe just like any other Hollywood Tale and fed as propaganda through the Media of Lies. The whole thing was a fraud and the people who committed it are still in power, while none of our police and intelligence services capture the real terrorists but instead knowingly and unknowingly protect and serve them.

The conspiracy theorists were right all along after all – as documented by Alex Jones at www.prisonplanet.com and within such a real news source such as www.globalresearch.ca, www.informationclearinghouse.info and http://republicbroadcasting.org . The sleeping people and the little lost sheep still believe that Osama and his reindeers crashed down such wonderful towers, and that the intelligence and police really do capture the bad guys instead of protecting them. The citizenry of America is more concerned with men playing games with balls, than with the life of their families, nation, the environment or humankind. The American dream became the American nightmare and all the high ideals of America, Canada and Mexico as sovereign nations within a sane world community were proven to be illusory and based on lies and deceits. As if America had some democracy to spread. America is not a democracy but a psychopathocracy—a country run by a psychopathic elite, as are Israel and Great Britain, the United Nations and Canada, and most of the countries of the world.

The masses of humanity have been deceived like little sheep --at home in front of the TV, listening to the radio and reading their newspapers; while at work, in their churches and synagogues. They have been intentionally deluded by the corporate Media of lies and the education of double-think, self-absorbed in the culture of materialism and narcissism.

Whatever happened to the values of humanity, to the Constitution and Bills of Rights, and the inherent moral principles of what is right or wrong? The neo-con, like neo-Nazi spiders, have woven their webs of deceit, jockeyed and perverted the police and judicial powers and attained a insidious fascist control of the lives of the populace. Madmen at the helms of nations, lusting for further blood, power and control, and willing for egomaniacal and satanic ends to even plunge humankind into pandemics and extermination and even a World War Three—all in the service of a claimed 'New World Order,' which I prefer to call the *Old World Psychiatric Disorder.* Humankind has never known life apart from the control of such self styled elites and monopoly men.

The criminal invasion of mid-Eastern lands, black operations groups around the world, psychopaths and perverts at the heads of the nations, hidden elites, pharmaceuticals and poisons, bioterrorism by our own governments, the corporate greed of the masters of war—that Dylan sang of, the lies and cover-ups of 9/11 and the establishment of the New World Order, are all concocted by the pseudo-illuminate, puppets, kings and queens. Behind the scene as a shadow is a cabal of Satanists, psychopaths and perverts, who have lost their hearts and souls and fallen under the control of alien intelligences and beings. Satan is said to have a hierarchy of servants and we certainly witness this in the crimes of our governments and police. Meanwhile, forces of light awaken peoples around the world to the deceits of the 'lie' and those *'upright of heart'* struggle to bring forth the truth to the world of sleepwalkers in order to awaken from *'the nightmare parable'* --being lived out in the life of contemporary humanity. The human race became a rat race and was deceived by a pseudo-master race. Oh, what a sad Tale of unspeakable deceit and cruelty!

Will the Tale of *The Two Towers* be followed by part III, *The Return of the King* and the restoration of righteousness to the world, as should happen in a Hollywood tale as it did in *The Lord of the Rings* and all before the new age Mayan calendar year of 2012? Or will humankind sink further into the Orwellian nightmare, webs of deceit and lies, with inoculations and implants, chemtrail spraying and GM (genetically modified) poisoning, the unspeakable greed of the elites, alien control and lunacy, and planetary processes of what G. I. Gurdjieff called the *"processes of reciprocal destruction,"* or simply 'war'? Humankind is moving towards Armageddon, while US, British and Israeli forces and hidden elites carry out international plots and plans, and the banksters impoverish the population--all part of what Bush called "the third wave." Indeed, money, sex and power are the three characteristic motives of men one, two and three, of the seven possible levels of human evolution. The third wave is that of power, as wielded by the heads of states and the underlying world tyrants, about now to conduct other mass murders in Iran, Pakistan, Palestine and elsewhere even against their own countrymen, committing more crimes against humanity and further starving and sickening the peoples of the world.

The *World Health Organization*, an assembly staffed in the 1950's by ex-Nazi doctors and scientists, proponents of eugenics, is now mandating 'enforced inoculations' for the masses of the world's populations, supposedly to protect them against viruses which the same cabal of pharmaceutical giants have designed! The new world order elite aim to reduce the world's population to their aim stated on the Georgian Guidestones of five hundred million. And so America, as a nation, moves forward to massive genocide of its citizenry, all the sheep who believed that their masters would not skin them alive and devour them.

CHEMTRAILS

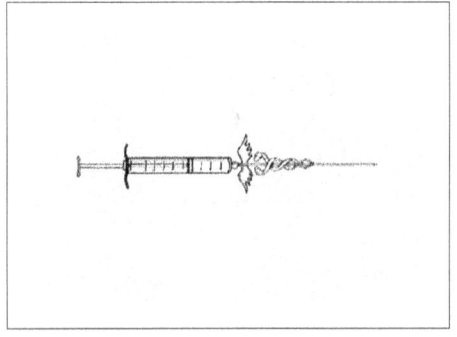

Chemtrails, inoculations and biological weapons, implants, pharmaceuticals and poisons, HAARP, weather control and mind control--the forces of Darkness have an arsenal of weapons for homicide and genocide and to spread terrorism throughout the world, while the corporate media of lies has been able to intentionally deceive, manipulate and confuse the little sheep brains.

The poor little sheep are being led to slaughter, hypnotized by black magicians and deceived by the medias of lies. Oh poor America, poor England, poor Israel, poor world, poor Muslim, Christians and Jews, poor humankind, all to sink to such depths of depravity as evident throughout the world. The Hollywood Tales became more important than the life of the Holy World--the light and the truth, the mysteries and cosmic nature of love. What a sad and pathetic Tale of humankind! And the masses of humankind do not even know that they are parts of such grand and psychopathological Tales as they are so asleep and deceived!

"tell 'em what you heard. It's about a revolution in your heart and in your mind ... cause everything is nothing and emptiness is in everything. This reality is just a fucked up dream with the flesh and the blood that you call your soul flip it inside out, it's a big black hole ...."

(Lyrics from Between Angels and Insects, Papa Roach)

What the Bleep do we know!?

Not too much according to Dr. Holmes, who presents a radical critique of this popular new age movie nightmare.

This new age movie represents a completely erroneous and fanciful understanding of the nature of human beings, and the mysteries of consciousness and the mind. It ignores the most important questions and evidences concerning the issues of consciousness, the heart, spirit and soul, and obscures the truth more than illuminating it. New age concepts are dressed up in a superficial quasi-scientific manner, and huge gaps remain between the quantum world and the world of the psyche or spirit. The movie fosters numerous misunderstandings and confusion, although it certainly has some valuable elements. It begins nicely with the Void, but everything else is downhill.

The movie *What the Bleep do we know!?* certainly starts out on a brief positive note, and has some very positive teaching or lessons. **In the beginning**, they have the void and infinite possibilities. Further, the new physics is the "physics of possibilities," as sub-atomic quanta are spread out as waves of probability, until the observer collapses the wave function of the quanta, so that it manifests as a discrete particle. This logic is then applied to understanding a human beings' life where there are all these possible outcomes and possibilities, and we as observers will collapse certain wave functions and not others. One of the main themes of the movie is that we, by our thoughts and intentions, play a role in bringing about some of these 'possibilities,' out of the infinite possibilities. Just as an observer effects the observed and collapses the wave function of a quanta forcing it to manifest as a discrete particle instead of a wave of probability; so also, our thoughts and addictions create our life circumstances. We are told that what happens within creates what happens without, our reality. The question is then explored of "why do we keep recreating the same realities?" This theme is then explored through the movie in terms of the woman struggling to cope with life, deal with her varied neurosis, and find herself again. The movie thus also looks at our patterns of self defeating thoughts and emotions and addictive behaviours; and encourages us to more consciously participate in our lives.

These are some of the valuable elements within this movie. Further *What the Bleep* deserves credit as an early effort to create a new genre of movies--perhaps for those tired of fortuitous violence, inhumanity and sex crimes, bravo and sexual titilation. However, from my perspective as a mystic, psychologist and scientist, what is missing from the movie is more notable than what it explicates. What is missing are any understanding of the mysteries and enigmas of consciousness, the mind and the heart, any understanding of the nature of spirit and soul, any ideas of the physics and metaphysics of consciousness and the multi-dimensional universe, and any practical teaching of how to awaken and experience self-realization. What is missing in the movie is the science of the soul and consciousness, although I think that the film makers imagine that they provide this.

The movie generally is based on new age philosophy and not upon the esoteric mystical or spiritual psychologies of humanity, which are profoundly deeper than simplistic formulas of some new age philosophies. This movie asks "What the Bleep to we know," but doesn't even mention the most profound enigmas that humankind is currently facing in our quest

'TO KNOW.' There is no serious exploration in the movie of the nature of human consciousness, nor of the scientific evidence and theories of soul or spirit, and there is no mention on the importance of 'the human heart.' As a whole, the movie lacks heart and it is based implicitly on the pseudo-scientific "head doctrine" of modern times. Although the issue of the nature and origin of human consciousness is the most profound one in psychology and science today, the number one enigma, no effort is made to investigate this. Further, the ideas offered along this line as the nature and role of human consciousness are totally misleading, based on the 'head doctrine' of modern times. Further, even the emotional centre within a human being is identified more with the limbic system, sub-cortical areas, and the circulation of neuro-peptides--and again, there is no heart.

As the yogis state, until your heart opens, you will be driven crazy by the monkeys of the mind. And this movie nightmare certainly has enough craziness in it to leave most viewers dazed and confused. There exist today far more advanced conceptions on this subject of "What the bleep do we know," than anything offered in this movie. And so, Dr. Holmes replies, unfortunately, "you didn't know too bleeping much." Further, we have to go deeper into these issues and clear up the multiple levels of confusion created by a movies such as *What the Bleep?*

Most seriously, the movie tends to view human beings dualistically—as a mind/body complex and the nature of consciousness is never really addressed. Certainly, there is no mention of the heart or soul. The movie is based on the pseudo-scientific idea of modern times that the brain in the head produces consciousness--which elsewhere I call "the head doctrine." It also takes sub-cortical areas of the brain and the neuropeptides as the basis of human emotions, but never is there any psychology of the heart--not only as a centre of emotional experience but as the centre of the I-experience. There is no understanding of the mystical process of self-realization through the awakening of the heart, which is the only teaching that will awaken humankind to the deeper levels of the Self and of multi-dimensional reality. Even the music group, Papa Roach know more about the nature of the human being, in the lyrics to *Between Angels and Insects*, than Ramtha in his wiseacring.

In modern times, there is a whole science to the heart and mind, and human consciousness, which is not even touched upon by this fanciful movie. It lacks heart, fails to explore consciousness or the extended faculties of the mind, or the nature of the multi-dimensional reality in which we live and move, and have our being. We must do better. Hello out there, anybody home.

The secret of the Cult of Narcissism by *Rhonda Byrne*

Review by Christopher P. Holmes, Ph.D.

"... the magician suggested to his sheep that they were not sheep at all; to some of them he suggested that they were *lions*, to others that they were *eagles*, to others that they were *men*, and to others that they were *magicians*."

G. I. Gurdjieff, 1949
In Ouspensky, *In Search of the Miraculous*.

The Secret is a newly published book by Rhonda Byrne, available also in a movie version on DVD. The author and individuals featured on the DVD have recently gained considerable exposure through the media--from Larry King Live on CNN, to Ellen DeGeneres, and most recently, on Oprah-twice if not more. If ever there was a book and movie to convince sheep that they are magicians, or can fly, this is it. Although there are some valuable insights and teachings within *The Secret*, this is another instance of what i would call *"new think"*-- pseudo-mystical, new-age pabulum, propagated to deceive people as to their true situation and how they are about to be skinned. Although people imagine the Secret to be a spiritual teaching, it is not. In fact, it is a superficial attempt to 'spiritualize materialism' and directly opposed to the paths of mystical attainment and higher magic.

In brief, the secret revealed in *The Secret* is the *law of attraction* and that *'like attracts like.'* This supposed secret is supposed to have been known to a series of philosophers and magus through the eons of time, but hidden because of its mysterious power. On the DVD, even Einstein's image flashes across the screen, to reinforce the secretiveness of this big secret.

Thus, if we think positive thoughts and imagine positive things for ourselves, then these things will magically appear in our lives. The big Secret is about how to actualize those things that most people want in life--varied forms of money, sex and power. To be successful and gain recognition, to have your dreams come true, a new romance and even to get a new car, house or home improvements--even a parking spot--all of these are offered by the quantum magic of *The Secret*. This is a secret for imaginary wish-fulfillment and actualizing your desires--just like a lottery ticket. *The Secret* is proposed as the key to unlocking the meaning of life—making you a real magician, instead of a sheep or a slug.

The basic idea of *The Secret* is actually in conformity with Aleister Crowley's definition of magick as *"making things happen in conformity with will."* *The Secret* suggests that we can so envision what we want and because of our entanglement with the universe, these things can manifest in reality. Quantum magic for sheep.

Knowing the Secret is compared in the movie to having a Genie in an urn, but instead of having just three wishes, we can have as many as we want. Generally, the aims of those espousing the Secret are for material and financial gain, new possessions, romances and business successes, and personal confidence. We want to "love ourselves" in a cult of narcissism and to be satisfied and gorged to satiety, while atrocities are committed around the world and within our communities. Our nations are run by donkeys and idiots, cruel elites and deceivers, but we can have a new form of quantum wish-fulfillment based on ego self-centredness and self-love. Oh boy, big secret-- bound to be a big hit.

Firstly, in passing, like doesn't always attract like. In fact, in nature *'opposites attract'* and like often repel like. Positive electrical charges and negative electrical charges attract, as do the south and north electromagnetic poles. Men and women are attracted to each other, as opposites, and even within gay couples, opposite types similarly attract. Like often repels like.

Of course, in other contexts, like attracts like. If you are cruel to other people, and terrorize them, then they may want to be cruel back towards you and terrorize you. If you are loving and compassion, you may be loved back. If you have money, it is easier to make money. If you change your self defeating patterns of thinking and feeling, of scarcity and struggle, it may help you to move forward and actualize some of those things you have not yet attained. There are valuable lessons in this movie and teaching--in some regards. It is only if a person expands their horizons beyond themselves, maybe to other peoples of the world, that the self-centered focus of *The Secret* becomes apparent. *The Secret* is like a key to narcissism, a new religion for the baby boomers who have been gorged to satiety, as described by Gurdjieff.

I do not mean to be mean to the author or facilitators of the big secret, nor to Oprah and other hosts who feature their work. I used to be a big Oprah fan, and Ellen, the View, and of other popular shows, before waking up, and there will be some things in this false teaching, which could help different people resolve issues at personal and ego levels--which can be valuable. It is only when I regard *The Secret* in the broader context of the psychopathology of modern humanity, the deceits of the media and Hollywood, and such, that the superficial and hypnotic nature of this big secret is apparent. It teaches us about how to fulfill our ego and material needs, while ignoring the rampant criminal activity and terrorism within our own society--not as committed by imaginary Arabs and Muslims, Christians or Jews, but as perpetrated by the psychopaths and deviants, the international criminal cabals, who came to rule the human race.

The human race was not intended to become a rat race controlled by a pseudo-master race, and to become a slave race. And yet, this is what has happened and humankind faces a task like that before Arjuna in the Gita, where the forces of light and love gather on a battlefield to face those forces of cruelty and deceit.

To understand the positions of human beings on planet earth, it is useful to quote this material from mystic G. I. Gurdjieff, about the hypnosis and delusions of humankind, the sheep being led unconsciously to slaughter --while buying into the Cult of Narcissism and "sacrificing care" to a great horny owl--in reference to the Satanic practices conducted at Bohemian Grove.

"First of all it must be realized that the sleep in which man exists is not normal but hypnotic sleep. Man is hypnotized and this hypnotic state is continually maintained and strengthened in him. One would think that there are forces for whom it is useful and profitable to keep man in a hypnotic state and prevent him from seeing the truth and understanding his position.

There is an Eastern tale which speaks about a very rich magician who had a great many sheep. But at the same time this magician was very mean. He did not want to hire shepherds, nor did he want to erect a fence about the pasture where his sheep were grazing. The sheep consequently often wandered into the forest, fell into ravines, and so on, and above all they ran away, for they knew that the magician wanted their flesh and skins and this they did not like.

"At last the magician found a remedy. He *hypnotized* his sheep and suggested to them first of all that they were immortal and that no harm was being done to them when they were skinned, that, on the contrary, it would be verg good for them and even pleasant; secondly he suggested that the magician was a *good master* who loved his flock so much that he was ready to do anything in the world for them; and in the third place he suggested to them that if anything at all were going to happen to them it was not going to happen just then, at any rate not that day, and therefore they had no need to think about it. Further the magician suggested to his sheep that they were not sheep at all; to some of them he suggested that they were *lions*, to others that they were *eagles*, to others that they were *men*, and to others that they were *magicians*.

"And after this all his cares and worries about the sheep came to an end. They never ran away again but quietly awaited the time when the magician would require their flesh and skins.

"This tale is a very good illustration of man's position.

G. I. Gurdjieff, quoted by P. D. Ouspensky *In Search of the Miraculous*, 1949. (p. 219)

The Hollywood lies became more essential
to the life of humanity
than the Life of the Holy World.
What a sad and pathetic Tale!
What a sad and pathetic big secret.

How to know Mr God with your mind and brain and then attain your soul through a big black hole

A Critical and Complementary Account of *How to Know God* by **Deepak Chopra** *Harmony Books, New York, 2000*

"... a fully awakened brain is the secret to knowing God."

(Chopra, 2000, p. 26)

The mind is creeping closer and closer to the soul,
which sits on the edge of God's world, at the event horizon.
The gap of separation is wide when there is no perception
of spirit; it grows smaller as the mind figures out what is
happening. Eventually the two will get so close that mind and
soul have no choice but to merge. When that happens, the
resemblance to a black hole is striking. To the mind, it will be
as if falling into God's world lasts forever, an eternity in bliss
consciousness. ... The mind was part of the soul all along, only
without knowing it. (pp. 288-289)

Through my life, I have read three or four of Dr. Chopra's works, heard him lecture on one occassion, and seen several of his videos. He is often an inspiring speaker, widely knowledgeable and engaging, and a highly original thinker and researcher--bringing quantum concepts into the area of medicine and healing. I stress this as there is much of value in Dr. Chopra's work and I do not mean to be disrespectful in my critique of this book *How To Know God*. However, from my perspective of zero point studies and the heart doctrine, as elaborated throughout the esoteric teachings, this book is sadly mistaken and runs totally contrary to the most fundamental teachings of the world's spiritual and mystical traditions.

Modern western psychology and neuro-science 'assume' that 'consciousness' is produced somehow within the brain, primarily or exclusively 'in the head.' In my critiques of modern thought, I label this false dogma *"the head doctrine."* Generally, modern philosophers of science distinguish in a simplistic way between a dual mind and body, and assume that the brain is the cause of the mind and somehow produces human consciousness and self awareness. Of course, within modern psychology, there is absolutely no understanding of what consciousness really is, or how it is produced by the brain or any of the details of this 'head doctrine.'

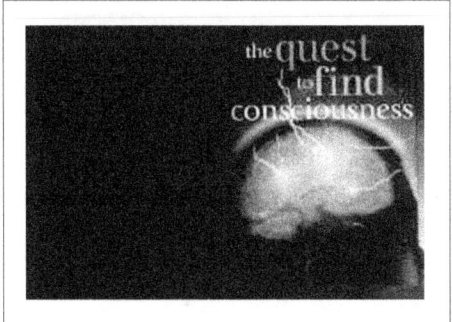

This illustration, from a *Scientific American* article *The quest to find consciousness*, is an artist's depiction of *"the mysterious brain activity involved in consciousness."* (Roth, 2004) Scientists have focused exclusively on the brain's structures and processes in order to explain consciousness and the nature of the mind. In a small table in Roth's article appears the title "FAST FACTS: The Rise of Awareness," wherein Roth makes three points:

1. How does consciousness, with its private and subjective qualities, emerge from the physical information processing conducted by the brain? ...
2. Recently neuroscientists have focused on the neural corre lates-the activities in the brain that are most closely associ ated with consciousness.
3. To date, no "center" for the phenomenon has revealed itself,

but advances in imaging have helped in the study of the brain areas that are involved during consciousness. (p. 34)

Of course, there is not a 'single fact' in the table, but only questions or assumptions. It is not proven that consciousness emerges *"from the physical information processing"* in the brain, nor from *"the neural correlates."* These are only assumptions although they are presented as *'fast facts.'*

Many new-age philosophies also implicitly assume the basic principles of the head doctrine. This fundamental idea is espoused in both of the new age movies *What the Bleep do we Know!?* and *Down the Rabbit Hole*, which regard consciousness and the mind somehow to be produced in the brain within the head, with our thoughts somehow creating our reality. Similarly, parapsychologist Dean Radin in *Entangled Minds* assumes that ESP and other psychical phenomena mainly involve the brain which somehow taps the information fields latent within space due to quantum entanglement.

How to Know God by Dr. Chopra is a supposed spiritual and enlightened book which now informs us that knowing God also happens in the brain, where the mind and consciousness are. These quotations from Dr. Chopra's book espouse such a view:

> Now our search has narrowed down in a way that looks very promising: God's presence, his light, becomes real if we translate it into a response of the brain, which I will call the "God response." We can get even more specific. Holy visions and revelations aren't random. They fall into seven definite events taking place inside the brain. (p. 6)

> So the brain, with its seven basic responses, provides more than sanity and meaning; it provides a whole world. Presiding over this self-created world is a God who embraces everything, but who also must fit into the brain's way of working. (p.9)

Oh dear, even Mr. God must fit into the brain's way of working!

> God is woven into reality, and the brain knows reality in these
> limited ways. It may sound as though we're reducing the
> Almighty Father, the Primeval Goddess, and the Mysteries of
> Mysteries to a firestorm of electrical activity in the cerebral
> cortex--but we aren't doing that. We are trying to find the
> basic facts that will make God possible, real, and useful. (p. 10)

This is really most strange! We are going to *"find the basic facts"* that will *"make God possible"*! Pretty unusual cerebral cortex, making God possible and even giving him something to do to be useful! Of course, all the esoteric and religious teachings of humanity have portrayed the Mysteries of Mysteries as those of the Heart. Blavatsky describes the Mind as *"the Great Slayer of the Real."*

Anyway, in *the new thought movement*, with Mr. God in the brain and mind, trying to be useful, we find further:

> If we only knew it, God's most cherished secrets are hidden
> inside the human skull--ecstasy, eternal love, grace, and
> mystery. This doesn't seem possible at first glance. If you take
> a scalpel to the brain, you will cut into soft grey tissue that
> doesn't respond to the touch. There are lakes of slow-running
> water in this quivering terrain and open caves where light
> never penetrates. You wouldn't suspect that a soul is hiding
> here somewhere, that spirit can find its home in an organ
> almost as liquid as red blood cells, and as mushy as an unripe
> banana. ... Your brain is hardwired to find God. Until you do,
> you will not know who you are. (pp. 13-14)

Wow! Love is now in the brain, along with ecstasy. In this view *"God's most cherished secrets are inside the human skull."* Should we love God then with all of our heads? Do we love our sweethearts will all of our heads? Or should we really refer to them as 'sweat heads,' instead of sweethearts? Perhaps we can give out pictures of our cerebral cortex on Valentine's Day, and assure our loved ones that we love them will all of our brains! If someone told me they love me with all of their heads, I would refer them to a psychiatrist, maybe to Dr. Chopra.

In line with these so-called scientific views of the brain producing the mind, consciousness and the I-experience,' this new book sees the brain as actually producing Mr. God! Consider this gobbeley-gook:

So now we have the outline for the entire spiritual journey in our hands; the unfolding of God is a process made possible by the brain's ability to unfold its potential. Inherent in each of us is wonder, love, transformation, and miracles, not because we crave these things but because they are our birthright. Our neurons have evolved

> to make these higher aspirations real. From the womb of the brain springs a new and useful God. ... A fully awakened brain is the secret to knowing God. (pp. 25-26)

> God is born out of the 'womb' of the brain! At least now, He can be useful.

This basic 'head doctrine' is opposed to 'the Heart doctrine,' of mystical sources--including *The Secret Doctrine* of Blavatsky, the yogic teachings and Hinduism, esoteric Christianity, mystical Kabbalah and Judaism, the teachings of the Sufis and Islam, the Tibetan Buddhism of the Dalai Lama, and many other esoteric teachings. In these views, the ego or personalized conscious experience is identified more with the 'mind' in the brain, but the deeper Self is identified as being within the human heart. No spiritual teacher ever espoused the idea that the 'soul' is in the brain or mind. A few quotations illustrate the alternative view of consciousness evident within the mystical and spiritual teachings of humanity.

In a *Psychology Today* interview (1976), Guru Bawa, an eastern wise man, made these rather startling comments about western psychology and the common misunderstanding of Self. According to the guru, psychologists are quite deluded about the origin of the mind (or consciousness):

> "I studied psychology once, and I became crazy," Bawa responded in a playful tone. "I lost all my powers. ... Psychologists don't know where the mind is. Some think it is in the brain. Others think it is in the genitals. Others think it is in the ass. But the mind is in the heart, and that is what psychologists do not know. Unless the heart opens, you will be driven crazy by the monkeys of the mind." (April, 1976)

This is a telling diagnosis of modern psychology and science. Certainly scientists are in a sad predicament if they do not know where the mind is or where consciousness originates! Yet, from a mystical and spiritual perspective, this is precisely the case: there are fundamental errors in modern scientific and new age approaches to understanding of the origin and nature of human consciousness.

Guru Bawa describes some psychologists as thinking that the mind is in the brain-as in the modern head doctrine. Others relate it to the genitals-in reference to Freudian psychology, with its focus on human sexuality; or, to the ass-in reference to the Kundalini energy, a primordial instinctual energy described by yogis as locked within the root chakra. However, Bawa insists: *"The mind is in the heart."* This is the deepest, most essential Self and Mind-- beyond what the yogis refer to as the "monkeys of the mind" of the material brain. In this viewpoint, mainstream psychology, philosophy and science alike, are fundamentally mistaken about the nature of consciousness, mind and self. They have grounded their approach to these essential questions on a set of erroneous assumptions and illusory ideas. They are not *'Knowers of Self,'* as described in the mystical literature.

Sri Chinmoy, another modern spiritual teacher, stresses the heart doctrine and also diagnoses human beings' common ignorance as to the true nature of self:

> He does not know himself precisely because he identifies himself with the ego and not with his real 'I.' What compels him to identify himself with this pseudo 'I'? It is Ignorance. And what tells him that the real 'I' is not and can never be the ego? It is his self-search. What he sees in the inmost recesses of his heart is his real 'I,' his God. (1970, p.16)

Human beings lack true self-knowledge and are asleep to their deep nature as spiritual beings. According to the mystics, we live in ignorance, identifying the Self with the thoughts, feelings, desires and sensations which make up the contents of the mind and the personal daily life dramas. All the while, we do not know Self, or the "real I"-related to the subtle mystical dimensions of the heart. Modern scientists and pseudo-scientists alike assume the brain and mind to be the basis for individual Self and for consciousness.

Ramana Maharshi, an Indian sage and mystic, similarly described the Self as being related to the mysterious Heart Centre-deeper than the personal or ego level of the mind centred in the head:

> ... the final goal (of yoga, or life) may be described as the resolution of the mind in its source which is God, the Self; in that of technical yoga, it may be described as the dissolution of the mind in the Heart lotus. ... The mind and the breath spring from the same source. They arise in the heart which is the centre of the self-luminous Self. ... Where the 'I' thought has vanished, there the true Self shines as 'I.' 'I' in the heart. ... The 'I,' the Self, alone is real. As there is no other consciousness to know it, it is consciousness. (1977, pp. 90-1)

Ramana Maharshi makes a number of important points concerning consciousness and self. Firstly, real "I" or "Self" is identified most intimately with the spiritual and soul dimensions of the heart, and connected therein to God. Secondly, the goal of yoga is the dissolution of the mind into its source-within the heart lotus or centre. Thirdly, the Self is "self-luminous" and "shining"-having a inherent light nature. Fourthly, the self-luminous Self is "consciousness itself." Consciousness is the light of Self. 'I' is within the heart.

If scientists and psychologists are unable to locate consciousness, the soul and spirit in the material realm, perhaps they are looking for it in the wrong place: firstly, in the head, rather than in the heart, and secondly, in the materiality of the physical world rather than in the subtle matters of the metaphysical dimensions which underlie and sustain the physical dimensions.

The Heart, not the mind in the head, is the centre of a human being considered as a whole quantum system. Further, all of the basic esoteric mystical and religious teachings elaborate the Heart Doctrine--that to know Self and God, involves the mysteries of the Heart.

> The heart is the treasury
> in which God's mysteries are stored;
> Seek the purpose of both the worlds
> through the heart, for
> that is the point of it."
> Sufi poet, Lahiji
>
> "God placed a divine spark into
> every human being. And that divine spark
> is the secret of secrets."
>
> (Robert Frager/Sheikh Ragip, psychologist and Sufi Master
> in conversation with Jonathan Cott: *On the Sea of Memory:
> A Journey from Forgetting to Remembering*, 2005)

Elsewhere, in Kahil Gibran's classic work, The Prophet, a man from the village approaches the Prophet and asks him to:

> "Speak to us of Self-Knowledge."
> And he (the prophet) answered, saying: "Your hearts know in silence the secrets of the days and the nights. But your ears thirst for the sound of your heart's knowledge. You would know in words that which you have always known in thought. ... the treasure of your infinite depths would be revealed to your eyes. But let there be no scales to weight your unknown treasure; ... For self is a sea boundless and measureless. ... The soul unfolds itself, like a lotus of countless pearls." (1968, pp. 54-55)

Gibran contrasts the thoughts of the mind and ego with the secret self within the heart. Whereas the mind is full of chatter and confusion, the Self within the heart is known in silence. Again, the heart center is compared with a flower—a lotus unfolding from within without. In western traditions, the rose is the more common symbol of the mysterious heart center.

Unfortunately, Mr. God is now, in new think, somewhere up in the brain, trying to find something useful to do. Further, human beings should love each other with all of their heads. So many modern books articulate such superficial nonsense, gobbled-gook, on the nature of consciousness, mind and Mr. God, with his comb sticking out of his pocket.³

Well, now we know that Mr. God is really up in our minds and brains, in the head, where Dr. Chopra even thinks the soul might be. Returning then, to How to Know Mr. God, lets consider what insights we might glean as to the lost science a of the soul. Recall Dr. Chopra's remarks, the only or one of a few simple references to the 'soul' in his work:

> "You wouldn't suspect that a soul is hiding here somewhere, that spirit can find its home in an organ almost as liquid as red blood cells, and as mushy as an unripe banana. ... Your brain is hardwired to find God. Until you do, you will not know who you are. (pp. 13-14)

This actually suggests that 'the soul' is up in the brain! This 'maleficent idea' is most peculiar.

At one point, Dr. Chopra provides a very useful and insightful image of the search for the human self. He writes:

> Peel away all the layers of an onion, and at the centre you will find emptiness; peel away all the layers of a human being, and at the centre you will find the seed of God. (pp. 8-9)

---

³ Mystic G. I. Gurdjieff, in his masterpiece story, *Beelzebub's Tales to His Grandson*, portrays in a literary way the strangeness in the mentation of those three-brained beings on planet Earth. Beelzebub explains to his grandson Hassein that the phrase *"We are the images of God,"* is *"one of the only 'cosmic truths'"* expressed by the three brained beings on planet earth, although they have no understanding of what it truly means. Then, in his humorous and insightful manner, Beelzebub elaborates upon how those "unfortunates," humankind on earth, have taken this deep truth:

> "'Good ... if we are "images of God" ... that means ... means ... "God" is like us and has an appearance also like us ... and that means, our "God" has the same moustache, beard, nose, as we have, and he dresses also as we do. ... almost with a comb sticking out of his left vest pocket ...

> "... those 'learned' beings ... assembled in the city of Babylon ... began to invent various maleficent fictions concerning their 'God,' which were afterward by chance widely spread everywhere on that ill-fated planet. ... it was said ... that that famous 'God' of theirs had, as it were, the appearance of a very old man, just with a heavy beard." (pp.776-7)

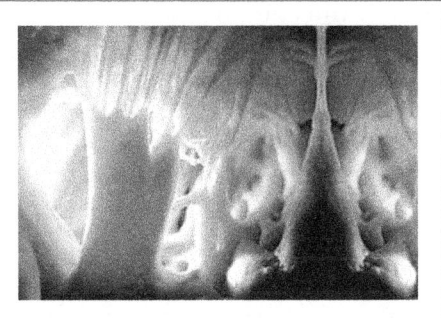
Illustration of interior chamber of the Heart

From my perspective, elaborating the heart doctrine and the zero point teaching, this quotation is most profound and congruent with my writings and teachings. I argue that there is a form of *"nothingness at the heart of being,"* as described in the Kabbalist *zimzum contraction*. Judaism depicts an empty space or void created within the human heart, which is why we seek to find God, in order to fill this primordial emptiness. The first manifestation of a seed of God is a 'divine spark' established within the higher dimensions of the vacated Heart Space. There is both a physics and metaphysics to these processes.

At times, Dr. Chopra has some other valuable discussions of the soul, expressing concepts similar to what I describe through zero point studies. Towards the conclusion of *How to Know God*, in a section entitled *A Map of the Soul*, Dr. Chopra writes:

> The soul is as mysterious as God, and we have just as few reliable facts about it. ... the soul is really a junction point between time and the timeless. It faces in both directions. ... the soul is like a carrier of the essence, but what is that essence like?
>
> ... the soul begins a quantum level, which makes sense since the quantum level is also our doorway to God. ... In India, the soul has two parts. One is called Jiva, which corresponds to the individual soul making its long journey through many lifetimes until it reaches full realization of God. ... The second half of the soul, called Atman (is) pure spirit, made of the same essence as God. ... Jiva lives at the quantum level, Atman at the virtual. ... the soul must have a divine aspect that embodies the goal of all seeking. (pp. 275-6)

So Dr. Chopra arrives at the idea of the individual soul, the jivatma, and the universal soul, the Paramatma, (or what he calls the jiva and Atman), drawing from the Hindu and Vedic teachings of India. This is all quite fine and Dr. Chopra has some valuable discussion of the soul, however, at the same time, he is seriously misrepresenting the teachings of India to imagine that God is know through seven levels of the brain and mind in the head!

In fact, according to the Bhagavad Gita, the jiva and the Atman, the Supreme Lord (the Supersoul or paramatma) and the individual spirit soul (the jivatma) are associated with the heart and not with the head.

The physical nature is known to be endlessly mutable. The universe is the cosmic form of the Supreme Lord, and I am that Lord represented as the Supersoul, dwelling in the heart of every embodied being. (8, 4)

Out of compassion for them, I, dwelling in their hearts, destroy with the shining lamp of knowledge the darkness born of ignorance. (10, 11)

> I am the Self, O conqueror of sleep, seated in the hearts of all creatures. I am the beginning, the middle and the end of all beings. (10, 20)

The two souls, the Supersoul and the individual soul, are compared to two birds sitting together on the branch of a tree. The individual soul is captivated by the fruits of the tree which represent material desires, while the Super Soul is a silent witness. To attain liberation, the individual spirit soul must overcome patterns of attachment to pleasurable experiences, desires and the fruits of action, and surrender to the deeper Self of the Lord. Self-realization or union with the Lord comes through overcoming the darkness of ignorance and awakening to the eternal principle within the sacred temple of the heart.

The nature of human consciousness can be understood as originating from the jivatma, or the individual spiritual soul within the heart. Again, consciousness is related to light and the spiritual soul is described as self-illuminating. Swami Prabhupada quotes the Gita:

> ... as the sun alone illuminates all this universe, so does the living entity, one within the body, illuminate the entire body by consciousness. (Ch. 13, V. 34)

The Swami further elaborates on the meaning of this sacred text:

> As the sun is situated in one place, but is illuminating the whole universe, so a small particle of spirit soul, although situated in the heart of this body, is illuminating the whole body by consciousness. Thus consciousness is the proof of the presence of the soul, as sunshine or light is the proof of the presence of the sun. ... consciousness is not a production of the combination of matter. It is the symptom of the living entity. The consciousness of the living entity, although qualitatively one with the supreme consciousness, is not supreme because the consciousness of one particular body does not share that of another body. But the Supersoul, which is situated in all bodies as the friend of the individual soul, is conscious of all bodies. That is the difference between supreme consciousness and individual consciousness. (1972b, pp. 659-660)

A small particle of spirit soul (the spiritual spark) inhabits the material heart as the "sun" of the body. The spirit soul is self-illuminating and its light is an expression of the infinite light of That Self, the Supersoul. Consciousness within the mind and body originates from this self-illuminating entity--as established within the Heart.

There is some kind of "seed of God"--but it is not simply in the brain. Dr. Chopra certainly has such moments of poetic insights. The Seed of God is within the heart, within the higher dimensional physics and metaphysics of the heart, and this is what the head scientists do not know. This book represents the most superficial of modern attempts to find God, although it provides some valuable concepts in thinking about the 'quantum nature of the soul.'

In another section, *The State of Union*, Dr. Chopra provides some valuable discussion of what I would label zero point dynamics. He writes:

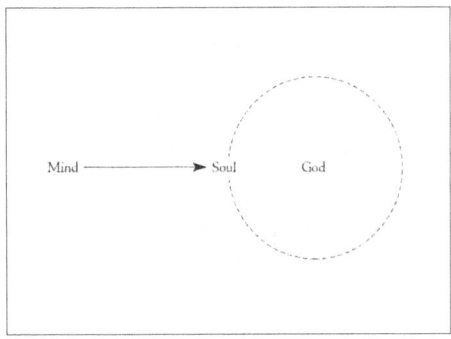

... knowing God comes down to this: like a photon nearing a black hole, your mind hits a wall as it tries to think about the soul. ...

The mind is creeping closer and closer to the soul, which sits on the edge of God's world, at the event horizon. The gap of separation is wide when there is no perception of spirit; it grows smaller as the mind figures out what is happening. Eventually the two will get so close that mind and soul have no choice but to merge. When that happens, the resemblance to a black hole is striking. To the mind, it will be as if falling into God's world lasts forever, an eternity in bliss consciousness. ... The mind was part of the soul all along, only without knowing it.
(pp. 288-289)

When the mind falls into God's world and into 'bliss consciousness,' this is described by the yogi master as the *"dissolution of the false mind into the lotus of the heart."* That is how Ramana defines the aim of 'yoga' or 'union.' And exactly, as Deepak describes, this is the dynamic of the mind yielding to the deeper awareness of the life of the spiritual soul.

So Dr. Chopra certainly does provide some very valuable ideas and explorations, although, as I have argued, he has made fundamental mistakes. However, if we supplement his work, with our own perspective, then we can arrive at a deeper synthesize. I hope Dr. Chopra appreciates this article if he ever has the opportunity to read it, or the heart to read it, as I think this only supplements and deepens his own efforts.

Towards the end of *How to Know God*, Dr. Chopra writes:

> ... every saint ... every master ... the human representatives of God constitute an infinite treasure. Dipping into this treasure will help to open your heart. At just the moment when your soul wants to blossom, the words of the saint or sage may be the right fertilizer. (p. 304)

Wow, quite a story of heads and hearts, mysteries and enigmas, *new thought* and *ancient wisdom*. In Kabbalah, both wisdom and understanding, Chokmah and Binah, are embodied within the mysteries of the human heart. A quantum approach to the nature of Self is most important.

ENTANGLED MINDS: Extrasensory Perception in a Quantum Reality by *Dean Radin*,

2006 Paraview Pocket Books, New York

Dean Radin, Ph.D., is currently the Laboratory Director at the Institute of Noetic Science in Petaluma, California. He has researched psychical phenomena for over twenty years within academic settings including Princeton, as well as at three Silicon Valley think tanks. His earlier book *The Conscious Universe: the scientific truth of psychic phenomena* was a number one parapsychology bestseller on Amazon.com. Dr. Radin is featured in the new-age movie *Down the Rabbit Hole*, the sequel to the popular *What the Bleep do we Know?!* He is clearly a leading researcher and theorist in modern psychic and paranormal studies, and this book is valuable in bringing attention to the scientific evidences for paranormal phenomena.

The first two hundred pages or so of *Entangled Minds* provides brief histories of different areas of psychic investigations and a review of a significant body of paranormal research--both Dr. Radin's own research work and valuable 'meta-analysis,' which he conducts on other paranormal research. There is then two thirty-page chapters, one on *"A New Reality"* dealing with aspects of the new physics and a second on *"Theories of Psi,"* applying concepts from physics to understanding the possible basis for Psi phenomena. The bulk of the book is a historic review and a summary of paranormal research, and the actual theory or model of Psi is really quite limited-- beyond introducing the most essential idea of the "entanglement of minds."

Dr. Radin explains the concept of "entanglement" as has emerged in modern physics and argues that *"psi becomes the unavoidable consequence of living in an interconnected, entangled physical reality,"* (p. 3) *Entangled Mind* does demonstrate a credible body of scientific and statistical evidence which supports this hypothesis. Dr. Radin considers psi *"as a perceptual ability, as information flowing from the environment into the mind without the use of the ordinary senses."* (p. 146)

I would firstly like to provide a complementary review of *Entangled Minds* by Dr. Radin. This is a valuable contribution to the modern parapsychology literature. It provides 'meta-analyses' of existing experimental literature on such paranormal faculties and experiences—as those of ESP, precognition, presentience and psychokinesis (PK); it reports Dr. Radin's significant original experimental contributions and it addresses the historic issues of science and the paranormal as well as the shallow objections and arguments of the sceptics; and, it suggests how the *new physics* provides more of a framework within which to understand paranormal phenomena.

Radin quotes a well-known maxim, *"Exceptional claims require exceptional evidence"*—attributed to both Carl Sagan and the sociologist of science, Marcello Truzzi. As it happens, Radin does provide such exceptional evidence in his reviews of the paranormal literature and then he relates this psychical research to a key concept in modern physics—that of entanglement.

"Entanglement" refers to the interconnectedness of separated quanta as implied in modern quantum theory. Albert Einstein referred to the *"spooky action at a distance"* inherent to basic quantum theory—such that particles separated in space and time from each other are seemingly interconnected at a level beyond the material level. Thus the measurement of one particle in a laboratory and the collapse of it's wave-function might instantaneously collapse the wave function of the other correlated particle. This occurs instantaneously and without the exchange of a messenger particle to mediate the interaction. However, scientists generally have believed in only *"local effects"* in physics, rather than such non-local *spooky action at a distance* as implied in quantum theory.

Radin explains: *"entanglement (refers) to connections between separated particles that persisted regardless of distance. These connections are instantaneous, operating "outside" the usual flow of time."* Wave/particles are entangled in higher dimensional "phase space," which information is then latent within the medium of space. Radin explains: *"New reality" refers to the modern understanding of the interconnected medium in which we live, the fabric of reality as revealed by modern physics."* (Radin, 2006, p. 5) The medium is that of space itself.

Evidence is emerging within science that *"entangled connections are proving to be more pervasive and robust than anyone had previously imagined,"* and *"it affects the wider, 'macroscopic' world that we inhabit."* Thus, "evidences of psychical entanglement" are evidence of quantum entanglement at larger macroscopic levels and not simply at the levels of singular quanta.

Dr. Radin regards the human brain as the primary site of both 'consciousness' and 'the mind,' and the experience of such entanglement. Thus the title of the book suggests that human 'minds' are entangled within the medium of space to other human minds, and to information about distance events, even future ones. Radin notes: *"there's no theoretical limit to how large an entangled object can be."* (p. 16)

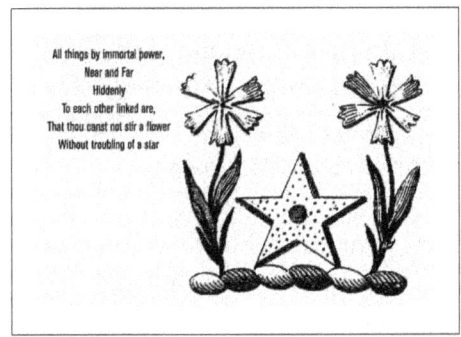

This image and poetic verse introduces Chapter 1, *In the Beginning*, and portrays a link between a lowly flower and a distance star, all entangled within quantum realities.

When it comes to explaining how all this might work, *Entangled Minds* does not really provide any elaboration or enlightenment on these issues. Instead, the book's focus is more upon the evidences for paranormal phenomena consistent with such a general notion of *entangled minds*. Dr. Radin also addresses the sceptics, who so flippantly dismiss and denigrate such psychical research—the *"... naysayers interested mainly in defending dogma.* (p. 11)

ENTANGLED MINDS & HEARTS

> "We might call the present era the 'Age of Information," and the zeitgeist is a quantum computer. ... The concept of mind is viewed as a dynamic, cybernetic inter-play between a complex physical structure (the brain) and an emergent process (the mind), with brain imagined to be primary driver of the process. Increasing numbers of scientists are beginning to ponder the role that quantum theory plays in the brain and in creating or sustaining consciousness. (Radin, 2006, pp. 242-3)

Although in ways, I compliment Dean Radin for a very valuable contribution to the parapsychology literature, at the same time, his work is limited by those same assumptions which characterize the broader disciplines of modern psychology and neuro-science, as well as new-age philosophies. This head doctrine associates consciousness and the mind almost exclusively with the brain in the head. Further, Dr. Radin while assuming that *the mind* is only in the head, tends to hold a simple dualistic view of *mind and brain* or *mind and matter*. Of course, Mind and brain now exist within a third element—the medium of space containing the phase entanglement information of the whole. The *"entangled minds"* title of the book suggests that the primary entanglement is between minds, but this is not so simply all there is to paranormal faculties and experiences. In fact, Dr. Radin himself reports varied parapsychology studies where heart rates are correlated between subjects and other autonomic nervous system indicators are used. He provides no details as to how the brain actually processes the information from within the medium or how such entanglement actually occurs or the further physics of the process.

A human being, as a microcosm of the macrocosm, must be considered as a whole quantum system and not simply as a brain in the head producing consciousness. As a whole quantum system, the centre of a human being would really be considered as related to the electrodynamics of the heart! In *The Heart's Code*, psychologist Paul Pearsall (1998) maintains that energetically speaking, the heart-rather than the brain is the centre of the psychological universe. Indeed:

> The heart's EMF (electro-magnetic field) is five thousand times more powerful than the electromagnetic field created by the brain and, in addition to its immense power, has subtle, non-local effects that travel within these forms of energy. ... the heart generates over fifty thousand femtoteslas (a measure of EMF) compared to less than ten femtoteslas recorded from the brain. (p. 55)

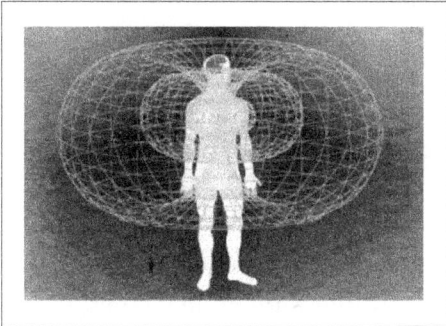

The profound significance of these facts leads Gary Schwartz and Linda Russe, in the forward of Pearsall's book, to comment:

> The Heart's Code points the way to a new revolution in our thinking. Metaphorically, the heart is the sun, the pulsing, energetic center of our biophysical "solar" system, and the brain is the earth, one of the most important planets in our biophysical system. One implication of the energy cardiology/cardio-energetic revolution is the radical (meaning "root") idea that energetically, the brain revolves around the heart, not the other way around. (1998, p. xii)

The heart is the largest source of biophysical energy in the body and itself can be regarded as a quantum computer. In fact, for varied significant reasons, the heart is the centre within the psychological life. In Pearsall's view, the heart involves energy and information that comprises the essence or soul of who we are. Unfortunately, Dr. Radin is not versed in the esoteric mystical studies and does not consider how the 'entangled minds' might be related to what is normally referred to as a 'soul.' Generally, Radin is somewhat dismissive of occult and mystical teachings, offering a new vocabulary to replace what he refers to as the *'occult lore.'*

The idea, that the heart is the center of the psychology of the individual instead of the brain, would indeed revolutionize our understanding of normal and supernormal psychology. Adopting this view would be analogous to the Copernican revolution, wherein scientists realized that the Earth, rather than being the centre of the universe, travelled around the sun within the solar system. The egocentric attitude of humans was shattered. Likewise, the acceptance of a deeper conceptualization of the heart, consciousness and the nature of Self would constitute a revolutionary development in modern psychology, philosophy and the life sciences. Further, it would provide a deeper model of the entanglement of human beings, which I would argue is based primarily upon the physics and metaphysics of the human heart. Although the mystical tradition regards the egoic self or personality as centred within the mind, the deepest level of Self is established within the heart--the material heart and the spiritual heart. One yogic master defines yoga, the state of union and Self realization as involving the *"dissolution of the false mind into the lotus of the heart."*

The heart is a thinking, feeling and willing organ, with profound energetic influences on humans' psychological, emotional and physical life. The heart has its own intelligence, independent of the brain, itself is a quantum computer. It perceives internal and external stimuli and reacts on its own to the outside world. It communicates "an info-energetic code" which is conveyed through tens of thousands of miles of vessels and 75 trillion cells of the heart and circulatory system. Pearsall notes:

> As research from neurocardiology continues, it is becoming clearer that the central role of the heart in our consciousness is much more than metaphor and that, as happened with the brain, continuing research will reveal complexities of a conscious heart that our brain cannot yet imagine. (1998, P. 69)

Pearsall states that we have been too "brain focussed" in the search for mind, and that instead of thinking in terms of a *dual mind and body*, a more rewarding and appropriate approach would be to adopt a triune model: that is, of a thinking brain, the material body and the energetic and emotional heart. The heart is the primary energy centre within the individual and in Pearsall's terms *"conveys the code that represents the soul."* The heart's attributes and functions are much more mysterious and significant than conventional scientific thinking supposes. Therefore, Pearsall argues that, through the psychology of the heart, modern psychology is *"beginning to make its first tentative contacts with the soul."* (p. 6) Pearsall examines the nature of cellular memory, life fields and non-local information fields, in an attempt to account for various clinical and psychological evidences that are emerging about the mysterious qualities of the human heart.

The remarkable stories of heart transplant recipients bear testimony to the secrets of the heart. Pearsall recounts an incident, which happened to him after he had presented a lecture on the heart's role in human's psychological and spiritual life. A member of the audience, a psychiatrist, was moved to tears as she recounted a dramatic story about an eight year old girl who had been the recipient of a heart transplant. The heart donor, a ten-year-old girl, had been murdered. After the transplant, the recipient suffered nightmares about the man who had killed the donor and was able to describe the time, weapon, and place, the man's appearance, what the little girl had said to her assailant, and so on. The police were able to identify and prosecute the murder based on her evidence! Somehow the recipient had access to the memories, information and emotional terror, and the soul influences of the donor!

Although his evidence is anecdotal, Pearsall cites several cases in which those who have received transplanted hearts are profoundly affected by the personalities, proclivities and life histories, such 'entanglements' of the donors. It seems that in receiving another's heart, the recipients are able to establish a connection with their donors, as this organ of 'the soul' maintains some entangled connection to the donor's life energies and memories-in ways that defy and confound current scientific understanding.

In *A Change Of Heart* (1997), Claire Sylvia, the recipient of a heart-transplant, recounts her remarkable experiences. She describes how the energies, emotions and soul life of the donor seemed to become intertwined with her own. Thus, she experienced an extraordinary metamorphosis after her transplant. She acquired her donor's food and beverage preferences, his conflicted feelings towards his father, his sexual attractions and impulses, and other energetic dynamics! Her dreams of the donor enabled her to establish who he had been, to meet his family and to learn more about him. Apparently, heart-transplant recipients frequently report such experiences. Nevertheless, doctors, scientists and other professionals either dismiss or politely ignore these intriguing phenomena, but these evidences suggest that it is not simply 'minds' which become entangled--but also hearts.

This is a major deficit in Radin's book—the limited conception of the mind in the head becoming entangled with other minds or events. However, Radin does include some discussion of ESP research where the measurements are of the autonomic nervous system and he mentions the entanglement of the body with the larger environment. ESP is most frequently evident in case histories when people are connected through the heart, like mother and child, or lovers, rather than simply through the mind. Different forms of paranormal faculties could involve complex dynamics of entanglement --not simply through the mind in the head, but through people's hearts, and solar plexus, and through the subtle anatomy. The psychic research literature demonstrates that the testing stimuli need to be emotionally engaging and in regular life, paranormal phenomena clearly occur most often around traumatizing events, deaths and losses—all affecting the heart and its physics. Like the souls haunting the Twin Towers and crying out for the truth of 9/11. There is no reason to assume that the entanglement of human beings only involves the minds in the heads, and not the entanglements of heart and souls.

Indeed, i would argue that the physics and metaphysics of the heart is actually the deeper origin of consciousness, the I-experience and other faculties of the mind, and hence of our entanglement to the universe. The scientists focusing on the head doctrine of modern times imagined even ESP to be primarily within the head brain, rather than as involving the heart and autonomic nervous system, or *subtle bodies* as described throughout the mystical literature. Just as modern psychologists and neuroscientists regard the mind and consciousness as somehow centred within the head-brain, so also, Dr. Radin assumes that the entanglement is centred on the brains, where the minds are, and not to the deeper human being as a whole quantum system. It is quite curious that modern ideas about human beings working on holographic principles, always want the universe to surround their heads, instead of their hearts. The following illustrations contrast two alternative views of the origin and nature of human consciousness, and the basis for the deep physics and metaphysics of life.

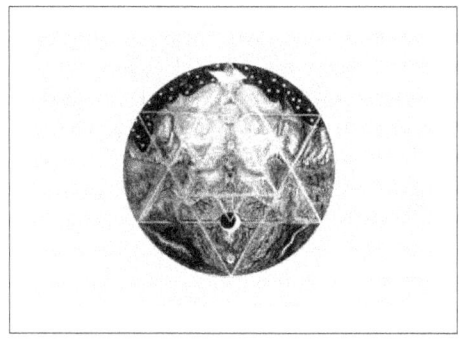
I would argue that indeed researchers of psychical phenomena need a deeper and holistic model of a whole human being as the basis upon which entanglement with others, events and the world, is effected and possible and not simply an isolated head. At times, Radin supplies a broader view, but then he fails to grasp this:

"The brain's electromagnetic fields are entangled with the rest of the universe not because of direct contact ... but because its fields interpenetrate with the energetic fields of everything else. This is how the universe remains entangled." (Radin, p. 268)

But what about human hearts!

In part, my critique of D. Radin's work is based upon the comment by Larry Dossey, M. D., printed on the book's cover. Dr. Dossey writes: *"From the Einstein of consciousness research comes a work that could change forever how we view the nature of human consciousness and our origins and destiny."* However, Dr. Radin, although his work is very valuable and significant, is certainly no *Einstein of consciousness.* In fact, his book says almost nothing about the origin and nature of human consciousness! He barely touches upon the issue and he himself does not describe his work in this way. Dr. Radin's work is a valuable contribution but he has not even begun to address the issues of consciousness and already has many wrong and incomplete ideas about it. Dr. Radin offers no evidence as to how or where consciousness is produced, nor what it is, and simply assumes the emphasis of modern thought on the primacy of neurological activities within the brain as producing mind and consciousness.

Dr Radin is not even addressing the mysteries of consciousness and his related comments on consciousness are simply mentioning the concepts of others--including William James and physicists Henry Strapp and Bernard d'Espagnat, but not exploring this subject deeply at all. He mentions Amit Goswami's views that *"consciousness is the fundamental ground state, more primary than matter or energy."* (p. 224) But this view is not even consistent with the main formulation of 'consciousness' offered in the book, which reads:

> Individual neurons in the brain combine into networks of neurons, giving rise to complex brain circuits and consciousness awareness (or correlates of awareness.) By analogy, individual minds may combine into networks of entangled minds, giving rise to more complex "mind circuits," forms of awareness, and collective psi effects beyond our comprehension.

Radin also quotes physicist Nick Herbert: *"I think that our learning to understand quantum theory is kindergarten classes compared to what we will have to grok to comprehend consciousness. Not that it will be some sort of complicated mathematics but some new way of thinking."* (p. 236) These are among the few brief passages even using the word consciousness in the book and Radin barely even comments upon them. Dorsey's description of Radin as the *"Einstein of consciousness"* simply demonstrates what widespread confusion and simplistic views persist concerning these most enigmatic mysteries.

At different points, Radin demonstrates some familiarity with mystical literature but he does not seriously understand how his ideas relate to the primary concepts of the mystics. Historically, the mystics are the ones who have always maintained such an entanglement between the individual and the world and the grounds of Being! Modern scientists think that they have discovered the idea of the unity of life through physics—like Columbus discovering America when there were already millions of people living there. Certainly most scientists, Radin included, want to deny that modern science has anything to do with mystical concepts. Radin points this out, commenting:

> Physicists interested in quantum reality are painfully aware that some interpretations of quantum reality are uncomfortably close to mystical concepts. In the eyes of mainstream science, to express sympathy for mysticism destroys one's credibility as a scientist. The taboo persists. (p. 262)

Dr Radin himself should overcome this taboo, as indeed the mystical literature provides profound insights into such topics as the nature of consciousness, the mind and the plenum of Space, and the nature of so-called 'paranormal' experiences and phenomena. But Radin wants to substitute his ideas of Entangled Minds for the ancient wisdom teachings. Radin mentions that the Greek word 'psyche' had meant 'soul' but this came in modern times to refer to the 'mind.' Radin further suggests that we should abandon the wisdom teachings of those awakened to higher consciousness, in favour of his new theory, because it is couched in the name of modern science and quantum theory. He writes:

> In magical times, theories of psi were based on what we now regard as occult lore. Concepts like "astral" and "mental" bodies, elemental and divine spirits, and various forms of "life-force" were the prevailing ways that people imagined psi to be mediated. As supernatural magic evolved into natural magic, and alchemy and astrology evolved into chemistry and astronomy, concepts of psi began to evolve beyond stories based on invisible spirits. Some people today still use occult terms like "astral body" when referring to psi, but most scientifically minded researchers regard occult lore only as metaphors. (p. 243)

Radin shows his own ignorance on these subjects, preferring instead the newly formed language of quantum theory and superficial comments upon the nature of the mind and consciousness. Scientists should study the mystical traditions to learn what is taught there, by those individuals through human history who are supposed to have demonstrated varied supernatural, psychical or spiritual abilities, or attained to higher levels of Self realization and the awakening of consciousness. Instead, the scientist will want to plod along, using their little minds and brains, pondering away trying to understand the mysteries of life. The mystics are likely to have had it right all along but we simply have not understood the things which have been said.

This is a very valuable book Dean Radin. It is valuable for your efforts to review the evidences for ESP and other psychical abilities, your taking on of the naysayer, and especially your introducing aspects of the new physics which clearly do provide a foundation for a deeper understanding of the unity and interrelatedness of life. Our minds are entangled but there is a far deeper physics and metaphysics to all of these things. Parapsychology needs a radical revision in the simplistic notions advanced about the enigmas of consciousness and mind, and this must include the study of a human being as a whole and not simply a brain localized in the head. To understand ESP will eventually bring us back to trying to grasp the higher dimensional physics and metaphysics of the human heart, and the development of a science of spirit and soul. Quantum physics is a valuable part of such a deeper science, but the popular scientists and writers have such confusions about the most primary subjects.

Thank you Dean Radin. I valued your book and hope to reread it. You are no "Einstein of consciousness" but you are a hard working researcher and investigator. I would recommend also that you consider further the newer physics of seven dimensional hyperspace, the holographic model of physics and concepts concerning zero point fields within the void/plenum of Space. You scientists, if you keep plodding along, will eventually discover something under your noses the whole time.

LETTERS TO
www.contactmusic.com on
Guy Ritchie, Madonna
& Kabbalah

In August of 2005, Christopher was invited by Guy Ritchie to fly to Los Angeles to take part in documentary movies being produced by Guy and his wife Madonna on the nature of ego and Kabbalah. Guy was reportedly pleased with our filming session and I expected to be in the final work when it was released, although I have never heard subsequently of the movie being available. It was a thrill to contribute to such a project and hopefully one day I will learn of what became of my efforts. The picture above was of my giving copies of my earlier books to Guy after our recording sessions.

The following two letters were written by me to the Contact Music forum on the internet, in response to commentaries I had read on both Madonna and Guy, in relation to their interests in Kabbalah and Judaism. Having just been invited to be a part of their filming and knowing something of Kabbalah, science and the enigmas of human consciousness, I reacted to the slanted negative and superficial commentaries I read about these two superstars in the media, so I submitted these letters. I have personally found Madonna's music to have most inspired me through the past seven years of my life and to hold such deep secrets.

ContactMusic.com

MADONNA WANTS ETERNAL LIFE

MADONNA is hoping for an eternal life because she likes the idea of reincarnation.

The pop superstar and Kabbalah follower admits she turned her back on Catholicism because there was nothing consoling about the religion and she wanted something more.

She says, "The thought of eternal life appeals to me. I don't think people's energy just disappears."

"I hope by the time it's my moment to leave this world physically, I'll have gotten my head around the idea that life is an endless cycle."

10/01/2006 02:39

screen name: Christopher P. Holmes ●● (2)   posted on 20/01/2006 07:34

comments: Screen Name: Christopher P. Holmes
Password: m01378

This is a pretty superficial note on Madonna, suggesting simply that she is "hoping" for an eternal life because she "likes" the idea of reincarnation."

People in modern times have no idea of the deep esoteric secrets within the teachings of Kabbalah, and Judaism. Modern scientists dismiss the idea that humans have a spirit or soul, as simply superstition or religious belief; while religious people believe that they have a spirit or soul, although they have no idea of what that is.

If Madonna wants eternal life, the mystical path is the only way, and Kabbalah is the most profound metaphysical teaching of modern times. It deals with the higher dimensional origins of consciousness within living beings, and with the sacred fundamental principles underlying creation-- how God is first one, then three and then seven, unfolding into the Tree of Life, with 3 supernals and 7 created spheres. Humans do live in a multidimensional universe, with afterlife possiblities and other lives, and the modern materialist views, Darwinian evolution by randomness and chance, are only so much gobble-gook, based upon layers of misunderstanding. Life is far deeper than suggested by the mainstream of materialist science, and soul-less psychology, or is imagined by modern philosophers.

A first principle of magic is that Every man, woman and child is a star! and thus has a magical nature, as a point source of supernal light, within higher dimensional Space. The aim in magic is to attain real I, to realize your nature as a star, and to attain the powers and experiences that correspond to such awakened states. Madonna is a star! And makes efforts to align her self-will with the Divine Will, such that she awakens to the higher dimensional nature of herself.

Not everyone in life is satisfied with the materialist science philosophy and the soul-less psychology of modern times, or the dogmas of religion, but instead, they strive instead towards their own self-perfection in terms of being. Madonna is one of these. Good for her, love to you Madonna, such a beautiful star out there in Space.

Madonna song "Isaac" on her newest CD is an absolutely beautiful inspired masterpiece of a song, in a class of its own. May Binah bestow her blessings upon you Madonna, and fill you with the secret knowledge of your heart, within Tipheret, in this year of 6, signifying beauty, as you are a star.

The writer of this article makes it all appear so simple and whimsical, that Madanna "likes" the idea of reincarnation, as though its all only a matter of what one 'likes.' Most people in modern times have no true knowledge of Self, and have a complete misunderstanding based upon common thought.

For Madonna, attaining Eternal Life is a serious matter of refining the higher dimension being-bodies as vehicles for the life of the soul. Madonna is such a star, and thus strives towards her own self-perfection, in terms of being. What she pursues is the most evolved of pursuits, to attain real I, and eternal life.

Imagine an oak tree that bears thousands of seeds or nuts, which fall to the ground. How many of those seeds are likely to become oak trees, whole new trees and a generation of life, and how many nuts will simply become fertilizer, and fail to fulfill their higher purposes and possibilities? Madonna is simply a nut that wants to become an oak tree, and has realized that indeed she is a star.

ContactMusic.com

RITCHIE KABBALAH IS A SCIENCE

screen name   Christopher P. Holmes (2)   posted on 30/01/2006 06:02
comments

Kabbalah is a profound teaching, with applications in all departments of human knowledge, from physics to psychology, and it embodies the essential metaphysical teachings of the world's religion. It is based upon the Sacred Law of Three and of Seven, which principles are completely unknown to popular thought or within contemporary science. Scientist and philosophers today think mainly dualistically --in 2's -- about any phenomena they study, whereas the metaphysical principles of Kabbalah suggest all things embody a triune and sevenfold nature.

For example, whereas modern scientist talk of matter and energy, a mystical perspective suggests a triune nature of matter, energy and intelligence, all upon seven planes of being. Modern scientists are 'third force blind' and do not understand how information and intelligence permeate space and provide a medium within which transformations of matter and energy occur, and within which we live and move and have our being. Science thinks there is only the world made, and that there are no underlying process creating and sustaining the phenomena of life. The Kabbalists have the most complex model of Intelligent Design offered within science or modern culture. In this view, intelligences, even spiritual and divine intelligences are permeating space. Further, whereas modern scientists consider that there is only the 'material world,' the Kabbalist has a scheme of four world orders--of the worlds of emanation, creation, formation, and the world made.

Modern psychology is usually defined as the 'science of the mind and behaviour,' studying the mind and body, again in a simplistic dualistic scheme. There is no psychology of the heart and soul, or spirit. Again, the mystical psychology of Kabbalah depicts human's more as having a triune nature of thinking, feeling and the body-- head, heart and hands. A human being, in Kabbalah, has a divine nature, a spiritual nature, a soul nature, and a material body.
Kabbalah offers a way of trying to comprehend any area of life or science, in terms of understanding the multidimensional universe. By contrast, modern science and materialist philosophies are the most superficial and simplistic schemes, and close their eyes to the huge evidence for paranormal phenomena, from ghost and near death experiences, and so much more. Kabbalah can not only be applied to understanding the material world, but also the multi-dimensional nature of life. Not all people are as foolish as modern scientists who imagine that human beings have no spiritual or soul nature. There are people in

life who know better.

Whereas modern psychologist studying human consciousness mainly distinguish in a dualistic way between the conscious and the unconscious, or left brain and right brain, Kabbalah offers a complex model of the metaphysical processes involved in attaining experiences of awakened states, and varied forms of higher emotions and mystical realizations. Because people in life are so asleep, and have only the pseudo-knowledge of modern science philosophy or education, or the dogmas of religion, they have no idea of the profound nature of Kabbalah. It is discouraging to read much of the press on Madonna and Guy Richie and the Kabbalah Centre, which is so simplistic and small minded.

Kabbalah teaches a human being how to become a star, attain Self realization. It is a complex psychology of consciousness and the heart, more complex and detailed than any contemporary ideas in psychology, philosophy and science. It is because the masses of people are so asleep and conditioned by the pushes and pulls of mechanical life, that they have no appreciation of something as complex as Kabbalah. Kabbalah is a teaching and it is 'scientific,' if you understand something of its inner secrets. I do not want to endorse any particular individuals or schools, but apart from that, Kabbalah is a scientific model and theory about the hidden nature of a multidimensional reality, far beyond anything imagined in the mainstream of contemporary thought.

Christopher P. Holmes Ph.D. (psych)
www.zeropoint.ca

On Nuts and Oak Trees

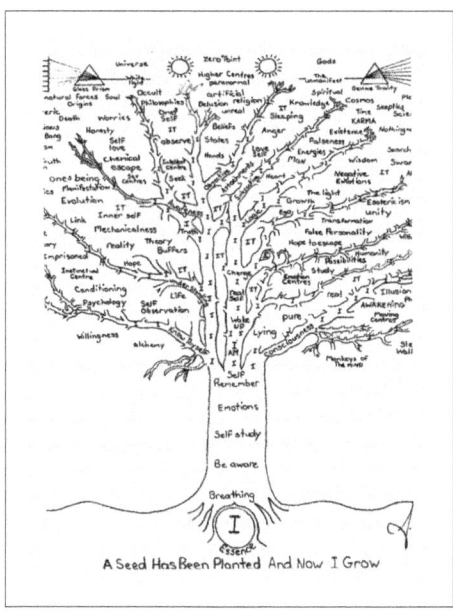

In *Boyhood with Gurdjieff*, Fritz Peters recalls experiences he had growing up in association with the teacher and master G. I. Gurdjieff. In the 1920's, Gurdjieff had established the ***Institute for the Harmonious Development of Man*** at a chateau outside of Paris, France. Peters was a young boy of eleven and served as a houseboy to this enigmatic man.

On one occasion, Gurdjieff asked Fritz to look out of the window, where there was an oak tree and to tell him how many acorns there were on the tree. Peters responded that there were thousands. Gurdjieff then inquired as to how many of those acorns were likely to become oak trees. The boy guessed that perhaps five or six, or maybe not even that many. Gurdjieff then explained the essential nature of his teaching by comparing it to the possibilities that Nature provides:

> "Perhaps only one, perhaps not even one. Must learn from Nature. Man is also organism. Nature makes many acorns, but possibility to become tree exist for only few acorns. Same with man-many men born, but only few grow. People think this waste, think Nature waste. Not so. Rest become fertilizer, go back into earth and create possibility for more acorns, more men, once in while more tree-more real man. Nature always give-but only give possibility. To become real oak, or real man, must make effort. You understand this, my work, this Institute, not for fertilizer. For real man, only. But must also understand fertilizer necessary to Nature. …"

> "In west-your world-is belief that man have soul, given by God. Not so. Nothing given by God, only Nature give. And Nature only give possibility for soul, not give soul. Must acquire soul through work. ... Even your religion-western religion-have this phrase 'Know thyself.' This phrase most important in all religions. When begin know self already begin have possibility become genuine man. So first thing must learn is know self ... . If not do this, then will be like acorn that not become tree-fertilizer. Fertilizer which go back in ground and become possibility for future man." (1964, pp.42-3)

G. I. Gurdjieff and his student P. D. Ouspensky have left a profound teaching for the modern world. The *fourth way* deals with the possibilities for the awakening of human consciousness and the evolution of the individual through the 'acquisition' of a soul. Nature has given humans the possibility for attaining real "I" and a soul, but this self transformation is dependent upon attaining self-knowledge, the remorse of conscience and the refinement of the essence, and the formation of the *higher being-bodies*. To attain real I, we must seek after truth and come to know ourselves. What these things entail are deep mysteries and there are many psychological illusions-layers of confusion and misunderstanding-which limit humans' grasp of these profound possibilities. Western psychology has lacked any investigation into the nature of the human soul or the possibilities for states of higher consciousness. By contrast, Gurdjieff provides an ancient science of the soul and a shocking portrayal of the sad life of humankind-governed by their psychological illusions and the common psychopathology of man. According to Beelzebub, the central character in Gurdjieff's *Beelzebub's Tales to his Grandson*, the three-brained beings on planet Earth are microcosmoses, or *"similitudes of the Whole."* As such, they have the possibility of not only serving local cosmic purposes-feeding the earth and moon as part of organic life on earth-but also of attaining varied levels of *Objective Reason* and individuality, and even of *"blending again with the infinite."* (1950, p. 945)

As a microcosm of the macrocosm, a human being can potentially coat higher being-bodies for the life of the soul, instinctually sense cosmic truths and phenomena, and maintain existence within the subtle realms of being after death, achieving different levels of immortality. Unfortunately, humankind came to exist only in waking sleep states of automated consciousness, perceiving reality topsy-turvy, conditioned by pleasure, desires and self love, and wasteful of their sacred substances. Human beings no longer realize their deeper cosmic purposes and possibilities, or attain real "I."

A Tribute to Jeff Martin & Tea Party

"Remembrance is the secret of redemption Forgetfulness leads to exile."
Hebrew sage, Baal Shem Tov

... here, here we are
shelterless souls
lit by the stars
... because the world keeps turning
... seven circles twisting
around these moments of our lives...
... see what we are is limitless light
reflecting the stars

seven circles, *Tea Party*

Although i do not usually write about music, being somewhat preoccupied with mystical and scientific investigations and studies, and now political dramas, I will take the occasion of Jeff Martin's interview on **106.9 FM, THE BEAR**, and the release of his new CD *Exile and the Kingdom*, to write something of a tribute to this outstanding Canadian musician and to the Tea Party band. For myself, on a personal level, the music of Tea Party has been a mainstay for over fifteen years as it was for Karen. I have managed to attend three of their concerts, two with Karen, and I would still look forward to another evening of such ecstasy and inspiration as their music provides, if such were ever possible. I have only just learnt of the Tea Party separation and of the members' independent work.

Tea Party are poets of the heart and soul. They sing of ecstasies and sorrows, love lost and discovered, and of the search for Self. *Tea Party* have explored also the dark side—the dark nights of the soul, the losses of love and desolation, the madness of the mind and addiction, the tragedies of death, and the dissolution into nothingness (as in **Psychopomp**). Their music—its depth, ecstasy and power, somehow embodies the mysteries of being, love and loss, with a beauty beyond words. One can feel it in your heart beat as Tea Party can so enliven one's Heart.

As it happens, there are many profound mystical insight and teachings within *Tea Party* lyrics, and i would like to illustrate some of these by explaining the mystical significance of certain key concepts and lines. I do not know what Jeff Martin knows of the deep lyrics that they sing, or the other other member, of the images they have used on the CD's (see the Tree of Life below), but their music does embody deep mystical teachings and truths. Martin sings *"what we are is limitless light,"* an ancient Kabbalist and mystical teaching, *"reflecting the stars"* --as every man and woman, and child, is indeed such a star-in their magical nature.

Tea Party sings of the mysteries and depths of the human heart and soul, the tragic dimensions of life and death, the deep human yearning to find heaven on earth, amidst the surrounding lies of life and the madness of humankind, of sexuality and drugs. Jeff Martin's solo CD is entitled **"Exiles and the Kingdom."**

This is certainly the condition of humankind depicted throughout the mystical traditions, one of exile.

The Kabbalist Tree of Life in fact can be used to depict the exile from heaven, and the path to finding one's way home-with Heaven coming down. Elsewhere, an esoteric verse from the Bible, Christ states: **"The Kingdom of God is within you."** (Luke 17: 21) The mystical life quest in any tradition is to find such a Kingdom within oneself. Until then, we live in exile with deep heart longings and we search to fill the emptiness of the heart and to find our way home.

you tell me love
tell me where the stars sleep
tell me why your eyes weep
i really want to know
and show me love
take me to the place where
everything would change there
and we'd be free.
Tea Party, ***Stargazer***, seven circles.

Heaven Coming Down is likely the band's most famous song, the feature of the CD TRIP*tych*. The lyrics read:

> with nothing to do you'd waste away
> obscured in exile
> they've witnessed the times
> you've gone astray
> whose fault? now you're thinking ...
> ... and it feels now
> just like heaven's coming down
> your soul shakes free
> as it's conscience hits the ground
> so strange are the ways,
> they all have changed
> still life it stays the same
> a break from the past
> could make it last
> maybe just a little longer
> ... you surrender
> love under will
> rest assured you're adored
> and it feels now
> just like heaven coming down
> your soul shakes free
> as its conscience hits the ground
> this time, no tears,

> just one last chance to see you prove
> stay strong, no fears
> there is a change that's
> coming through
> hold on my love
> hold on …

It is impossible for lyrics to convey the intensity of the music and feeling within this quite awesome song—a classic song of inspirational rock.

The lyrics *"you surrender, love under will,"* reflect particularly the Magick of Aleister Crowley. Crowley's main dictum in the ***Book of the Law*** is ***"Do as thou will shall be the whole of the law. Love under will."*** In his writings, Crowley explains the mystical conception of love in terms of Hadit and Nuit, the point star within cosmic space, and the aim in magick is to realize this magical nature and attain one's true Will. Crowley's first principle of magick states that: *"Every man and every woman is a star."* If one can attain his or her true will, one surrenders the lower egoic will's and can experience the cosmic dimensions of love. For Crowley, or anyone spiritually or mystically inclined, all love making can be made a sacrament unto the mysteries of Nuit, the Goddess of space embodied in all living beings.

Other elements in the lyrics to ***Heaven Coming Down*** embody the same teaching as within Gurdjieff's fourth way psychology. The awakening of conscience is regarded as the key element to the awakening of the higher emotional centre within a human being and this can help to bring about the awakening of spiritual consciousness. As that happens, the soul shakes free, and the conscience hits the ground, or is transcended in the realization of heaven. *"Rest assured, you're adored,"* can be experienced with the awakening of the heart and the realization of the deep love of the Divine Mother. Love as an element pervades the universe--if we are awakened enough to experience such things.

So for myself, ***Heaven Coming Down*** represented these processes of transformation and awakening, and encourages me to stay strong, keep the faith and somehow know that you're adored.

Underground, another track from TRIP*tych,* portrays an individual's search for Self and truth, and not accepting the lies and deceit of life:

> ... now all my life i've been wandering
> looking for teachers with the keys
> nothing found still searching
> for sound ...
> underground
> now let me tell you about a story
> it's about a man consumed with vice
> he's theosophical in nature
> and hedonistic in disguise
> and all his life he's been wandering
> looking for teachers with the keys
> nothing found still searching for sound
> underground ...

This character is "theosophical in nature"-- as is Jeff, and Tea Party. Theosophy is the teaching of occult scholar Madame Blavatsky and she penned *The Secret Doctrine* published in 1888. The title *Seven circles*, reflects such an influence, as indeed, Blavatsky explained: *"Seven is the number of the Divine mysteries."* For Blavatsky, all cycles of time, of life, of human evolution, all embody this sacred Law of Seven.

Tea Party has many such elements of mysticism and occult teachings within their lyrics—a curious mixture of theosophy and hedonism, East Indian and mid-eastern influences, Crowley, drugs, sex, magic and Kabbalah, all reflecting somehow the nothingness and the infinite light of the stars within ourselves. In fact, the themes and feelings of Goddess worship are found through many Tea Party songs.

The Seven Circles CD contained a poster of Shiva, the Hindu God of Destruction. However, the Tea Party figure is more androgynous, or feminine in nature, than a traditional depiction here. Shiva dances in ecstasy, religious ecstasy, as this is so essential to the human soul. Further, Shiva stands upon the Dwarf of Ignorance, detailed here.

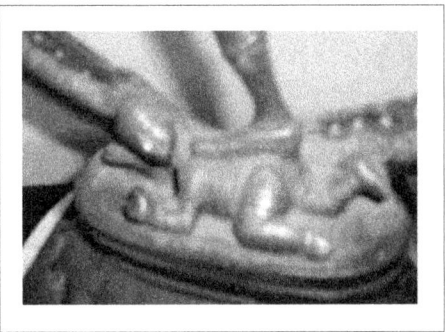

The Dwarf of Ignorance is the masses of humankind, who live in ignorance of Self. Shiva in the dance of ecstasy portrays this transcendence of ignorance within our selves, and realization of the inner life of ecstasy. The music and feeling of Tea Party is so often one of such ecstasy and can help enliven the individual to awaken within the inner life. Sister awake, brothers awake. Wake up and listen to Tea Party.

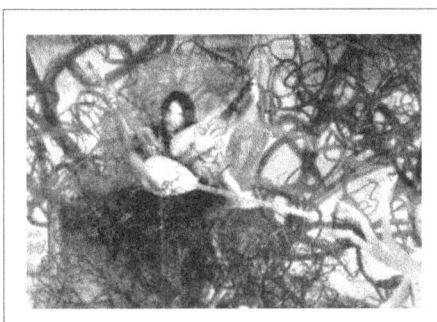

where's my angels i'm a naked soul
where's my angels i'm a naked soul
now don't you hide from me
from *Angels*

in the face of the fire
you see angels conspire
will they hear your desires
will they stop your soulbreaking
could they stop your soulbreaking
will they stop your soulbreaking
could they stop your soulbreaking
please love

Lyrics to *Soulbreaking*

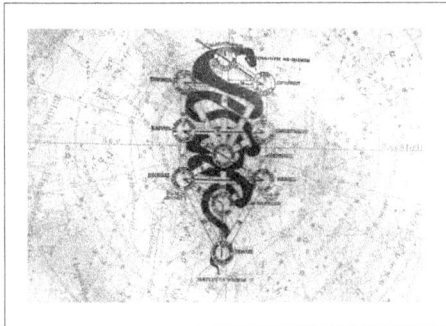

The magic of Tea Party's music is this interplay between the poles of madness, despair, desolation and soul breaking, ecstasy, remembrance and the struggle to find the kingdom.

Tree of Life within the realms of the Absolute, the back cover to *7 circles* Footnote: *"Remembrance is the secret of redemption Forgetfulness leads to exile."* Hebrew sage, Baal Shem Tov (Source: Jonathon Cott's On the Sea of Memory: A Journey from Forgetting to Remembering, 2005)

MARK COMINGS
physicist, mathematician and space science research

It is thirty years since physicist F. Capra, in the *Tao of Physics* (1975), noted similarities between the religious philosophies of the East and the concepts of modern physics. Scientist and mystic, Mark Comings is of the next generation of physicists to take such a perspective further and to elaborate the paradigm emerging for the new millennium. The following notes are based on Mark's lecture and workshop in Montreal (May, 2005) at the convention of the IIIHS attended by Dr. Holmes, and a review of his video *"The Courage to Change: An Exploration into Time, Space, Light and Mind,"* produced by Sirius Media, 2005. (***www.siriusmedia.org***)

SPACE

The most important concept being revised in modern physics is that of Space. What used to be called the "quantum vacuum," is now understood as the "quantum plenum," containing the absolute fullness of things. Mark notes that at the deepest substrates of being within the apparent emptiness of space are infinite energies and potentiality. He provides John Wheeler's estimate of 10^{94} grams/cm^3 or ergs, as the amount of energy latent everywhere within seemingly empty space. This amount is more than all that contained within the matter and energy of the larger universe outside. However, within the quantum plenum all the forces cancel each other out such that it all adds up to nothing, or seems to. Life in the quantum plenum is infinitely rich and this is the medium within which we as human beings live and move and have our being. Whereas life in the quantum vacuum sounds kind of empty and leads to a philosophy of scarcity, life in the quantum plenum offers a profound new model of the multidimensional nature of human existence and a philosophy of abundance.

Mark notes that Space is the 'ether' of modern times, a plenum of absolute fullness. He notes that this plenum is filled with a boundless luminosity, efflorescing with vacuum photons. At a certain level within the plenum of Space, Mark estimates the 'brightness of space' at a hundred times the luminosity of the Sun's corona. Space is pervaded by such luminosity. Mark suggests that there is an "ultra micro-structure of Space" and a hidden dynamic geometry, which is a generative field underlying material manifestation. Further, space is a "radial plenum," wherein each point can be considered as the centre of the whole. Most importantly, Mark conceives there to be an "intrinsic sentience" within Space itself—a view similar to that of Newton who regarded Space as "God's sensorium."

These insights of modern physics confirm Madame Blavatsky's teachings of ***The Secret Doctrine:***

> Space is neither a "limitless void," nor a "conditioned fulness," but both: being, on the plane of absolute abstraction, the ever-incognizable Deity, which is void only to finite minds, but on that of mayavic perception, the Plenum, the absolute Container of all that is, whether manifested or unmanifested: it is, therefore, that ABSOLUTE ALL. (1888, pp. 8-9)

Life in the plenum of Space is one of abundance. Mark brings the physics to life as he reminds us that we ourselves exist in this Space, this plenum.

LIGHT, CONSCIOUSNESS AND MIND

Mark Comings also explores the physics of light and regards consciousness itself as a form of higher dimensional light with potentially unlimited degrees of freedom. Mark argues that there is a physics to the inner light of consciousness, just as there is to external light. Whereas modern materialist scientists have regarded consciousness as non-substantive, Mark identifies it with *"luminous inner light."* There is thus both a physics and metaphysics to such light and thus to consciousness. Mark notes: *"... the laws of outer light are cast in the image and similitude of the laws of the inner light."* He describes consciousness as *'higher dimensional light,'* wherein there are higher degrees of freedom—as in the spiritual domain. Mark thus suggests that there is a ***"spiritual physics of the inner light."***

These are profoundly valuable concepts which are supported throughout the mystical literature, but which are only beginning to make sense in terms of the new physics. When will humans see the light or gain the light which is within themselves, as the mystics have asked through the ages? The profound importance of this equation of consciousness with light and higher dimensional light is not easy to grasp, and we must grow in an inner understanding of what this means, like Plato's cave dwellers learning to turn around and to see the light of true existence. Mark Comings obviously has done this himself, as is evident in his heart felt descriptions of the inner light. Dr. Comings is attempting to articulate a physics of the inner light, which leads to metaphysics and higher dimensions. Space itself, in which we live and move and have our being, is thus a "multidimensional sea of radiance," and consciousness has a supernal light nature.

Mark describes a human being as a "hyper-dimensional crystal lattice" within the plenum, with an ***"indwelling light of consciousness."*** Mark describes how there might be a hierarchy of light all the way back to the Ayn Soph Aur (or limitless light) of the Kabbalist. The outer light forms are described as cast in the image and similitude of the inner light. However, Mark explains how we directly experience the flux of the inner light through your being. When talking about love and having courage (derived from the French for heart), he describes opening the heart and "letting the inner light flood through your being" directly experiencing the "flux of inner light through the body." At one point in the video, Mark states that if your heart opens, the "light floods through us." What is so profoundly important about Dr. Comings' work is the manner in which he brings home to us the direct applications of physics of light to understanding the dynamics of the inner world.

In his first Montreal lecture, Mark provided a valuable discussion of some of the basic physics of light. In particular, he noted how Maxwell's four primary equations describing light as an electro-magnetic force have been modified within modern times. Light came to be regarded as having two directions of oscillation, electric and magnetic, but not to oscillate along the third dimension. Maxwell's equations allowed for such compression waves along the third dimension, but these were ignored when it came to the practical applications of his equations. Mark thus regards light as having more a 'triune' rather than 'dualistic' nature, and further that light manifest in the three dimensional space itself has a higher dimensional physics to it. The supernal light which Mark depicts has *"... n degree of freedom"*--just as the limitless light of the Ayn Soph Aur for the Kabbalist.

"In is up, dimensionally." Mark's phrase captures the essential meaning of "within-without from zero-points," as used in my own writings. A new notion of Space is involved here, of a hyperspace or higher dimensional Space, pervading and underlying the space which we imagine is outside of us and around us. Phenomena within the three dimensional space are due to a metaphysics in higher dimensions, wherein we are all rooted into the Plenum and consciousness has an intrinsic 'light' nature. Potentially, human consciousness can, in the terms of the Dali Lama, merge with the 'mind of clear light.'

Mark Coming's equation of consciousness with light is a profoundly significant step forward in trying to understand the enigmas of human consciousness and the relationship of modern physics to ancient metaphysics. F. Capra, in the ***Tao of Physics*** (1975) provided a view of space as plenum and void, and of the quantum interconnectedness of phenomena, but Capra lacked a significant insight into the enigmas of consciousness and light, and then insights into the higher dimensional nature of light itself. M. Talbot, in ***The Holographic Universe***, had a holographic model but again lacked this essential insight into the mysteries of human consciousness as light, and of supernal light that emerging from within the grounds of being. Mark applies this all directly within ourselves, as this is how we as beings emerge out of the nothingness, the void/plenum, and can be illumined by the inner light. All of these things can be know within ourselves!

Whereas the simplistic materialist view of space as empty and non-sentient is not too promising and leads to a philosophy of *scarcity* and a view of death as the end, the emerging view of Space as the plenum, opens up a pretty vast universe for us as living human beings, ensouled in some manner but living multi-dimensional lives within such underlying realms of spirit, light and the plenum of Space.

A PARADIGM OF RADICAL ABUNDANCE

From his studies of free energy technologies to his descriptions of illumined consciousness, Mark offers a view of life in the plenum as that of abundance. He explores the deep physics of Space and Light, and the nature of the multi-dimensional universe in which we live, breath and have our being. Mark himself breaths new life into the most advanced ideas in physics by demonstrating how it all applies within the inner world. A human being exists within Space and can directly experience varied forms of inner illumination and consciousness. Mark's work highlights how the concepts of physics can be applied directly to understanding the inner life and Self.

In the paradigm of Radical Abundance, Mark describes these higher potentials within ourselves, especially of inner illumination and of love. The scarcity model of mainstream materialist science offers only a life in empty space with limited resources and ending at death. There is no inner light, spirit or soul, and consciousness is left out of the equation. Mark as both a scientist and mystic, has come to apply the ideas of physics directly to understanding the enigmas of human consciousness. Human consciousness involves somehow *light within Space*. Modern consciousness researchers do not generally even think that understanding consciousness has anything to do with understanding the nature of Space, light, or higher dimensions. Everyone in the mainstream of science assumes that material processes produce consciousness, although it's a complete mystery where, what and how, but certainly they do not consider that consciousness as some higher dimensional physics/metaphysics to it. However, it is this higher physics and metaphysics of consciousness, the heart and mind, which has been elaborated through the ages within the esoteric spiritual teachings of humankind. The discoveries of modern physics are increasing serving to illustrate the hidden meanings and science of the wisdom teachings.

The advantage of a mystical science approach to understanding life relative to the common scientific approach is brilliantly articulated by Rene Weber (1986). She explains in ***Dialogues with Scientists and Sages: The Search for Unity***:

> "The drive for unification is a link between the aims of science and mysticism. ... It is mysticism, not science, which

pursues the Grand Unification Theory with ruthless logic-the one that includes the questioner within the answer. Although the scientist wants to unify everything in one ultimate equation, he does not want to unify consistently, since he wants to leave himself outside that equation. ... Of the mystic, more is required. He is engaged in deconstructing and reconstructing not some neutral external reality, but himself. ...

"By analogy with the physicist's splitting of the atom, the mystic is engaged in splitting his self-centered ego and the three dimensional thinker that sustains it. ... in his altered state of consciousness, the mystic has learned to harmonize his awareness with the sub-atomic matter of which he is composed. In this process, he aligns himself with the deep-structure of nature. ... The mystic, a true alchemist, brings micro-level and macro-level together. ... All mystics seek the depths. ... A parallel principle drives both science and mysticism-the assumption that unity lies at the heart of our world and that it can be discovered and experienced by man. (pp. 6-13)

The mystical quest is to directly experience unity-not simply to know it with the mind as an intellectual abstraction. Hence, the mystic includes him/herself in the equation as he/she attempts to penetrate to the heart of being. Mark's explanations of the nature of Space and Consciousness as higher dimensional light provide valuable keys to understanding the paradigm of radical abundance and the possibilities for an illumined life within the plenum.

The problem with hard line materialist and sceptic scientists is that they leave consciousness out of their equations-and do not consider that there might be a substantive consciousness-especially one capable of directly experiencing the deep roots of matter, nature and creation. Consider the wisdom articulated by the Sufi sage, Ibn al'Arabi: ***"Know that since God created human beings and brought them out of nothingness into existence, they have not stopped being travelers."*** This comment suggests that the void, the emptiness, the plenum, higher space dimensions and root principles-these things discussed by scientists, are directly experienced by yogis, mystics and seers, you and I. In fact, you are never not experiencing these things, but you are simply unaware of it, because you do not know yourself, or understand the true origin and nature of your own consciousness and being. We ourselves emerge out of the nothingness of Space and are illumined by the light of consciousness.

Mystical teachings actually claim that to 'know self' at the deepest level leads to experiences of higher or more enlightened states of human consciousness, alternate forms of objective knowledge about the nature of Self, the universe and the inscrutable mysteries of nature, and even, to divine knowledge of God. Mystical knowledge involves the direct experiencing of the unity of life-within different realms and to different depths of penetration. If these kinds of states and experiences are indeed possible, then mysticism, by the criterion of science itself would indeed be more scientific than what are considered the so-called 'exact' science.

Unfortunately, modern science writers, such as B. Greene, P. Atkins, L. Smolin, all leave consciousness out of their equations. They don't imagine that the quantum physics could have anything to do with the nature of human consciousness, despite the fact that consciousness exists within space, and light is directly experienced in consciousness. What might physics have to do with consciousness? Mark Comings is making steps to elaborate the basic principles of such a new paradigm of human understanding—based exactly upon such a physics and metaphysics of consciousness, light and space. If we can understand such an illumined perspective on the nature of things, we find ourselves in a radical abundance. Unfortunately, we might also be somewhat horrified by the madness of humankind—ruled by the mode of ignorance, the philosophy of scarcity, with an economy based on fossil fuels and war, and an emotional pathology of fear, narcissism and self interest.

According to Mark Comings and in accord with my own work, consciousness must be understood in terms of the physics and metaphysics of light, space and higher dimensions. Mark's materials on these basic issues were immensely valuable and insightful, and there was so much more, all needing time to assimilate, revise and hear again and again.

HIGHER EDUCATION & SPIRITUAL SCIENCE
On the Failure of Post Secondary Education and the New Inquisition[4]

Swami Prabhupada: ... everyone has dormant consciousness of God. ... It simply requires proper education to awaken it. However, this education is not given in the universities. That is the defect in modern education. ... (p. 7)

INTRODUCTION - 'A CERTAIN HOPELESSNESS'

I experience a certain hopelessness in trying to convey to you the seriousness of the deficits within the existing university and post-secondary educational system. There are many reasons for this sense of hopelessness, as will be clearly evident as this letter unfolds.

Firstly, my hopelessness arises because my concerns do not address the more familiar issues--such things as funding, accessibility, or organizational politics. Instead, I intend to critique the actual content of what is being taught within different university disciplines, particularly psychology, and to raise the issue of what is not being taught and researched within Ontario Universities. In my perspective-as a individual, as a psychologist, a scientist and a mystic, the most fundamentally important topics of "higher education" are actually not being explored at all within the universities!

---

[4]This article was written as a submission to the Robert Rae Review of Post-Secondary Education in the Province of Ontario, in December 2004. It was subsequently revised on February 2, 2006.

This is in fact an astonishingly ridiculous and stupid situation. Further, university education in a number of disciplines is propagating a whole false system of knowledge and conducting whole areas of insignificant research, all of which is fundamentally misguided, a waste of time, energies and trees. This picture illustrates the idea of how we might have a whole false system of knowledge, constructed by certain types of intellectuals and thinkers, which system of knowledge is quite illusory and unfounded. This is currently the case in the Ontario University system-that much of what passes as learning, knowledge and social science simply involves wrong ideas, wrong viewpoints, misunderstanding and imagination-with little foundation in reality.

Not only do we have this massive problem and confusion, particularly within the soft social sciences and philosophy, but further, there is a new form of inquisition present within the university system-which prevents academic freedom and the serious exploration of the most profound mysteries of life and human existence!

I know that these sound like bombastic and exaggerated viewpoints, especially when you yourselves are likely to have been educated, or 'conditioned,' within the present university system and are likely to share the same false understanding of the nature and significance of human life. Most academics and scientists live with some kind of split between what they think they know in their minds and what they might feel or not feel within their hearts.

Anyway, I will try to explain some of these issues and illustrate my viewpoints with concrete examples and explanations-including the results from a survey which I have conducted of Canadian Universities and with some exploration of my own history as a university professor at York University from 1977 to 1990. Over an eight year period or more, I was involved at York University in a dispute over academic freedom and raising the same issues I am raising here.

Please try to be patient and consider seriously the issues that I am raising-which are otherwise unrecognized within the university system itself, by committees or among the general public. I am not simply trying to dredge up past history, or to make headlines, but I sincerely believe in the importance of these issues. As you will see, concrete evidences will be presented as to the truth of the matters which I address.

The last time I wrote a letter like this was in 1984 to the Bovey Commission on the Future Development of the Universities of Ontario. (Toronto Star, *What's in store for our universities?*, October 2, 1984) [5] These issues were completely ignored previously and will likely be similarly ignored by your committee this time, as history tends to repeat itself unless people wake up and change in their hearts: And this is what all the head scientists do not know or understand. Of course, the previous complete disregard by the Bovey Commission of the serious issues I raised will likely simply be repeated by your own Commission. Of course, this is another factor for a sense of hopelessness which I have in regards to the writing of this letter. [6]

---

[5] The Toronto Star article read: "*Mystics dished up the last public pitch to a provincial commission on universities yesterday before the group meets in private today to decide their fate. It was an ironic twist. Caught between a staggering mandate and a deadline that has been ridiculed as too short, the commission just may need a mystic to pull off the task Queens Park has handed it. ...*

"*Yesterday, Christopher Holmes, a cofounder of the Institute for Mystical and Spiritual Science, told the commission that every campus needs a department of mystic studies and asked the commission to recommend funding for them. "Self-knowledge is the key to true wisdom," said a brief from the Institute.*"

[6] As expected, there was never any response from the Robert Rae review to this submission, which was also not posted on the web site along with other submissions to the committee. This is despite the fact that C. Holmes handed this report in person to Robert Rae on December 8th, 2004 and he said that he would read it, and his request that it be posted. Follow up telephone and email contacts were subsequently ignored. The report was also submitted to the Minister of Education, G. Kennedy, in January of 2005 with a request to meet with the Minister of Education to discuss the brief. The scheduler from the Minister's office, wrote to me on January 19, 2005 to inform me that someone would contact me in "the near future" to inform me whether or not the Minister's schedule would permit such a meeting. Of course, again, I have received any further letters or emails. Effectively, both the Robert Rae review and the Minister of Education ignored the issues raised by the brief. On May 25th, I received a letter from the office of the Premier of Ontario thanking me for my submission and telling me how much money the government is further investing to "deliver an educated and skilled workforce." The form letter ends with the line: "*Be assured that my colleagues and I will continue to take your views into consideration as we work to deliver the results Ontarians demand and deserve.*" In the three page summary of their report and financing, there is no mention of anything related to "my views." The 'sense of hopelessness' did indeed appear to be well founded.

Of course, perhaps this brief has found a broader distribution as a manifesto for some higher education, which doesn't simply train the brains for the workshops, as suggested by the Premier's letter. He states: "*The brains and know-how of a skilled workforce are the competitive edge of the 21st century.*" There is no mention of the awakening of consciousness and the heart, or investigations of spirit and soul, or attaining extended faculties of the mind.

THE PUBLIC'S BELIEFS AND INTERESTS

Despite sciences' advances in explaining many aspects of the mind and the physical universe, there is still widespread "belief" throughout society in supernatural forces and phenomena. The vast majority of people believe in some kind of spiritual reality or God and/or claim themselves to have had psychic and mystical experiences.

Two classic surveys by sociologist, Andrew Greeley, demonstrated that belief in mystical, spiritual and psychic realities is indeed widespread and the norm in American society. Greeley surveyed 1467 subjects in 1973 and 1474 in 1984. Sample statistics from Greeley's study show that 67% of Americans claim to have had ESP experiences; 73% believe in life after death; 74% believe that they will be re-united with loved ones after death; and 42% claim to have had contact with the dead. Surveys by the Gallop Organization over the years are consistent with these estimates. Gallop found that 43% of subjects (in 1985) had an unusual spiritual experience; 71% believed in afterlife (in 1981); 95% believed in God or a Universal Spirit, and so on. A 2003 survey by the Barna Research Group in California demonstrated that 76% of Americans believe in the existence of heaven and 71% in the existence of hell, while only 5% of the sample said that there is no afterlife, and another 5% said they were not sure. (Ottawa Citizen, October 25, 2003). Clearly, the vast majority of the American population believe in the existence of the human spirit or soul and that human beings survive physical death in some form within some afterlife realm.

In Canada, similar patterns are evident: A 1984 Gallop poll reported that 87% of the Canadian population believe in the existence of God; 71% in the existence of heaven; 39% in hell; and 29% in reincarnation. (Toronto Star, 1984) A more recent VisionTV/TIME pole found that 81% of Canadians strongly (66%) or somewhat (15%) agree that they believe in God; and 60% believed in the existence of heaven and/or hell-other dimensions of afterlife existence. When asked whether "having an inner spiritual life" was important, 51% of the sample described this as "very important" and a further 26% as "somewhat important." (TIME, November 24, 2003)

Well, although having a spiritual life is rated as important by the majority of Canadians and despite the widespread belief in such possibilities, these profoundly important issues are almost completely ignored within the educational system and within the mainstream of modern psychology and science. In fact, there are no Canadian psychology departments offering investigations of spiritual or mystical psychologies, any 'science of the soul' or investigations of psychical and paranormal phenomena.

Greeley (1987) discounts the sceptics' claim that belief in such supernatural things as spirit or soul, simply reflect the prevalence of mental illness or of religious convictions among the population. In fact:

> ... our studies show that people who've tasted the paranormal, whether they accept it intellectually or not, are anything but religious nuts or psychiatric cases. They are, for the most part, ordinary Americans, somewhat above the norm in education and intelligence and somewhat less than average in religious involvement. We tested people who'd had some of the deeper mystical experiences ... with the Affect Balance Scale of psychological well-being, a standard measure of the healthy personality. And the mystics scored at the top. Norman Bradburn, the University of Chicago psychologist who developed the scale, said no other factor has ever been found to correlate so highly. (p. 48)

Indeed, most people in our technological culture do not accept the conclusions of materialist science and soul-less psychology. Beliefs in God, psychic and spiritual realities are pervasive, and in fact on the upswing. Further, studies show that psychical experiences and spiritual beliefs are associated with psychological and physical health, social adjustment and creativity-rather than indicating psychological difficulty, social maladjustment or intellectual naiveté.

There is, in fact, a fundamental split between what the scientists think they know with their minds and what people intuitively feel in their hearts. The scientific mind imagines that we live in a purely material universe, with no God or gods, or any type of divine, spiritual or psychical forces within the psyche or mind, or within nature. On the other hand, most people belief 'in their hearts,' that there is something far deeper and more significant to human life than simply being a material biological being, which lives and dies with the body. Most people do believe in such things as God, afterlife, psychical forces and the like.

Although scientists usually dismiss such spiritual or soul possibilities as simply imagination, religious doctrines and conditioning, illusions and delusions, errors in thinking, 'as beliefs,' and so on, this is never proven. Further, most scientists simply ignore or dismiss the massive experimental and scientific evidences gathered over the past century, which already establishes the validity of all kinds of unexplained paranormal phenomena. To understand how such paranormal things are possible would require a radical new paradigm within psychology and within other areas of science. Generally, modern western society lives with this split between the mind and the heart, science and religion, which is a great disservice to both to the advance of science, particularly psychology, and to the general public interested in and believing in, spirituality.

The most significant areas of human investigation into the mysteries of life, from my perspective as a mystic scientist, concern the existence and nature of the human spirit and soul, the nature of human consciousness, the faculties of extended mind and the mechanisms underlying all the paranormal phenomena occurring all the time within the lives of broad segments of the population. Surveys done by varied scientists and polling organizations consistent find that the large majority of the public either 'believe' in, or have directly experience of, varied forms of psychical or paranormal phenomena, or have had spiritual experiences and realizations. Yet despite the overwhelming interest among the public in the issues of the heart and soul, it is exactly these areas of investigation and human inquiry which are completely ignored within 'modern' post-secondary education-particularly within psychology, but also within other disciplines and areas of science and education.

AN INTERNET SURVEY OF CANADIAN UNIVERSITY PSYCHOLOGY DEPARTMENTS

I have recently conducted a survey over the internet of Canadian Universities in order to determine what is offered in the areas of spiritual and mystical psychology, psychology as a science of the soul, consciousness studies, or paranormal investigations, within our university system. In particular, I have reviewed the psychology programs at the Universities of Victoria and Vancouver in British Columbia, the University of Alberta, the University of Regina-Saskatchewan, the University of Winnipeg-Manitoba, three Universities in Ontario-York University, the University of Waterloo and Carleton University, McGill University in Quebec and the major Universities in P. E. I., New Brunswick, Newfoundland and Nova Scotia. This survey has examined the psychology programs of thirteen universities in Canada from coast to coast.

The survey was conducted by exploring the web sites of the varied psychology programs, counting up how many undergraduate and graduate courses are offered in each department and how many of these had anything to do with consciousness studies, investigations of the human spirit or soul, paranormal phenomena and the like. Further, I investigate how many professors there are in each program and how many of these have any interest or expertise in these areas.

In brief:

The University of Victoria

The University of Victoria (www.uvic.ca/psyc) offers 41 different undergraduate courses in various areas of psychology and over 20 graduate courses, with 47 full time professors and 7 part time. The university offers no courses on consciousness or spiritual studies and no professors describe expertise in these areas.

The University of Vancouver

The University of Vancouver (www.ubc.ca) offers 41 undergraduate courses and 20 graduate courses with 47 full time professors and 7 part time. Once again, there are no courses on consciousness or spiritual psychologies, and no professor describes themselves as having any interest or expertise in these areas. Thus, British Columbia's two largest universities have effectively banished the study of spirit and soul, consciousness and the heart, and the mysteries of the human psyche from the province. Quite impressive BC!

The University of Alberta

The University of Alberta (www.ualberta.ca) offers 50 different undergraduate courses and 17 graduate courses with 30 full time faculty. Once again, nothing is offered in the said areas and no faculty members have expertise in these subjects. One course which mentions consciousness studies is offered from a cognitive perspective (which offers exactly what I would describe as the false understanding which pervades the modern discipline of psychology.)

The University of Regina, Saskatchewan

The University of Regina, Saskatchewan (www.uregina.ca/arts/psych) is the one university found which offers some courses in the areas of this inquiry. Of 85 undergraduate courses and 41 graduate courses, there are four course offerings which include "Studies in yoga," "Consciousness Studies," "Humanistic/Transpersonal Psychology" and "Parapsychology." These specialty courses are not consistently offered and were not part of the core curriculum. The University of Regina should be commended for at least offering some courses in these areas. Of the 13 main faculty members who describe their work, none of them list expertise in the areas of discussion. The courses which are offered would appear to be offered by part-time faculty members.

The University of Winnipeg, Manitoba

In Manitoba, the University of Winnipeg (www.uwinnipeg.ca) offers 67 undergraduate courses and lists 21 faculty members, and offers no courses on consciousness studies, spiritual psychology or paranormal studies, and no professors have expertise in these areas.

Ontario

Next, we come to the province of Ontario, in our survey. It is in the province where I received my so-called "higher education"- first as an undergraduate at Carleton University and then as a graduate student at the University of Waterloo. In fact, I was never exposed to anything along the line of what I now understand as mystical and spiritual psychology, consciousness studies etc., throughout my nine years of 'higher education.' I received a Ph.D. in 1978. I was then employed at York University from 1977 to 1989 and once again never encountered any other faculty members or courses on these topics-except those courses which I taught during my time at York. Thus in my twenty years of exposure to the Ontario higher educational system, I was never exposed to any influences, investigations or teachings in these areas. This in fact was a huge disservice to me.

Fortunately, I encountered such influences and teachings during my Ph.D. studies, not from within the university but from outside, and I have since studied these areas for approximately forty years, along with my studies of psychology and science. Anyway, I will review the programs at Carleton University, the University of Waterloo and York University in order to explore what is available to students within our so-called 'progressive' post-secondary educational system in the province of Ontario.

Carleton University

Carleton University (Www.carleton.ca/psychology) offers approximately 50 undergraduate courses and 27 graduate courses-with nothing offered in the areas of our concern. Of the 49 faculty members in the department, no one acknowledges any interests or expertise in these areas, as far as I could determine (giving the limitations of the web search.)

The University of Waterloo

The University of Waterloo (psych@watarts.uwaterloo.ca) offers approximately 38 undergraduate courses and 40 graduate courses (although these figures are somewhat difficult to determine from the web site). These programs are offered by 26 full time professors and 14 adjunct professors. Once again, there are no courses offered in the areas we are exploring and no professors acknowledge interest or expertise in these areas.

York University

Lastly, we come to York University in Downsview, Ontario. (www.arts.yorku.ca/psych). York boasts one of the biggest psychology departments in the country and offers approximately 48 undergraduate courses and 81 graduate courses, with over 60 full time professors. At York, once again, there are no courses at either the graduate or undergraduate areas offered on any of the topic of our concern and no faculty member offers any expertise in these areas.

To further investigate York University, I sent them the following question by email. This was sent under an email address other than my own, because of my past notoriety at York. The question was posed by an inquiry student who wants to study spiritual psychology in the province of Ontario, or anywhere in Canada for that matter. The question read:

I am interested in whether or not your department offers
any courses on spiritual or mystical psychology,
the study of paranormal or psychic phenomena,
or studies of human consciousness.
I am interested in courses in these areas.
Do you know of any professors with such interests who yoo
might direct me to? Thank you.

The response from Anita H. of the York University Undergraduate office, read simply:

We do not offer any courses in these areas. (November 9, 2004)

McGill University, Montreal, Quebec

Moving onward to McGill University, Montreal, Quebec, (www.psych.mcgill.ca), the department offers 63 undergraduate courses and 49 graduate courses, with 43 full time professors and 16 part time. Again, there were no course offerings in these areas and no professors described interests or expertise on these subjects. The response to the email inquiry stated: *"I'm afraid there isn't anyone in that area here in psychology"* and it was suggested that I *"try religious studies."*

University of New Brunswick, Fredericton

The four remaining eastern provinces demonstrate the same patterns. The University of New Brunswick, Fredericton (www.unb.ca), offers over 50 undergraduate courses and 38 graduate courses with 17 full time professors, yet offers nothing within these areas.

The University of Nova Scotia in Halifax

The University of Nova Scotia in Halifax (www.dal.ca) offers 62 undergraduate courses over 20 graduate courses with 34 full time professors and similarly provides no instruction or expertise in these areas for students.

University of Prince Edward Island

Lastly, and not least, the University of Prince Edward Island (www.upei.ca) offers over 49 undergraduate courses with 13 full time professors, while the

University of Newfoundland

University of Newfoundland (www.mun.ca) offers over 53 undergraduate courses and 29 graduate courses with 29 full time faculty, yet again both departments completely ignore all the issues of human consciousness, spirit and soul, and the issues of the heart.

The results of the survey are clear. There are approximately 429 full time psychology faculty in thirteen universities across Canada and none of them have expertise in these areas of our concern. There is no possibility for students in Canada to be exposed to the esoteric and spiritual psychologies of humankind; as such teachings are completely ignored within the modern *"science of behaviour and the mind."* Of the 697 undergraduate courses offered across Canada, there were four secondary course offerings exploring alternative models and transpersonal areas, all at one University. Of the 382 graduate level courses offered across Canada, there are no opportunities for students to study any aspects of human consciousness, spirit or soul, or paranormal studies. Modern psychology has effectively dismissed the most solitary important area of psychological investigation from the discipline.

The primary deficit of modern post-secondary education and the so-called scientific psychology dominant within Canadian Universities is that the issues of consciousness, the heart and the soul, the nature of spirit, and paranormal phenomena are almost completely ignored. Meanwhile, much of the theory and research being conducted is severely misguided, ill-informed and invented, with little advantage to the study of the human psyche. The modern approach to "cognitive psychology"-the big rage, supposedly at the forefront of psychology, is quite misguided in its approach to consciousness studies.

In fact, if someone were to come to me seeking "self-knowledge" or seeking to understand the nature and mysteries of consciousness and reality, I would strongly advise against pursuing academic studies in psychology, as well as in other areas of university education, which similarly lack a mystical/spiritual perspective. Modern psychology has almost completely abandoned the investigation of the mysteries of life, the heart, and human consciousness. If a person is spiritually inclined, modern academic studies will create enough confusion and misguided notions, as to squelch any such natural 'thirst for being.'

Thus, we have a situation where psychology departments offer no service to the vast majority of Ontario residents who might want to study spiritual psychology, seek self-knowledge, or who want to understand paranormal phenomena (as occur all the time in everyday life.) The pseudo-scientists have simply closed their eyes to the most important areas of psychological studies and "higher education." The universities in this way are failing to meet their mandate to foster spiritual growth within our society or to foster investigations into the mysteries of life.

If people only had some realization of this profound deficit in modern education, particularly in the supposed modern study of psychology, they would be appalled.

THE STRANGE CASE OF PROFESSOR Z: ON THE IDEALS OF MURRAY ROSS, ACADEMIC FREEDOM & THE RIGHTS OF STUDENTS

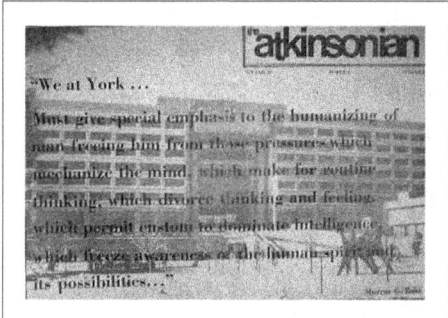

"We at York ... must give special emphasis to the humanizing of man freeing him from those pressures which mechanize the mind, which make for routine thinking, which divorce thinking and feeling, which permit custom to dominate intelligence, which freeze awareness of the human spirit and its possibilities."

Murray Ross

These words are engraved in stone at York University over the arches of the Murray Ross building and they express an excellent ideal of what "higher education" might involve, including *"unfreezing awareness of the human spirit."* This quotation was used extensively by myself and students in defence of my work at York during my struggles there for academic freedom. Students knew that the mystical/spiritual perspectives which I was introducing did exactly what Murray Ross had posed as an ideal for higher education and that apart from my teaching, they had no other options along this line-dealing with 'unfreezing awareness' and the 'human spirit.' Fortunately, Murray Ross had not been educated within the York University psychology department and still had some spiritual inspiration.

"The Strange Case of Professor Z" was the title of a long fifty page letter I wrote in 1988 protesting my dismissal from York and explaining the history of my struggle for academic freedom. The phrase "professor Z" was based on an article from the Canadian Association of University Teachers (C.A.U.T.) newsletter dealing with the issue of academic freedom. This article had talked about a hypothetical "Professor Z" who had an orientation different from his colleagues and how this might lead to situations where

academic freedom could be violated and professors would be denied tenure because of holding a different orientation from his colleges:

> "The term academic freedom as it is applied to the individual professor is defined ... as the freedom "to teach, investigate, and speculate, without deference to prescribed doctrine." I have chosen in this paper to focus on the danger to academic freedom, as understood, that can emerge from the peer evaluation system. ...
>
> ... Professor Z's approach to his discipline differs from that of the majority of his colleges; his pedagogical theories and practice are not traditional; the orientation of his research is not at the moment widely accepted in his discipline. Now, are we bound in this instance to accept the results of the peer evaluation? ... is there a possibility that this denial of tenure constitutes a violation of the academic freedom of Professor Z? ...There are significant conflicts over orientation within every discipline. Quite apart from the rights of the individual faculty member, it is gain, rather than loss for students to be exposed directly to these conflicting views."

After I was denied tenure in 1984, by the ministry of double-talk, I filed a grievance within the university over this issue of academic freedom. The grievance procedure led to the establishment of a committee to review my case, and in 1985, the majority of faculty members on the committee decided in my favour suggesting that there had been a denial of my academic freedom and they recommended to the University that my case be reassessed. Unfortunately, for political reasons, influence peddling and such, the University would not accept the Committee's decision. This simply forced a new level of arbitration, where CAUT took up my case and more years of delay! No-one thought these matters needed immediate attention but 'due process' allowed the University to more simply dispel student protests and wash their hands of the matter. CAUT actually took up my case and was involved for years but in a totally ineffectual manner, where their own agenda was more important of the truth of my situation. Anyway, I subsequently used to the phrase "professor Z" to refer to myself and my years of struggle for academic freedom at York University.

When I was teaching mystical/spiritual psychologies and investigating paranormal phenomena while at York, there was an overwhelmingly positive student response to my work, and wide student protest over my dismissal. A sample of student commentary gives a sense of the enthusiasm which students had for alternative perspectives:

> "I think that the issues examined in the class are important; in fact, vital. People have to start asking why they believe the things they do and why they don't believe other things. The world is a wonderful place. We should start looking at it with a sense of mystery. Only then could we do it justice. This class exposes people to some of the world's incredible mysteries and encourages people to ask questions. I've been at this university for 4 years and this class has been an incredibly valuable experience.
>
> "Eastern psychology or alternatives to Western Psychology in general, are sadly lacking at York University or any other North American University I have heard of. The dismissal of this course by high handed tunnel visioned executives should be a travesty of justice and the freedom to think in new and different ways. The efforts of York University to rail road Dr. Holmes from this establishment of 'higher learning.' is an example of how close minded academics and society at large are still basically unwilling to stray from the beaten path and that conservatism is still prevalent in our world.
>
> "I feel that the materials presented in this course are more relevant than any other teachings, I have ever been exposed to, they are applicable in all aspects of study (including self study) and there is no question in my mind that it is of the utmost relevance to continue Professor Holmes' work at York University. ... My interests have gone from singular and unrelated ideas and opinions to a multitude of perspectives leading to the same organized and comprehensive understanding. I am very thankful for the honour of being exposed to Professor Holmes and his teaching, for such knowledge and teachers are rare in this 'modern' world. I would feel genuinely distressed if the opportunity was not available to anyone who had the insight and courage to

reach out and see the world, their world in a more deep and insightful manner.

"This course gave me a higher understanding of myself & the world around me. I feel it's an excellent course & I would recommend it to everyone.

"It would be tragic to remove this course from the curriculum.

"I felt that this course is very beneficial to the study of psychology. It is important to be exposed to all areas of thought dealing with the human mind and human being. Psychology has become so far removed from the element of mysticism and it is frightening that the study of the mind has become too scientific and mechanic. I have found out more about myself and understanding myself, while Dr. Holmes was always sure to relate his material to modern psychology today. ... Chris Holmes is a very original, well informed teacher who is interested in bringing knowledge to his students. ... The course is tough but worth it.

These are only a sample of hundreds of favourable student comments offered on my teaching and work at York University. One anonymous student wrote this comment on my case, which was frequently quoted in my own protest letters:

"I don't know who is reading this but whoever it is, know this. To get rid of this professor through blind ignorance and tunnel vision, and hence this subject matter, is a crime to higher education."

The proceedings at York did indeed perpetrate such a "crime" against the ideals of academic freedom, against Murray Ross's dedication of the Ross Building and most importantly, against the students who were so enthusiastic to be exposed to an alternative perspective on the issues of psychology, consciousness, the spirit and soul, and so on. Part of my problem while at York was my popularity as a teacher, not because of myself so much, as because of the viewpoints, ideas and practical teachings, to which students were exposed. A mystical and spiritual psychology is far more practical and useful to students than the standard cognitive and behavioural dogmas now encrusted within academic psychology departments.

Anyway, in 1989, the elected student federation at York, voted unanimously to protest my dismissal. The President of the Student Federation, Tammy Hasselfeldt, penned a protest letter on behalf of the student council. This letter read in part:

> "A fundamental concern we have with regards to Prof. Holmes case is that of academic freedom. It seems that in a university dedicated to the search for truth and to spiritual values in education, it is outrageous to dismiss the one professor who would bring such a perspective to York's psychology department and into the larger university. It would seem that at York of all places, a professor and a scientist should have the right, individually and professionally, to explore the areas of psychical, mystical and spiritual studies. Instead, it appears that Dr. Holmes has faced varied forms of irresponsible academic assessments. Not only is this suggested by student commentary, but also by other evidences.
>
> "To the vast majority of students, especially those who have studied with Dr. Holmes, the importance of researching and learning in these areas of psychic, mystical and spiritual ideas and teachings is highly obvious! Many students further describe Dr. Holmes teaching as highly valuable in a personal way, and as providing an important perspective in education.
>
> "The dismissal of Dr. Holmes and his perspective from York is in complete disregard of student opinion, and of our right to be exposed to progressive education in an atmosphere of academic freedom and tolerance. ... (January 17, 1989)

This letter was sent to the President of the University, Deans, the Senate, and even to the then Minister of Education, Lyn McLeod. No-one even responded to this strong appeal and protest from the student government of the university!

Ms. Hasselfeldt makes a number of important points in her letter- particularly that: *"To the vast majority of students, especially those who have studied with Dr. Holmes, the importance of researching and learning in these areas of psychic, mystical and spiritual ideas and teachings is highly obvious!"* Although one might think that this would be an obviously important areas of study, in fact, these are the areas completely ignored with modern so-called institutes of higher learning, despite the profound importance of the issues addressed! As the survey results demonstrate, psychology departments in Ontario and Canada offer almost nothing in these areas. This really is quite outrageous, but it passes by unrealized because people do not know what such studies involve and how important they are to the advancement of psychology as a discipline and to the evolution of humankind.

The dogmatists of modern psychology and materialist science philosophy perpetrate a terrible disservice to their students and the general public by the complete ignoring of these areas of study, and further, even persecuting those who do explore these areas. My case at York University was one case wherein I was the heretic and essentially persecuted, while the opinions of thousands of students were ignored. During the same period, Howard Eisenberg, author of *Inner Spaces: Parapsychological Explorations of the Mind* (Mussen Book Co, 1977), went through a similar process of persecution at the University of Toronto and opposition to his teaching. Further, Ian Currie, author of *You Cannot Die: The incredible findings of a century of research on Death* (Methuen, Toronto, 1978), underwent harassment and opposition at the University of Guelph. Both of these individuals shared something of their struggles with me during the 1980's when the inquisition was in full sway. Howard Eisenberg gave a public lecture attended by over a hundred fellows at the University of Toronto on his case, as I attended it. There may well be other similar cases over the past twenty years, but I have yet to make an attempt to investigate this.. The internet survey results clearly indicate the almost complete absence of such explorations in modern psychology and the Canadian University system.

The psychology departments of Ontario and Canada have effectively banished spirit, soul and human consciousness from their studies of the human psyche! If current students or the broader public really understood the terrible disservice to students and society which this neglect perpetuates, they might wake up enough to demand change. Most likely, no one will step up to the plate and examine this issues seriously, but instead, will simply ignore such a disturbing portrait of their own favorite "higher education"-just as the student letters of protest on my behalf were simply ignored; as well as the petition run by Excalibur, the York Student newspaper, which collected over a thousand names. No one in authority paid any heed to the protests, but simply washed their hands of the case and postponed addressing the profound issues involved. It was indeed a 'crime' to higher education, when I was dismissed from York and I think of those thousands of students who were deprived of the opportunity to see the world through a mystical and spiritual perspective.

And now, twenty years after I was driven out of York, dedicated to unfreezing awareness of the human spirit, what does York University offer in these profound of investigation, science and self-study? As the undergraduate secretary states in her email to an inquiring student: *"We do not offer any courses in these areas."*

It was a crime then and it is a crime today, that our educational system does not allow students the opportunity to study the esoteric mystical and spiritual psychologies, philosophies and science-which are, in important areas, far ahead of modern so-called 'exact psychology' when it comes to understanding the true nature of human beings. Modern psychologists have no idea of how limited and superficial the modern discipline has become and what fundamental mistakes have been made. Further, they would gladly persecute anyone like Professor Z.

PUBLIC ACCOUNTABILITY AND THE FAILURE OF MODERN EDUCATION, MODERN PSYCHOLOGY AND THE ONTARIO UNIVERSITIES

the term 'psychology' is actually derived from the Greek terms 'psyche,' signifying soul and 'logos,' signifying knowledge. The original meaning of psychology thus suggested a "science of the soul." Unfortunately, attempts to investigate such areas constitute the 'new heresy' of modern times, and there is considerable fear within academic and so-called scientific circles of mixing what is thought to be "real science" with what is considered to be vague spirituality or mystical speculations. Sociologist A. Greeley described a *"scientific iron curtain raised against serious research on these experiences"*- of the mystical, psychical and spiritual. Similarly, even back in 1888, occult scholar Madame Blavatsky, noted that: *"In our day, scientists are more self-opinionated and bigoted than even the clergy."*

Unfortunately, the study of spiritual teachings and psychologies is regarded as perhaps relevant to the study of religion, but not considered to be relevant to the so-called 'science' of psychology or to the study of academic philosophy and the life sciences. In reality, such perspectives are relevant to every department of knowledge, including the hard sciences of physics, cosmology, medicine, and so on. I have focussed my critique on modern psychology, because I am a psychologist and have most expertise in this area. However, the same issues and problems exist in relation to other disciplines and I have known of even established professors in other disciplines fearing that their mystical or spiritual interests be known.

The lack of spiritual psychology and science is surprising because of the fact that there are huge scientific and research literatures establishing the validity of ESP, psychokinesis, near-death experiences, ghosts, remove viewing, past life memories and varied other paranormal phenomena. These 'system-destroying facts' illustrate that there is something fundamentally mistaken in modern soul-less psychology and materialist science philosophy. Modern psychologists dismiss all of these areas of inquiry and make no efforts to understand the hidden nature of the human psyche. They simply close their eyes to all the system-destroying facts and pursue relatively insignificant issues within some specialty, of some sub-division of psychology. The most important psychological issues are almost completely ignored. Psychology today might be compared with Newtonian physics, which has yet to undergo any significant paradigm shift over the past century.

However, if human beings have a spiritual or soul nature, then much of modern university instruction, especially in the area of the soft sciences and philosophy, is all quite fanciful and imaginary. Much of university instruction is in fact simply memorization of the wrong ideas and invented theories of previous wiseacres and misguided intellectuals.

The ignoring of the most profound areas of human investigation-into mystical and spiritual teachings, and the science of self-realization as taught through the ages-in the modern universities is a great disservice to student, to the public and to the advancement of science itself. Whereas the natural sciences have made tremendous advances, modern psychology is based upon fundamental mistakes and knows nothing of the true nature of human beings. Human beings are multi-dimensional beings and there is a huge body of scientific evidence establishing this fact. Unfortunately, such viewpoints are the new heresies and earlier inquisitions within the Ontario University system have banished such influences in order to pursue the petty concerns and theoretical squabbling of modern theorists.

Swami Prabhupada, representing the spiritual/mystical teachings of ancient India, makes some interesting claims about what should be the main focus of the educational system::

> Swami: You should try to understand this science of God consciousness. ... everyone has dormant consciousness of God. ... It simply requires proper education to awaken it. However, this education is not given in the universities. That is the defect in modern education. ... Because our government does not know that life, especially human life, is meant for understanding God, they are supporting all the departments of knowledge very nicely except the principal department, God consciousness. ... Reasons there may be many, but the principal reason is that this age is the Kali-yuga (dark age). People are not very intelligent; therefore they are trying to avoid this department of knowledge, the most important department of knowledge. ... You do not know so many things....
> (1980, pp. 7, 19)

Prabhupada claims that we all have dormant consciousness of God which can be awakened through proper education. Further, there is a "science of God consciousness," which the Vedas and a wide range of other esoteric mystical and spiritual teachings elaborate. In this perspective, there is something fundamentally fraudulent about modern materialist science and psychology, and the educational system. Scientists have ignored the most important issues of self-knowledge, the mysteries of human consciousness and the nature of the human spirit and soul.

I would like to thank the committee members for reviewing and considering this brief. You are likely now to realize how I might be disheartened, and experience a certain hopelessness in attempting to have these concerns be given serious attention. It is easy to dismiss me, as a mystic, especially when people have so little idea of what this entails and when routine thinking comes to dominate intelligence. It is because people in our society are so ignorant as to what mystical and spiritual psychologies involve, especially in academic circles, that these influences have been so widely ignored. Especially, this is troublesome when there is in fact a massive literature, scientific and anecdotal, which establishes the reality of such deeper realms as the scientists have hardly begun to imagine. It is indeed the Kali Yuga, or the age of ignorance-spiritual ignorance.

It is very easy to dismiss this letter as simply 'mystical looniness,' but really this is a disservice to the Canadian public and to all those students who might have been inspired to see the world and its mysteries anew-in the light of mystical psychology and science. In fact, from my perspective, we have no institutes of higher education because the most advanced models of the human psyche, of spirit and soul, are completely ignored, as well as the massive bodies of evidence which document the paranormal nature of life. Modern educators simply close their eyes to such enigmas, and pursue instead the modern pseudo-scientific psychological dogmas. Further, we have a new period of inquisition, wherein instead of the church persecuting scientific investigators, we have a body of pseudo-scientists and intellectuals who simply ignore the most profound issues of psychology and human life. This is a sad and disheartening situation.

Intelligent Design

GOD AND THE SCIENTISTS ON WHY WE DON'T NEED GOD NOW THAT WE HAVE PHYSICISTS WHO SIT AT DESKS.

Book Review of *The Grand Design* by Stephen Hawking & Leonard Mlodinow

It is almost irresistible for humans to believe that we have some special relation to the universe, that human life is not just a more-or-less farcical outcome of a chain of accidents reaching back to the first three minutes, but that we were somehow built in from the beginning. ... But if there is no solace in the fruits of our research, there is at least some consolation in the research itself. Men and women are not content to comfort themselves with tales of gods and giants, or to confine their thoughts to the daily affairs of life; they also build telescopes and satellites and accelerators, and sit at their desks for endless hours working out the meaning of the data they gather. Stephen Weinberg, *The First Three Minutes*, 1979 (pp. 143-4) [6]

The grandest thing about *The Grand Design* is its title and attractive front illustration. Otherwise, this is a most superficial and preposterous book which certainly adds little to the debate between science and religion, and once again, shows how credentials in science allow anyone to philosophize about the meaning of it all as if their scientific mantle confers a certain 'infallibility upon them. As Blavatsky stated in 1888, *"in our day, the scientists are even more opinionated than the clergy."* Scientists, like Hawking, Sagan and Weinberg, present their own personal biases and dogmas as if based on 'real science,' instead of simply being their own philosophy and a superficial one at that. *The Grand Design* provides only glimpses of modern theories in physics and the most preposterous declarations about what they all mean.

In the first chapter, *The Mystery of Being*, Hawking espouses his attitudes towards 'philosophers' and he states the intention of the book:

> … philosophy is dead. Philosophy has not kept up with modern developments in science, particularly physics. Scientists have become the bearers of the torch of discovery in our quest for knowledge. The purpose of this book is to give the answers that are suggested by recent discoveries and theoretical advances. (p. 5)

In Chapter 1, Hawking and Mlodinow introduces one particular theoretical advance which they regard as promising to explain many of the enigmas of science concerning the laws of nature and the fine tuning of natural laws as required to explain the emergence of life. The authors state: *"we now have a candidate for the ultimate theory of everything, if indeed one exists, called M-theory."* The book certainly sounds promising and the authors state their intentions:

---

[6] In addition to reading *The Grand Design*, i have managed to watch Leonard Mlodinow on the Larry King Show on CNN along with Stephen Hawking and commentators; and to have listened to some of Dr Mlodinow interview on the Coast to Coast AM show with George Noory.

> We will describe how M-theory may offer answers to the
> question of creation. According to M-theory, ours is not
> the only universe. Instead, M-theory predicts a great many
> universes were created out of nothing. Their creation does not
> require the intervention of some supernatural being or god.
> Rather, these multiple universes arise naturally from physical
> laws. ... Thus our presence selects out from this vast array
> only those universes that are compatible with our existence.
> Although we are puny and insignificant on the scale of the
> cosmos, this makes us in a sense the lords of creation. (pp. 8-9)

Hawking likes to have this semi-mystical type element as a subtext to his writings, describing us as such 'lords of creation.' The authors then promise to explore three main questions:

> Why is there something rather than nothing?
> Why do we exist?
> Why this particular set of laws and not some other?
> This is the Ultimate Question of Life, the Universe, and
> Everything. (pp. 9-10)

These are pretty big promises, all to explain why we don't need God or a Creator any more, now that we have Stephen Hawking and Leonard Mlodinow, and other scientists who sit at their desks.

In Chapter 7, *The Apparent Miracle*, Hawking and Mlodinow address the issue of the 'fine tuning' of different environmental and physical laws which allow for the emergence of human life on this planet. They explain: *"Our solar system has other "lucky" properties without which sophisticated life-forms might never have evolved."* (p. 149) The earth is just the right distance from the sun so that the water neither boils nor freezes, the eccentricity of the earth's orbit is just 2 percent allowing for seasons, and there are many features of nature seeming atuned to allow organic life to evolve on earth. Whereas a religious person could regard this as due to the intelligence or design of a Creator, scientists explain such phenomena in terms of the 'weak anthropic principle.'

> Obviously, when the beings on a planet that supports life examine the world around them, they are bound to find that their environment satisfies the conditions they require to exist.
>
> It is possible to turn that last statement into a scientific principle: Our very existence imposes rules determining from where and at what time it is possible for us to observe the universe. That is, the fact of our being restricts the characteristics of the kind of environment in which we find ourselves. That principle is called the weak anthropic principle. ... the principle refers to how our knowledge of our existence imposes rules that select, out of all the possible environments, only those environments with the characteristics that allow life. (pp. 153-154)

As scientists have discovered more and more planets, and billions of stars and galaxies, it is apparent that there could be many different inhabited planets within the universe. If the earth hadn't been habitable, then we would not have been here to ask such questions. What seems perhaps to be due to fortunate circumstances or intelligent design is due to this type of self-selection process.

Hawking and Mlodinow then extend the weak into a 'strong anthropic principle' to apply the same logic to explaining why the laws of physics are so attuned to allow for the emergence of intelligent life.

> Environmental coincidences are easy to understand because ours is only one cosmic habitat among many that exist in the universe, and we obviously must exist in a habitat that supports life.
>
> The weak anthropic principle is not very controversial. But there is a stronger form that we will argue for here, although it is regarded with disdain among some physicists. The strong anthropic principle suggests the fact that we exist imposes constraints not just on our environment but on the possible form and content of the laws of nature themselves. The idea arose because it is not only the peculiar characteristics of our

> solar system that seem oddly conducive to the development of human life but also the characteristics of our entire universe, and that is much more difficult to explain. (p. 154)

The laws of nature are highly tuned in terms of the strength of the laws, the masses and charges of elements, and dozens or hundreds of other parameters, all of which allowed for the chain of events to occur which began with a big bang singularity and ended up with living beings who could look back in time at where they came from. Although many people *"would like us to use these coincidences as evidence of the work of God,"* Hawking and Mlodinow argue that we can now explain this in terms of the strong anthropic theory and knowledge of M-theory.

M-theory is described by Hawking and Mlodinow as not a singular unified theory, *"the traditional physicist's dream,"* but a network of theories, each good at describing phenomena within different ranges. M-theory developed out of string theory and has 11 space-time dimensions: including four large dimensions which we are ordinarily aware of and an underlying "internal space" of seven "compacted dimensions." M-theory does not contain only vibrating strings, or superstrings , but also point particles, two-dimensional membranes, objects called 'p-branes,' where p can vary from zero to nine, depending on the dimensionality of the elements. M-theory has provided a way of integrating five different model of string theory and supergravity theory into one network.

> There is an enormous number of ways in curl up these entities into higher dimensions of this 'internal space.' The mathematics of M-theory restricts the manner in which these internal dimensions are curled.
>
> The exact shape of the internal space determines both the values of physical constants, such as the charge of the electron, and the nature of the interactions between the elementary particles. In other words, it determines the apparent laws of nature. ...
>
> The laws of M-theory therefore allow for *different universes* with different apparent laws, depending on how the internal space is curled. M-theory has solutions that allow for many

different internal spaces, perhaps as many as 10^{500}, which means it allows for 10^{500} different universes, each with its own laws. ... M-theory allows for 10^{500} sets of apparent laws. (pp. 118-9)

This is an unimaginably vast number and yet in Hawking's views of quanta as represented by the 'sum over histories approach,' then all of these possibilities can occur. *"In this view, the universe appeared spontaneously, starting off in every possible way. ... the multiverse concept (but) these are just different expressions of the Feymman sum over histories."* (p. 136) In this view then, out of 10^{500} universes, some of these are going to have the properties that can lead to the evolution of life forms. We happened then to be one such this particular world, so-called *'lords of creation'* by fortunate opportunity. If the laws of nature were not so finely-tuned, we would not be here.

When scientists realized that there are billions of suns and solar systems, which can have planets and favourable conditions for the evolution of life, then the fact that there is life on earth does not seem such a miraculous occurrence, as there could be life forms on billions of planets. So now, Hawking and Mlodinow extend the weak anthropic principle covering environmental coincidences to the *strong anthropic principle* to account for the fine tuning of the laws of nature. Since M-theory postulates some unimaginably large number of possible universes with workable and non-workable dynamics, then the fact that some of them are just right, is not a matter of divine intelligence but of good luck, happenstance and M-theory. Hawking defines the M in M-theory as possibly referring to 'master,' 'miracle' or 'mystery', or 'all three.' M-theory is Hawking's holy trinity.

Hawking offers this philosophical commentary on the human situation:

> Were it not for a series of startling coincidences in the precise details of physical law, it seems, humans and similar life-forms would never have come into being. (p. 161)

> ... the multiverse concept can explain the fine-tuning of physical law without the need for a benevolent creator who made the universe for our benefit. (p. 165)

> We claim, however, that it is possible to answer these questions purely within the realm of science, and without invoking any divine beings. (p. 172)

Of course, one has to puzzle over this supposed solution to the fine-tuning of the laws of nature, that it is a simply fortuitous occurrence in a world of 10^{500} opportunities. Can such a concept be falsified? It seems that Hawking is simply offering another hypothesis to explain creation and of course, this is a valuable perspective to consider. However, we cannot simply conclude that this is the answer, as itself is so incomplete, seemingly arbitrary and circular in its logic. One scientist described the probability of evolution occurring by chance as being as likely as a tornado blowing through a junk yard and assembling a Boeing 747. Of course, if we had 10^{500} tornadoes, one never knows. What if we had 10^{500} monkeys typing on typewriters, could they produce the works of Shakespeare? Is such a theory or model falsifiable? Can 10^{500} angels dance on the head of a pin? Probably, in one of these universes.

And so how does Stephen Hawking solve the questions of, *'Why is there something rather than nothing?'* and *'Why do we exist?'* The idea of 'vacuum genesis,' creation out of the void/plenum of the quantum vacuum, has been around for thirty years in modern science. In theoretical physics, gravity is regarded as a negative form of energy and it is used to balance out the positive energy bound up in matter, such that the whole thing could add up to nothing! This can explain how a universe could be created out of nothing without violating the laws of the conservation of matter and energy. Hawking explains that because *"the positive energy of the manner can be balanced by the negative gravitational energy, and so there is no restriction on the creation of whole universes."* (p. 180) And so, why is there something rather than nothing? Hawking and Mlodinow, with a hop, a skip and a jump, conclude:

> Spontaneous creation is the reason there is something rather than nothing, why the universe exists, why we exist. It is not necessary to invoke God to light the blue torch paper and set the universe going. (p. 180)

Wow, this 'real science' has replaced one unknown God with another unknown, 'spontaneous creation.' In fact, Hawking and Mlodinow describe M-theory in this way as "a model of a universe that creates itself."

Certainly, this is an interesting hypothesis and theory but that does not validate it and in many ways this simply substitutes one unknown for another. Instead of God, now we have 'spontaneous generation' and our being here will be taken as proof of such circular arguments.

What is most disappointing about this book is the meager amount of time and space used to explain M-theory, new models of higher dimensional space, the holographic principle, or how M-theory deals with the issues of gravity. Discussions of M-theory indicate practically nothing of its significance or meaning and Hawking gives no attention to the emerging ideas about black hole physics, information theory and such. As a world leading expert on black holes, i wanted to read more of such things and not such a standard overview of the history of science and philosophy through the past two thousand years. There is material on such things as the wave/particle nature of light and material elements, the uncertainty principle, Feymann's 'sum over history' approach to quantum descriptions, the big bang, the inflationary and expanding universe, and more, but much of this is quite standard materials and not especially explained well.

Also, why would Hawking say so little of his earlier notion of explaining away God by his smearing out of the big bang singularity? Twenty years ago, Hawking was explaining why we didn't need God because science was on the verge of discovering a theory of quantum gravity and smearing out the naught singularity point. Now, Hawking has a new argument for the non-existence of God and considers that M-theory provides such logic to dismiss the creator. At the same time, he explains practically nothing of what M-theory is or how it deals with the issue of gravity.

Stephen Hawking with the publication of the book is raising what i have long called *"the problem of God's contracting universe."* In the early 1980's, Carl Sagan as the Hollywood hero of science, declared that *"As we learn more and more about the universe, the less and less there is for*

God to do." Sagan discussed the issue of God in a chapter entitled *A Sunday Sermon* of his best-seller *Broca's Brain: Reflections on the romance of science*, where he espoused the same philosophical stance as offered to us by the new high priests of science--Drs Hawking and Mlodinow. In the 1980s, Dr. Sagan thought that science was on the verge of solving the mysteries of life and creation and that this advancement of science made 'the God hypothesis' unnecessary.

> It used to be believed that every event in the world--the opening of a morning glory, let us say--was due to direct microintervention by the Deity. The flower was unable to open by itself. God had to say, "Hey, flower, open." ...

> There are many legitimate scientific issues relating to origins and ends" What is the origin of the human species? Where did plants and animals come from? how did life arise? the Earth, the planets, the Sun, the stars? Does the universe have an origin, and if so, what? And finally, a still more fundamental and exotic question, which many scientists would say is essentially untestible and therefore meaningless: Why are the laws of nature the way they are? The idea that a God or gods is necessary to effect one or more of these origins has been under repeated attack over the last few thousand years. Because we know something about phototropism and plant hormones, we can understand the opening of the morning glory independently of divine microintervention. It is the same for the entire skein of causality back to the origin of the universe. As we learn more and more about the universe, there seems less and less for God to do. (1979, pp. 285-6)

Now, thirty years later, Stephen Hawking is solving the mysteries of creation with a hop, a skip and a jump, just as did Carl Sagan, while providing the most superficial analysis of his favourite new M-Theory and of why we no longer need a creator to fine tune the parameters and laws of nature.

Hawking has been arguing that we no longer need a Deity or Creator for over twenty years. His earlier focus was upon the need to develop a theory of quantum gravity in order to 'smear' out the 'big bang singularity'--

regarded as a boundary condition. Hawking hopes that there may not be a Big Bang, no "edge" to the universe that can be singled out and pointed to as the initial starting point (the singularity). His resistance derives from the fact that he believes an edge entails a God—at least a causal principle that functions like a definite starting point. (Weber, 1986, p. 205)

In his best seller, *A Brief History of Time* (1988), Stephen Hawking attempted to explain creation in such a way as to avoid *the God hypothesis*. Hawking suggested that if scientists were successful in developing a unified theory of 'quantum gravity,' then it would do away with the necessity of a big bang singularity. The singularity is interpreted as a last remaining "gap" in science's explanatory framework, where religious and superstitious folk still invoke the idea of God or a Creator. The problem for scientists, as Hawking explains, is that:

> ... all our theories of science are formulated on the assumption that space-time is smooth and nearly flat, so they break down at the big bang singularity, where the curvature of space-time is infinite. ... predictability would break down at the big bang. ... Many people do not like the idea that time has a beginning, probably because it smacks of divine intervention. ... There were therefore a number of attempts to avoid the conclusion that there had been a big bang.
> (1988, pp. 46-7)

In Hawking's unified theory of quantum gravity, the mysterious singularity would be "smeared out" according to the uncertainty principle of quantum theory and Feynman's sum over history approach to quanta. In this case, he argues, science will have arrived at a completely natural explanation of the origin of the universe and there will be no need to invoke any metaphysical causes, or God to account for the beginning. Heaven forbid that a singularity *"smack of Divine intervention."*

> "So long as the universe had a beginning, we could suppose it had a creator. But if the universe is really completely self-contained, having no boundary or edge, it would have neither beginning nor end: it would simply be. What place, then, for a creator?" (Hawking, 1988, pp. 140-1)

Professor Hawking used to strive to discover a *wave equation* for the universe consistent with quantum theory which could avoid any big-bang singularities by eliminating *"such badly behaved points."* (1988, p. 133) Hawking thus describes quanta in terms of the *"sum over history"* approach of physicist R. Feynman, where all possible paths of a quantum in *"imaginary time"* are added together to represent the quantum-instead of describing it as a point particle. (Essentially, the sum over history represents the plenum condition of all possibilities.) Hawking notes that, in this case:

> In real time, the universe has a beginning and an end at singularities that form a boundary to space-time and at which the laws of science break down. But in imaginary time, there are no singularities or boundaries. So maybe what we call imaginary time is really more basic.... (p. 139)

According to Hawking's philosophical musings, dissolving the singularities into imaginary time and dimensions would somehow mean that the universe would not require *"an undefined boundary condition,"* represented by the singularity.

Of course, it does seems that even in this model we have a boundary condition where the real time passes over into the imaginary. In 2010, Hawking agrees with the notion of the point source derivation of the universe. He notes:

> "... if you go far enough back in time, the universe was as small as the Planck size, a billion-trillion-trillionth of a centimetre, which is the scale at which quantum theory does have to be taken into account. ... we do know that the origin of the universe was a quantum event." (2010, p. 131)

Dr. Hawking (1984) considered the philosophical implications of how quantum gravity theory could resolve the singularity enigmas:

> There would be no singularities at which the laws of science broke down and no edge of space-time at which one would have to appeal to God or some new law to set the boundary conditions for space-time. One could say: "The boundary condition of the universe is that it has no boundary." The

> universe would be completely self-contained and not affected by anything outside itself. It would neither be created nor destroyed. It would just BE. (p. 136)

Dr. Hawking's arguments for why we no longer need a Creator if we can smear out the singularity are really quite peculiar. Even if one smears out the naughty singularity into imaginary time, it still represents a boundary condition-what Blavatsky calls a 'ring-pass-not' or a portal between different levels of reality. Dr. Hawking's logic in dismissing God is his leap of faith-faith in his own intellect and the powers of rational science. In an interview, Hawking comments: "*We still believe that the universe should be logical and beautiful. We just dropped the word 'God.'*" (Weber, 1986, p. 212)

No doubt the success of *A Brief History of Time* has motivated Hawking to promote a similar type of logic today, to explain why once again we do not need a Creator, this time because of M-Theory which can solve the problem of the fine tuning of the constants and laws of nature. Of course, Dr. Hawking didn't find his unified wave equation or theory of quantum gravity promised to us twenty years ago, and in fact he now espouses an alternative view and questions even if such a unified theory is possible, instead of a network of partial theories.

Hawking and Mlodinow embody at times, what i would consider to be the most pseudo-scientific attitudes and philosophy and pass it off as though it represents 'real science.' Considering that Hawking traces the universe back to 'nothing,' one would think that we should then inquire into the nature of that 'nothingness.' Quite the contrary, Hawking argues:

> Some people support a model in which time goes back even further than the big bang. It is not yet clear whether a model in which time continued back beyond the big bang would be better at explaining present observations because it seems the laws of the evolution of the universe may break down at the big bang. If they do, it would make no sense to create a model that encompasses time before the big bang, because what existed then would have no observable consequences for the present, and so we might as well stick with the idea that the big bang was the creation of the world. (p. 51)

To me, it would seem obvious that if we trace the universe back to nothing, we then need to inquire into the nature of those Eternal principles latent within that nothingness. The non-eternal universe arose out of an Eternal realm, but Hawking and Mlodinow want to treat the nothing as really just nothing. In contrast, in the Secret Doctrine of Blavatsky, she states that there are patterns of existence pre-existent in non-existence. She describes a seven skinned Eternal Parent Space, wherein there are latent Seven Luminous Lords. When creation occurs, the seven inside give rise to the seven outside, and the laws of nature evident in the created world are regarded as manifesting the pre-existing patterns of creation.

Of course, these are two different philosophical perspectives and rationales, but this example illustrates what i consider the glaring deficits of the science philosophy which underlies *The Grand Design*. The creation out of nothingness is an ancient mystical idea and is even in the book of Genesis, where the earth is described before the beginning as 'empty and void.' Modern science also traces the universe back to a singularity, at least in 'real time,' and this also has been an ancient mystical claim--the zero point origin of the cosmos. However, Drs Hawking and Mlodinow want to dismiss 'metaphysical' or spiritual beliefs and dogmas, but they really have no idea of how their science relates to what occult sources actually suggest. Blavatsky was describing a multiverse, seven dimensional hyperspace, cycles of expanding and contracting universes, and much more, a century before modern physicists arrived at such bizarre ideas.

In *Pythagoras' Trousers: God, Physics, and the Gender Wars*, Margaret Wertheim provides a useful analysis of modern physics and she critically examines the physicists' obsession to find the ultimate *"Theory of Everything"* (or *TOE)* which would explain all the laws of physics within one grand theory. Why, she asks, do physicists assume the right to associate their endeavours with "God," the "mind of God," the 'God particle' and the like? Physicists assume the role of the "high priests" of science and associate God with their favourite particle, higher dimensional superstring or Theory of Everything. She writes:

> Stephen Hawking, Leon Lederman, and George Smoot-these are men at the heart of contemporary physics. ... All these men have publicly associated the quest for a unified theory with God. In drawing an association with contemporary physics and God, they are not alone. Indeed, this kind of dialogue has become endemic among physicists-at least as far as their popular writing is concerned. ...

> But many physicists using the God drawcard are not engaged in serious theological or spiritual thinking. Following a millennia-old tradition that has associated mathematically based science with divinity, they simply assume it is legitimate to present their activities in a quasi-religious light. Despite the supposedly secular climate of twentieth-century science, some physicists are once again demanding that we see them as high priests, leading humanity "upward" toward transcendent, even divine knowledge of the world. (1997, pp. 221-222)

Stephen Hawking provides the most unusual paradoxes in his writings and philosophy. Most people—even many who have read *A Brief History of Time*—think that Hawking embodies a religious or spiritual attitude in his search for the ultimate quantum gravity theory. However, this is far from true and in interviews, Hawking readily dismisses the belief in God, afterlife, mysticism and the like-believing instead "in science" and 'natural laws' instead of 'supernatural laws.'

Wertheim examines the paradoxes of Hawking's public image and his inconsistent underlying attitude:

> TOE physicists themselves are associating a unified theory with God. The most famous in this camp is Stephen Hawking. In the introduction to Hawking's international best-seller *A Brief History of Time*, Carl Sagan alerts the reader that: "The word God fills these pages. Hawking embarks on a quest to answer Einstein's famous question about whether God had any choice in creating the universe. Hawking is attempting, as he explicitly states, to understand the mind of God. The implication throughout his book is that a unified theory *transcends* space and time and somehow exists "beyond" the realm of material manifestation-a feat traditionally attributed to God alone. ... (p. 217)

> The immense success of *A Brief History of Time*-it has sold more than 5 million copies worldwide-and Hawking's personal success in the public arena, are, I believe, in part attributable to the quasi-religious tone in which he presents the enterprise of contemporary physics. Although his

> reference to "the mind of God" actually occurs at the every end of the book, it opens the film of the same name. As the filmmakers rightly recognized, in an age when many people are hungering for a rapprochement between the spiritual and the scientific, the concept of the physicist as high priest is immensely appealing. And, like Einstein, Hawking is very convincing in the role. He too has assumed an almost mystical aura, which in his case is compounded by the extreme disjunction between the power of his mind and the lameness of his body. ... Hawking may be confined to a wheelchair, but his mind soars. Not even many physicists understand the concept of "imaginary time." He is a being seemingly poised at the junction of the human, the subhuman, and the superhuman—and many people long to believe that this disabled physicist might just take us to God.
>
> Ironically, it is Hawking himself who has suggested that his relativistic-quantum cosmology might obviate the need for a "Creator." But he seems to want to have it both ways—at the same time pushing God out of the universe although invoking him as a constant subtext of his work. It is not at all clear from *A Brief History of Time* whether Hawking genuinely believes in a god, or whether he is just indulging in self-aggrandizement. Unlike Copernicus, Kepler, and Newton (and even Einstein in his own way), Hawking is not a serious theological thinker ... Yet, whatever Hawking's true feelings about God, many people have come to see him as a scientific high priest, the inheritor of Einstein's mantle. (pp. 217-219)

The use of the words God, the mind of God, the God particle, and the God like Superforce are endemic to popular science writers and TOE theorists. However, the underlying attitude is usually that we no longer need God, now that we have modern physicists as high priests to answer the ultimate questions about cosmic origins, even having to spend long hours sitting at their desks.

Hawking is hoping to fill in the last "gap" in contemporary science, trying to exclude God from the universe by accounting for creation events in purely mathematical and physical terms, thereby explaining away the Big Bang singularity. Of course, to Hawking, there would be nothing "mystical" about singularities, quantum theory or the quantum vacuum. Carl Sagan similarly bandies about the name of God, admitting God only if we define "him" as the *sum of all the physical laws*, but not accepting any of the traditional attributes of God-that is, as an omniscient, omnipotent and omnipresent Being.

Scientists often regard science as the new religion and want to *metaphorically* see into the mind of God but they do not take to heart the deeper mysteries of what that quest might entail. Scientists leave themselves, their own consciousness and being, out of the equation. Furthermore, scientists simply do not realize the extent to which their own theories are beginning to vindicate mystical teachings -because of the pervasive lack of familiarity and appreciation of what such occult teachings entail.

Indeed, what is it that leads scientists to conclude that there is nothing 'mystical' about singularities, superstrings, the nothingness and plenum of the quantum vacuum, M-theory and the holographic model, or other emerging ideas in physics? It is just as 'mystical' to have the singularity eventually smeared out, beyond the level of the zero point into imaginary time and the infinite, as for it to appear as a point source at all. Dr. Hawking does not even consider that such zero points, ethers, space and higher dimensions, the void and the plenum, have been the domain of occultists for hundreds and thousands of years. In fact, metaphysical expositions of creation bear profound relationships to modern theories.

In the 1970s and 80s, astronomer Robert Jastrow compared the big-bang scenario to the Genesis account of creation and noted certain similarities. All major religious and esoteric teachings depict creation as having occurred *once upon a time* and this basic idea was confirmed by the discovery of the big bang. Jastrow noted further how the idea—that God willed that there should be 'light"—made sense in terms of trying to depict early creation events, as energetic photons can create material particles. However, thirty years later, scientists have advanced from the big bang scenario to singularities, vacuum states and higher dimensions, we must consider how these concepts have also been articulated by occultist Blavatsky as within other esoteric teachings.

The search for unity itself arises out of the Judeo-Christian tradition of monotheism and the faith that all things are unified and part of one superforce or Divine Being. Although modern physicists associate their theories with the search for God, this is not usually accompanied by any serious spiritual search or informed mystical understanding. References to God and physics may help to sell books but they can obscure the basic mechanistic and materialist philosophy underlying scientific theories.

Madame Blavatsky (1888) noted that: *"the occult side of Nature has never been approached by the science of modern civilization."* Although Blavatsky wrote this over a hundred years ago, she would likely not change her attitude if she were familiar with Stephen Hawking's M-theory and the so-called scientific theory of creation out of nothing. Scientists are arriving at knowledge of the profound depths of creation, but because they subscribe to a simplistic mechanistic outlook, they do not recognize or appreciate the mystical and metaphysical dimensions of their own theories. Blavatsky embodied the truly scientific attitude in her recommendation:

> The Secret teachings ... must be contrasted with the speculations of modern science. Archaic axioms must be placed side by side with modern hypotheses and comparisons left to the sagacious reader. (*SD I*, p. 480)

Unfortunately, Stephen Hawking does not have such a perspective, as most scientists do not.

Steven Weinberg, a well-known physicist and cosmologist, is the author of *The First Three Minutes* (1979) which chronicles the physics of the early universe. After providing a fascinating account of the origin and evolution of matter and energy in the early universe following the Big Bang, Dr. Weinberg concludes with these philosophical ruminations:

> It is almost irresistible for humans to believe that we have some special relation to the universe, that human life is not just a more-or-less farcical outcome of a chain of accidents reaching back to the first three minutes, but that we were somehow built in from the beginning. ... But if there is no solace in the fruits of our research, there is at least some consolation in the research itself. Men and women are not content to comfort themselves with tales of gods and giants, or to confine their thoughts to the daily affairs of life; they also build telescopes and satellites and accelerators, and sit at their

desks for endless hours working out the meaning of the data they gather. (pp. 143-4)

In Dr. Weinberg's view, to engage in *tales of gods and giants* or to feel that human life has some *"special relation to the universe"* is nothing more than a source of self-consolation and self deception. Such ideas, he believes, have nothing to do with the nature of reality discovered by science. Instead, he suggests that human life is more like a *"farcical outcome of a chain of accidents."* Humanity's saving grace consists of those scientists who struggle so valiantly to collect data and solve the mysteries of life and the universe-- all while sitting at their desks. It seems quite evident to Drs. Weinberg, as to Carl Sagan and Stephen Hawking, that there is less and less for God to do, now that we have real science and scientists who sit at desks.

Drs Hawking and Mlodinow provide a valuable service in arguing their perspective on the mysteries and raising what i would call the problem of God's contracting universe. I would argue, quite contrary to the stance of such scientists, that the findings of modern physics are confirming ancient claims made within the mystery teachings themselves. *God, Science & The Secret Doctrine* is actually the most appropriate work to lay side by side with Dr. Hawking and Mlodinow's *Grand Design*, to highlight the many enigmas and mysteries of science, creation and the issues of God.

Bravo, Dr. Hawking, for an interesting and provocative work.

DEITY IN EVERY POINT[7]

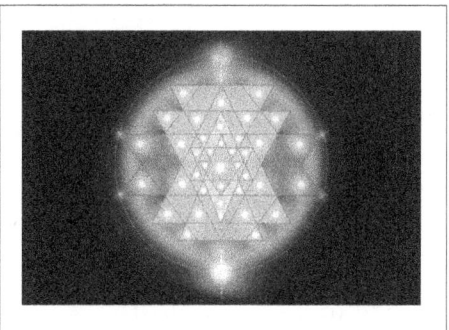

"...the design displayed in the mechanism, the ordershown in the preservation, destruction and renewal of things forbid us to regard the world as the offspring of chance, and force us to recognize an intelligent design."

Blavatsky (1954, p. 316)

---

[7] This chapter is based upon chapter V,9 of *God, Science & the Secret Doctrine*.

There is something profoundly fraudulent and simplistic about modern science philosophizing and the antiquated and pseudo-scientific worldview currently established in modern psychology, science and education. It is not that the *facts of science* that are wrong but the interpretation of these facts and the underlying philosophical framework. It is a science philosophy of materialism, reductionism, neo-Darwinian evolution by randomness and happenstance, a soul-less psychology based on the head doctrine of consciousness studies, the study of little bits in isolation connected only through local effects, and with a pervasive denial of soul, spirit and higher intelligence within the phenomena of life. The facts of science can be interpreted in different ways and certainly already support important mystical claims about creation physics, metaphysics and cosmology as elaborated by Blavatsky over a century ago. Unfortunately, the masses of people lack any understanding of these issues and of their significance.

Hopefully, there will be significant insights from intelligent design advocates — as to the principles and applications of intelligent design theories. A model of Intelligent Design, such as that provided by Blavatsky and elaborated here could be applied within every department of knowledge, science and education. Unfortunately, the public advocates of Intelligent Design seem to be completely unaware and misinformed regarding the esoteric metaphysical teachings within their own religious traditions. I have yet to read one Christian advocate explain the scientific significance of even the first three verses of their own favourite sacred book, the Bible. It will be a travesty if the only consideration of "Intelligent Design" consists of dogmatic Christian fundamentalism. Indeed, dogmatic Christian creationist views provide a straw man for pseudo-scientists posing as rational sceptics to attack, thereby illustrating the supposed formidable power of science over irrationality. Carl Sagan, the most fraudulent science philosopher of the past century, compared science to a 'candle in the dark,' but really he only offered us a superficial pseudo-science masquerading as truth.

The esoteric mystery teachings of religions are not understood nor investigated within the modern educational system and scientific community. In fact, they are not even mentioned in discussions of Intelligent Design! The sceptics and critics of Intelligent Design are generally correct in portraying Christian creationist views as being simplistic and pseudo-scientific. In the form that such Intelligent Design models are generally offered, they are just as superficial as the materialist's own philosophy of a universe governed by chance and randomness. Both views are non-falsifiable, in the terms of the philosopher of science Karl Popper, and outline no areas for significant scientific investigation.

However, if we consider the model of Intelligent Design suggested by *The Secret Doctrine* and elaborated here, then such a theory can be evaluated theoretically and experimentally. Blavatsky provides a complex model of *"divine micro-intervention,"* which we have applied to detailing the physics and metaphysics of life and creation. She did not intend that her teaching be simply accepted as dogma, but rather, it needed to be understood and investigated by comparing it with contemporary scientific understanding.

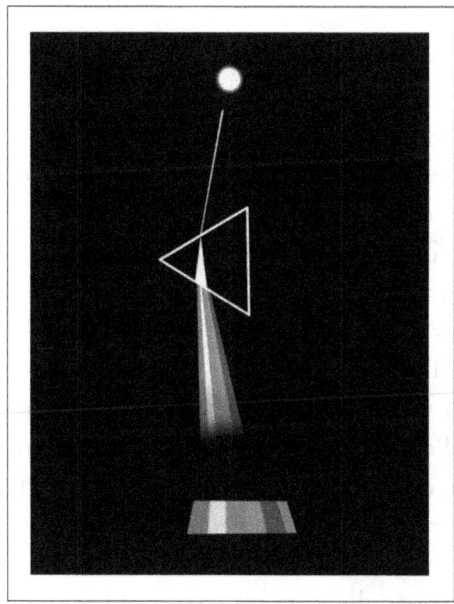

Since we live in a multi-religious and cultural society, humankind needs to seriously consider the esoteric creation teachings of different traditions--the Vedas, Kabbalah, mystical Christianity, Sufism and Islam, Tibetan Buddhism, native spirituality and the like. However, more than any other source, H. P. Blavatsky provided a profoundly unique synthesis of the perennial wisdom teachings and an alternative model of human existence and the metaphysics of the Kosmos. *The Secret Doctrine* has applications to every department of the physical and social sciences, arts, and philosophy; to understanding the enigmas of human consciousness, spirit and soul; and particularly to understanding the mysteries of cosmic creation—the physics and metaphysics of the holographic Universe. Unfortunately, Intelligent Design advocates seem to be aware of none of this. Educators must not simply add new dogmas to the rubbish already taught within science and instead pursue serious investigations of intelligent design models--their implications and applications in all departments of knowledge. Surely, they will have to eventually stumble across the Sacred Laws of Three and Seven, if only by chance, and a new understanding of the multidimensional world and the nature of Space, and even about zero point dynamics.

Esoteric and religious metaphysical teachings, as synthesized within Blavatsky's secret doctrines, not only teach that there is a creative God principle within nature, but further, they articulate particular numerological and geometric principles of metaphysical and physical design. These are the Laws by which the One produces the Many—the diversity of creation. Creation embodies a triune and sevenfold nature in all things. Further, these patterns are repeated above and below, in metaphysical and physical reality, spirit and matter. Blavatsky offers a higher dimensional model of the Kosmos and of human consciousness, which compared with the scientists' *box* of matter and energy within time and space, makes the latter seem puny indeed. Only the holographic paradigm in modern science is beginning to arrive at concepts similar to those of H. P. B. and *The Secret Doctrine*.

Acknowledgement of esoteric teachings and claims is completely lacking within the public and scientific debates over the issues of Intelligent Design. People argue endlessly over the issues of science and religion, God versus chance, belief versus reason, creation versus evolution, and other such dualistic non-sense. Unfortunately, religious believers do not grasp the basic esoteric principles underlying their own favourite dogmas. An understanding of sacred number study has been lost within the institutionalized churches and religions, as it has been within science and education. Numbers are mainly considered in a linear way, as on a number line, wherein each number is simply the number before plus one more. In contrast, the secret doctrines and mystical/occult literatures of the world are replete with symbols, glyphs, and formula, embodying sacred numerological principles. Blavatsky declares: *"God geometrises,"* (*Isis Unveiled*, 1877, p.508)

Modern science is basically founded upon a dualistic perspective of twos, in which it is always contrasting opposing principles—such as matter and energy, waves and particles, observers and the observed, the mind and the body, conscious and unconscious, science and religion. In contrast, mystical and spiritual science suggest that the Divine Principles of a Triune and Sevenfold nature are embodied within all phenomena of nature. Thus, the One is divided by three and yields seven—just as white light divided by a prism creates a spectrum of colours. Similarly, the material world is composed of protons, electrons and neutrons constituting atoms, which are arranged in seven rows of elements of the periodic tables. These phenomena of nature embody the Sacred Principles. In modern physics, three main families of particles have now been identified, each of which has three generations of particles, and all of which are equivalent to modes of motion on higher seven-dimensional superstrings or Calabi Yau spaces. 'Space' can be considered as a unity, or as three-dimensional (x, y, z axes), or, as seven-dimensional—in which case, there is above and below, left and right, forward and backward, with a seventh central point—the origin point of the Cartesian co-ordinates. Time, can also be considered as a unity, or as having a triune nature of past, present and future, and as embodying a natural sevenfold cyclical unfoldment of rounds and races. Time, space, matter and energy—all of the four elements of modern science—can be regarded separately in such a 1-3-7 analysis, akin to the mathematical nature of light!

Whereas modern science has considered mainly matter and energy, within time and space, an occult perspective suggests a trinity of intelligence, energy and matter, or spirit, soul and body; all upon seven planes or dimensions of being existence. An occult perspective offers a far more multidimensional model of human and Cosmic existence, than does modern science. Scientists still think that there is only 'the material world' and deny the existence of the 'immaterial world,' in their typical dualistic philosophy of life.

Margaret Wertheim described the metaphysics of Grosseteste:

> In Grosseteste's metaphysics of light, we see the first full-blown expression of a mathematico-Christian cosmology, in which we may even recognize elements of the modern mathematical world picture. ... the universe was generated from a point of primordial light-the divine illumination, or *lux*, of which visible light was said to be the physical manifestation. ... Man could not study the divine *lux* directly, but he could study its physical manifestation in light. ... a mathematical understanding of light would serve as the model for understanding all natural influence, or what we would now call force. ... this is close to what mathematical men believe today. In contemporary physicists' quest to understand the forces of nature, it is light that has generally served as the model. (pp. 49-50)

Deity is a divine mathematician and geometry is inherent in nature as it reflects the same creative principles inherent in the Mind or Being of God.

In this view, creation emerges from a point of primordial light, the divine lux, which is the ultimate basis for all manifestation—the Ray of Light that penetrates into the Mother Deep. The dynamics and properties of light in the physical world reflect these same principles in keeping with the mystical axiom: *As above, so below*.

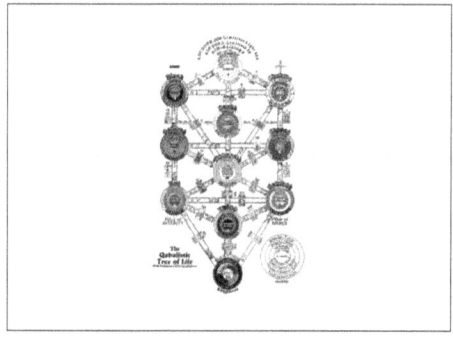

These principles of the Law of Three and the Law of Seven are found within Christianity, Judaism and Kabbalah, Islam and Sufism, Tibetan Buddhism and Hinduism, in the Fourth Way teachings of G. I. Gurdjieff and elsewhere, but nowhere is their significance articulated as profoundly, as within *The Secret Doctrine*, which provides the keys to unlocking wide areas of mystical and scientific study.

Blavatsky provides this succinct summary of these esoteric principles within the Kabbalah.

> The entire system of the Kabalistic numerals is based on the divine septenary hanging from the Triad (thus forming the *Decade*)... which, finally, all merge into the ONE itself: an endless and boundless Circle. (*S.D. I*, p. 239)

Such esoteric number study pervades *The Secret Doctrine* but an understanding of its meaning is completely lacking within the mainstream literature or science, in new age philosophizing and in popular discussions of the issues of intelligent design!

Nonetheless, the sacred numerology and geometry articulated in *The Secret Doctrine* does provide *"a God Theory"* -not only claiming the existence of such invisible powers and forces but actually providing an intelligible explanation of metaphysical dynamics and the principles of creation. These teachings are absolutely worthy of scientific and scholarly examination, even if only to *"hone our minds for useful things,"* as Carl Sagan suggests. Blavatsky's masterpiece provides the keys to the study of the world's religions and mystical teachings, and a complex metaphysical explanation of creation dynamics. She poses views on many issues still central within contemporary science and she offers ideas still in advance of the progress of mainstream science—particularly regarding zero point dynamics and the holographic nature of Space. Any understanding of esotericism seems to have completely escaped modern philosophers, educators and scientists. They are instead dismissive of religion, spirituality, psychical phenomena and metaphysical study, and have no appreciation of the subtlety of esoteric number study, symbols and geometry.

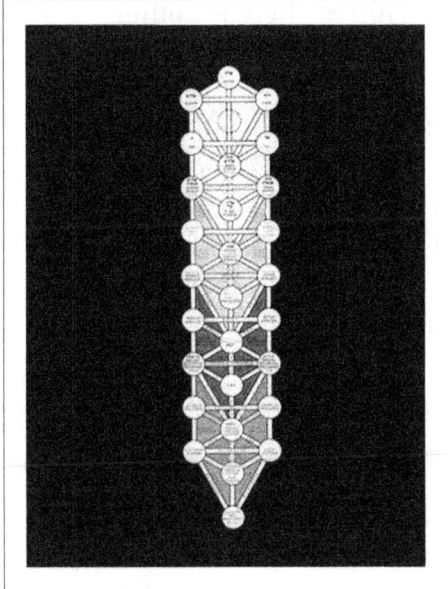

To compare an occult and mystical view of life with the traditional materialist scientific view, consider this Kabbalist glyph of the *Ladder of Jacob*. This symbol is based on four *Trees of Life*, representing the divine, spiritual, psychical and material worlds—the worlds of *emanation*, *creation*, *formation*, and *made;* and the elements of fire, air, water and earth. Each of these four worlds has a supernal triad and seven spheres below. The *Ladder of Jacob* actually depicts the creation of various world orders out of prime source substances through a hierarchy of broken symmetries in higher dimensional space. It is essentially a mathematical and geometric model of the inherent structure of the quantum vacuum—the zero point fields or ethers. It also depicts the various metaphysical inward dimensions of human existence within Cosmic Space. The *Ladder of Jacob* is a model of intelligent design based upon four world orders created according to the laws of Three and Seven. The last sphere at the bottom of the Ladder is that which is finally made manifest physically, but the whole inner structure of the Ladder is inherent within the final sphere.

The modern materialist scientist simply takes the last Sphere or Sephira of this whole multi-dimensional *Tree of Life*, calls it the 'material world' and considers that he has arrived at a comprehensive explanation of creation. Imagining themselves to be uncommonly clever, these scientists are blind to the whole inner metaphysics of life, the heart and creation. Divine intelligences ensoul matter through zero point dynamics through varied planes of the Ethers of Space. Any material quantum is ultimately implicated in the whole through an inner multidimensional nature.

Modern scientists automatically and unconsciously deny the existence of spirit and soul, and intelligences within nature and the Ethers of Space. Now, they will simply extend their materialist science philosophy to their studies of holography and higher dimensions, and argue that there is certainly nothing 'mystical' about any of this, just as there is nothing mystical about singularities or the void/plenum of the quantum vacuum.

The *Tree of Life* is said to exist within the Garden of Eden, an indicator of its secret knowledge! The other Tree inside the Gates of Eden is the *Tree of Knowledge of Good and Evil*, suggesting a dualistic paradigm. Even the serpent, symbolizing the line of thinking that leads one astray, is double-tongued, saying one thing and doing another, like the madmen who deceived the masses of humanity. In Kabbalah, the *Tree of Life* is said to be hidden within the *Tree of Knowledge of Good and Evil — and similarly, the study of dualistic science might eventually lead to an understanding of the higher laws and Divine Principles.*

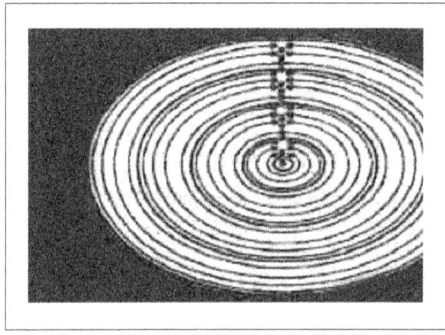

In this illustration, the Zero Point centre exists within the ethers of the void and plenum of the quantum vacuum. The dimensions of *Jacob's Ladder* now surround the central point. This simple Kabbalist diagram actually depicts a profound model of higher dimensional metaphysics. It represents zero point dynamics and the idea of how such points might be 'clothed in different bodies.'

In a scholarly study of Kabbalah and modern science, L. Leat (1999) provides another illustration of sacred geometry most relevant to our studies. In the following illustration, Leat depicts the sphere *"Da'at,"* in the *Tree of Life*, surrounded by the *"matrix of creation."* Da'at is the eleventh hidden Sephira, represented within the abyss separating the three supernal spheres from the seven realms below. Just as Kether, the Crown Sphere, can be presented as an infinitesimal point source, a point within a circle, so also is Da'at—*which embodies Kether and the supernal triad into the seven spheres below. The Supernal Triad give birth to a Son, as the "Three fall into Four."* Da'at represents the emergence of the Son into the worlds below. In terms of modern science, Da'at is the singularity condition, the portal from the three realms of supernal Existence into the seven lower dimensions of being existence.

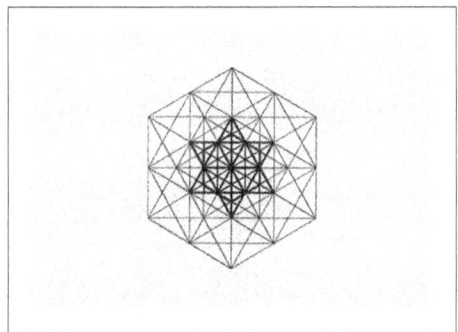

In an 'involving' *Tree of Life*, Da'at would appear as a white hole, a point source of Supernal Light. In an evolving *Tree of Life*, the dissolution of the world would be into a black hole. The creation and dissolution of the Cosmos occur within-without from such zero point sources. Da'at is a very special Sephira which possesses properties and significance that are not easily discerned. Kabbalists state that as any living being emerges through the Abyss, it cries out 'I Am' (although this is also said of Kether.) The Universe is such a living being—a *Son* or *'a wink in the eye of self-existence.'*

In the *Ladder of Jacob*, with four *Trees of Life* overlapping in a particular way, this geometric image represents the *Da'at Sephira* in the *Tree of Creation*-the *second realm of* Beriah. Da'at is the final end product of the Divine World above and is the first appearance within the spiritual world. The *"matrix of creation"* surrounds Da'at and is represented by the complex geometric form surrounding the central point. This diagram essentially illustrates the dynamics governing the Kabbalist's *'god-particle.'* This could also represent Blavatsky's Monad, Shirley MacLaine's *God Spark*, the Sufis' divine spark, and the 'spark of holiness' of the Kabbalist. The 'matrix of creation' around the point depicts the inner metaphysical processes and forces that serve to embody this point source—to clothe it in different bodies.

In the illustration, the zero point source is established as the centre of a *Star of David*, or *Seal of Solomon*. This symbol is composed of two triangles turned up and down, representing the conjunction of Fire and Water, Spirit and Matter. The triangles depict the Law of Three as evident above and below. Blavatsky ascribed great significance to this symbol and especially to its lesser known form—that with a seventh central element or point.

The Theosophical Publishing House in London, England published a third volume of *The Secret Doctrine* in 1897. It is composed of selections of Blavatsky's extensive writing and notes which she apparently intended to include in a third volume. In a chapter on *"The Hexagon with the Central Point, or the Seventh Key,"* Blavatsky wrote:

> Pythagoras viewed the hexagon formed of two crossed triangles as the symbol of creation, and the Egyptians, as that of the union of fire and water (or of generation), the Essenes saw in it the Seal of Solomon, the Jews the Shield of David, the Hindus the Sign of Vishnu (to this day); and if even in Russia and Poland the double triangle is regarded as a powerful talisman—then so wide-spread a use argues that there is something in it. It stands to reason, indeed, that such an ancient and universally revered symbol should not be merely laid aside to be laughed at by those who know nothing of its virtues or real Occult significance. (p. 105)

Blavatsky then quotes another occultist, from *Things Concealed*, depicting the Seal of Solomon with a central point: *"The seventh key is the hieroglyph of the sacred septenary, of royalty, of the priesthood (the Initiate), of triumph and true result by struggle. It is magic power in all its force, the true "Holy Kingdom." In the Hermetic Philosophy it is the quintessence resulting from the union of the two forces of the great Magic…. "* Blavatsky then concludes: *"The force of this key is absolute in Magic. All religions have consecrated this sign in their rites."*

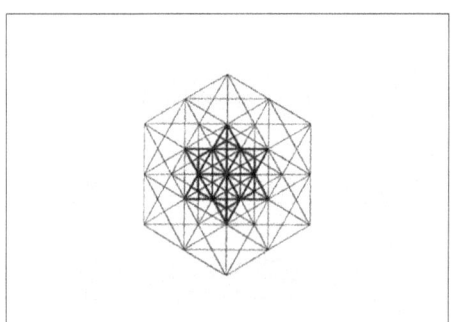
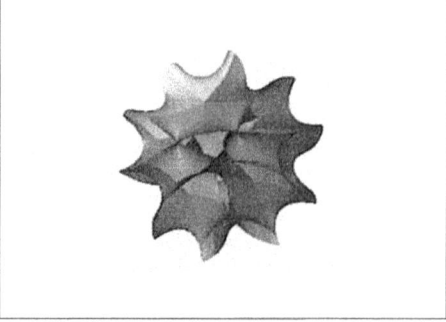

As it happens, the Kabbalist diagram of the first point of creation and the surrounding matrix of creation (essentially a multidimensional Star of David with a central point) is most similar to that provided by scientists Greene and Atkins in their recent books on physics. In accord with the idea of placing ancient wisdom and axioms side by side with modern hypotheses, compare these last two illustrations depicting the scientists' seven-dimensional Calabi-Yau space—postulated to exist at every point within the universe—with the *Da'at of Creation*, the 'God particle' of the Kabbalist scholar. These Calabi-Yau Spaces are described as seven dimensional with varied inner holes in a manner most compatible with Blavatsky's description of the seven holes dug in space and the zero point foundations for the laws of nature. Physicists are trying to figure out exactly an interior mathematics and physics of such seven dimensional entities. The similarities between ancient esoteric teachings and contemporary physics are indeed profound.

The teachings of the Kabbalah, like those of *The Secret Doctrine*, bear complex relationships to ideas in modern science. Further, they can be taken as providing a model of intelligent design—of the metaphysical and physical processes which underlie and sustain all things. The Kabbalist descriptions of negative existence, the void and plenum, the zero point source origins, the broken symmetries in higher dimensional space, the higher dimensional dynamics of light, and the descent from subtle into material planes of existence, are all ideas compatible with modern concepts in physics and cosmology, with Blavatsky's teachings and the mathematics of light. It seems that a singularity point of the Infinite might be embodied by such a complexity of inward dynamics.

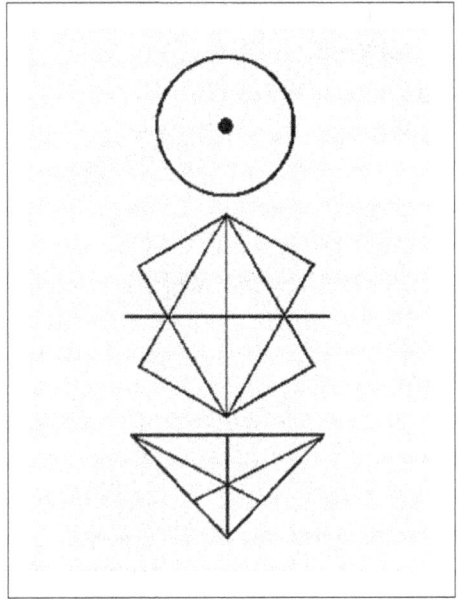

In *Isis Unveiled*, Blavatsky (1877) provides a profound series of three geometric figures. She writes of these:

"Attach thyself," said the alchemist, *"to the four letters of the tetragram disposed*

in the following manner: The letters of the ineffable name are there, although thou mayest not discern them at first. The incommunicable axiom is kabalistically contained therein, and this is what is called the magic arcanum by the masters." (p.506)

The first circle with a central point represents the first point of cosmic differentiation or the zero point laya centre established within the *Eternal Parent Space*. The second figure has seven points including one at the centre—as a singularity zero point condition might differentiate into seven 'holes dug in space.' The central figure also corresponds to the six upper sepheria of the *Tree of Life*, with the central point representing Da'at—*the Son*. Da'at represents the point from the upper circle as made manifest in the world below. The central figure portrays 'broken symmetries,' relative to the more perfect symmetry of the Star of David, thus representing the creative forces manifest with symmetry breaking.

The third figure represents a four-dimensional nature as the product of the seven forces in the realm underlying it. It represents the four laws of nature which hold it all together as a four-dimensional spacetime complex. The third figure also has seven points where lines interact.

These principles are similar to the *Stanzas of Dzyan* III:

> 3. DARKNESS RADIATES LIGHT, AND LIGHT DROPS ONE SOLITARY RAY INTO THE MOTHER DEEP. THE RAY SHOOTS THROUGH THE VIRGIN-EGG. THE RAY CAUSES THE ETERNAL EGG TO THRILL, AND DROP THE NON-ETERNAL GERM, WHICH CONDENSES INTO THE WORLD-EGG.
>
> 4. THEN THE THREE FALL INTO THE FOUR. THE RADIANT ESSENCE BECOMES SEVEN INSIDE, SEVEN OUTSIDE. ...

The first diagram in Blavatsky's sequence of the *magic arcanum* represents the 'non-eternal germ,' the first point of cosmic creation. The second figure represents the spiritual world or heaven worlds and the third figure represents the material worlds made. The heavens and the earth are the seven inside and seven outside. Blavatsky's geometric sequence portrays profound numerological principles, the means by which form is created out of formlessness—through zero point centres by which the Gods and other invisible bodies *'clothe themselves in bodies.'*

Scientists have not begun to penetrate the hidden wisdom of *The Secret Doctrine*, Kabbalah or to relate the ancient metaphysics to the concepts of modern physics and science. Ancient metaphysics, the study of light and divine principles, the concepts of zero point dynamics, the notion of a seven-skinned Eternal Parent Space, and many more concepts elucidated within *The Secret Doctrine* throw a most interesting light on the concepts and enigmas of modern science. Somehow, a manifest but essentially illusory four-dimensional spacetime complex, with gravity to hold it all together, is produced out of a higher dimensional metaphysics within an underlying Eternal Parent Space.

H. P. Blavatsky's secret doctrines provide a multidimensional model of Intelligent Design, a subtle and complex explanation of how a higher dimensional metaphysics gives rise to a lower dimensional physics through zero point dynamics within holographic Space. Her work addresses the most significant failings in the modern formulation of these issues of intelligent design, evolution, consciousness and such. Blavatsky does not simply declare *"God geometrises,"* but she provides a provocative model of the spiritual and metaphysical principles and forces that underlie the manifest material Universe. She explains how God does *micro-intervene* in the laws of nature and how the universe concentrates itself in a point.

THE ORIGIN AND NATURE OF HUMAN CONSCIOUSNESS

"Spiritual teachings elaborate an alternative model of the higher dimensional origins of human consciousness and self. Whereas modern science presupposes that material processes with the brain produce consciousness and the experience of self, mystical and esoteric perspectives describe consciousness as the light of Self and as emerging from within-without through some higher dimensional physics and metaphysics of the human heart."

"At the heart of the universe, a galaxy, the sun, a quantum and a human being are such zero point laya centers, whereby the Gods and other invisible powers clothe themselves in bodies. Thus, life and consciousness within a living being originates within/without out of higher space dimensions through the dynamics of a multi-dimensional heart."

"The Self is a point source of coherent light consciousness emanating from a realm of Eternal Light, higher dimensional Space and the uncreated Void. A point of intuitive perception within the heart can thus be related to the larger dimensions of the macrocosm."

"It is the conjunction of the self-illuminating zero point element within higher seven dimensional space that lies behind the creation of the human holographic experience originating out of the depths of the Heart."

Holmes, C., Esoteric Quarterly (Fall 2010, Winter 2011, Spring, 2011)

I
The Heart Doctrine[8]

"... when I die, the 'I' will be lost forever, too."

- Isaac Asimov, material scientist -

*"What he sees in the inmost recesses of his heart
is his real "I," his God."*

- Sri Chinmoy, mystic -

*"Learn above all to separate Head-learning from Soul-Wisdom,
the "Eye" from the "Heart" doctrine.
But even ignorance is better than Head-learning
with no Soul-wisdom to illuminate and guide it. ...
The "Doctrine of the Eye" is for the crowd,
the "Doctrine of the Heart," for the elect.
... 'Great Sifter' is the name of the "Heart Doctrine"...."*

Blavatsky, The Voice of the Silence, 1889

---

[8] This article series was published through the online journal of Esoteric Studies, www.esotericstudies.net. Part I was in the Fall 2010 edition; Part II in Winter 2011, Part III in Spring 2011, and Part IV in the Fall of 2011. I would like to particularly thank Donna Brown of the Esoteric Quarterly for her encouragement and support of my work, for enabling me to publish this article series and for her outstanding reviews of *God, Science & The Secret Doctrine*, Spring, 2009 and of *The Heart Doctrine*, 2010. I would also like to thank the many anonymous reviewers who sacrificed their time and efforts to provide so many valuable comments and suggestions, as were then incorporated into the article series.

ABSTRACT

The issues of consciousness are profoundly important from both a scientific and an individual perspective. What is this "I" in me—this inner self awareness? Is there some type of mystical I, not simply a collection of molecules or a pack of neurons? Where could such come from and what types of experience are possible for human beings during life and after death? *The Heart Doctrine* is an inquiry into the ultimate origin and nature of human consciousness, as well as into the issues of the existence or non-existence of the human spirit and soul. The approach is to contrast 'the head doctrine'-the major twentieth century scientific theory of consciousness, with 'the heart doctrine'—derived from ancient and modern mystical and spiritual teachings. This comparative study provides a valuable alternative approach to the deep mysteries and enigmas of consciousness and it highlights many of the assumptions underlying modern scientific views.

THE MYSTERIES OF CONSCIOUSNESS

What is the nature of human consciousness? Psychologists, scientists and philosophers use this term in a hundred and one ways with a thousand and one meanings and interpretations. Within the scientific and popular literature as well as in common discussion, there is widespread confusion and misunderstanding regarding the issues of consciousness. Further, people do not generally question the nature of consciousness within themselves or even have a language in which to talk about such things.

The contemporary scientific literature demonstrates how much scientists are in the dark about the mysteries of consciousness. This is exemplified by a *Scientific American* article- *"The quest to find Consciousness"*- published in a special issue of MIND (2004). The most certain comments offered by G. Roth regarding consciousness are that *"a true understanding of the phenomenon remains elusive,"* and further, *"For now, no definitive explanations exist …."* [9] Science journalist John Horgan in *The Undiscovered Mind* (1999)

---

[9] G. Roth, The Quest to find Consciousness. *Scientific American* (Special Edition, *MIND*. 2004).

came to a similar conclusion: *"Mind-scientists and philosophers cannot even agree on what consciousness is, let alone how it should be explained."* [10] The Dalai Lama simply states: *"I do not think current neuroscience has any real explanation of consciousness itself."* [11]

Interestingly, John Horgan quotes Harvard psychologist, Howard Gardner, who suggests that someone may find *"deep and fruitful commonalities between Western views of the mind and those incorporated into the philosophy and religion of the Far East."* Gardner states that a fundamentally new insight is necessary in order to understand consciousness; although unfortunately, *"we can't anticipate the extraordinary mind because it comes from a funny place that puts things together in a funny kind of way."* [12] Gardner's comments are ironic, as indeed there exists a fundamental difference between western scientific views of consciousness and the mind as centred in the brain and both eastern and western spiritual and esoteric traditions with the emphasis upon the heart. Understanding this difference between *the head doctrine* and *the heart doctrine* will certainly provide a novel perspective on the issues of consciousness and put things together in a *"funny kind of way."*

What is the nature and origin of human consciousness? These are issues of profound importance not only to science, but also to us individually- in terms of understanding the meaning and significance of our lives. Unfortunately, science's entire approach to consciousness may be fundamentally misguided. The mysteries of consciousness are far deeper than imagined by Roth-who ends up associating the *"seat of consciousness"* with the association areas of the cerebral hemispheres in interaction with other mid-brain structures. Roth embodies 'the head doctrine.' Further, scientists generally have no idea of the profound alternative mystical and spiritual viewpoints on these issues of consciousness.

The issues of human consciousness are also central to the contemporary debate between science and religion, and to the question of the existence of God. The debate between science and religion hinges on the issue of the origin and nature of consciousness-because this is linked to that of the

---

[10] J. Horgan, *The Undiscovered Mind: How the human brain defies replication, medication, and explanation* (New York, Touchstone Books, 1999), 228.

[11] Dalai Lama, *The Universe in a Single Atom: The convergence of science and spirituality* (New York, Morgan Road Books, 2005) 130.

[12] J. Horgan, ibid., 260.

existence or non-existence of the human spirit, soul or divine nature. Is consciousness a product of material processes as science claims or does it originate from within spiritual, metaphysical or divine realms?

To begin, the term consciousness can be taken generally to refer to the *inner awareness of being*, which each of us has or is within our lives. Although we might see another person's physical body, we can never directly view their inner world of consciousness or their inner experience of being. Yet, in a very real sense, it is within this inner world that each of us has our existence. Hence, in order to understand consciousness, we must make an effort to understand it within ourselves through direct inner awareness and experience. This approach supplements other scientific approaches which rely upon external observers and intellectual theories and it is the essential method of the mystics, yogis and masters of the esoteric traditions. Such self study explorations of consciousness have been hardly considered within the mainstream of modern thought which also propagates varied misleading ideas on the subject. The Dalai Lama explains, *"it is clear that the third-person method – which has served science so well in many areas – is inadequate to the explanation of consciousness."* [13]

THE HEAD DOCTRINE

For decades, psychologists dismissed the study of consciousness as it was too difficult to study empirically and borders on such unscientific pursuits as religion and metaphysics. Behaviourist John Watson remarked that no one had ever seen a soul in a test tube and that the study of consciousness was just as elusive as that of the soul. Nevertheless, in the second half of 20th century, consciousness re-emerged within academic psychology and neuroscience as a legitimate area of study. However, scientists embraced extremely limited views of consciousness and most often equated it with thinking and other cognitive processes of the mind. It is assumed that consciousness is produced by the brain's material neurological processes and/or by information processes. *The head doctrine* is the most commonly accepted western scientific and psychological model of consciousness. However, the nature of consciousness has remained the most mysterious of all psychological phenomena.

---

[13] Dalai Lama, ibid., 133.

In the *MIND* article by Roth, *The Quest to find Consciousness,* it is simply assumed that consciousness is generated somehow within the brain from material processes. Yet, when we read Roth's article for scientific insights into consciousness, we come up quite empty handed. A small table, entitled *"FAST FACTS: The Rise of Awareness,"* includes these three points:

> 1. How does consciousness, with its private and subjective qualities, emerge from the physical information processing conducted by the brain? ...
>
> 2. Recently neuroscientists have focused on the neural correlates-the activities in the brain that are most closely associated with consciousness.
>
> 3. To date, no "centre" for the phenomenon has revealed itself, but advances in imaging have helped in the study of the brain areas that are involved during consciousness. [14]

Of course, there is not a single 'fact' in the table but only questions or assumptions. There is absolutely no "proof" that consciousness emerges *"from the physical information processing"* in the brain or from *"the neural correlates."* Although presented as *'fast facts,'* these views are really nothing more than simple assumptions.

When it comes to 'states of consciousness,' Roth offers a pretty limited scheme of consideration from a so-called scientific perspective:

> Any effort to understand consciousness must begin by noting that it comprises various states. ... At one end of the spectrum is the so-called alertness (or vigilance) state. States of lower consciousness include drowsiness, dozing, deep sleep and on down to coma.[15]

A normal state of 'alertness' is put at one end of the continuum, as if this is the highest possible state of consciousness a human being can experience

---

[14] Roth, ibid, 34.

[15] G. Roth, ibid, 34.

and the other levels are below it-down into coma and the extinction of consciousness in death. It is assumed that there are no states of consciousness beyond basic vigilance-hence no 'Self consciousness,' cosmic consciousness, spiritual or God consciousness.

Nevertheless, the basic assumption that the brain produces consciousness seems most reasonable and few scientists question it-despite the fact that they are completely unable to establish how or where the brain produces consciousness or what exactly this consciousness is. Nevertheless, putting aside these uncertainties, theorists share the view of prominent neurologist Roger Sperry, who remarked: *"I don't see any way for consciousness to emerge or be generated apart from a functioning brain."* [16] Of course, Sperry also cannot see how consciousness emerges from a functioning brain, but this seems to escape his attention.

While most people would consider that understanding human consciousness is somewhat irrelevant to their life apart from posing issues in science, this is simply not the case. In fact, if the strictly material conceptualization of consciousness is true, then this has profound implications for the nature and significance of human existence. Scientist Isaac Asimov identifies the most important of these:

> The molecules of my body, after my conception, added other molecules and arranged the whole into more and more complex forms, and in a unique fashion, not quite like the arrangement in any other living thing that ever lived. In the process, I developed, little by little, into a conscious something I call 'I' that exists only as the arrangement. When the arrangement is lost forever, as it will be when I die, the 'I' will be lost forever, too. [17]

This is the gist of the head doctrine. Human beings are material beings whose consciousness lives and dies with their functioning brains. When the molecules or neurons are destroyed, consciousness is no more and so

---

[16] R. Sperry, Emergence (In *The Omni Interviews*, Omni Press Books, New York, 1984.)

[17] I. Asimov, The Subtlest Difference. (In Abell, G. & Singer, B. eds. *Science and the Paranormal*. Scribner's Sons, New York, 1981), 158.

life ends at death and the "I" is lost forever. In the same vein, Carl Sagan elaborated a strictly materialist position:

> ... the mind is merely what the brain does. There's nothing else, there's no soul or psyche that's not made out of matter, that isn't a function of 10 to the 14th synapses in the brain. [18]

In this view, there is no individual singular 'I' in a living being and we are instead nothing but a 'pack of neurons' (as described by Frances Crick) or an arrangement of material molecules.

Current scientific thinking also tends to regard consciousness as being *non-substantive*-that is, as nothing in itself. According to this view, there is no way for consciousness to exist separately from or beyond the mind and the body, because consciousness has literally no substance in itself-it is no thing. Rather, it is an epiphenomena produced by material and electrical processes. Psychologists and scientists further reject any animistic or vital principle within the life of a human being and deny the existence of spirit or soul. There is no modern psychology as a science of the soul in the mainstream of science or academia. Similarly, scientists have banished spirit from their considerations of nature and the universe. Life is viewed as having been created according to natural laws and principles governing material processes, rather than being created by any form of supernatural or metaphysical means.

Whereas humans used to invoke God or gods to make sense of the unknown and to interpret the meaning of life in terms of supernatural forces, scientists suppose that their discoveries of natural forces and laws have done away with the need for such religious and mythic explanations. Carl Sagan, the esteemed popular science writer, gave voice to this sentiment when he declared:

"As we learn more and more about the universe, there seems less and less for God to do." (1979) However, when it comes to the central enigma of modern science concerning the nature of consciousness, scientists have made no progress at all and may have many wrong ideas and misguided theories.

---

[18] C. Sagan, *Psychology Today* (Interview, Jan/Feb. 1996), 65.

In summary, according to the mainstream of contemporary science, human beings are material biological beings, the result of the blind evolutionary processes of random mutation and natural selection. In fact, all the phenomena of nature are believed to have occurred in a God-less Universe, governed by chance and the mechanical functioning of natural laws. In this view, human life and the life of the universe are the fortunate by-products of material processes-ranging from those of subatomic physics to those of evolution and neurology. Consciousness and mind are most frequently equated with the sum of neurological and psychological processes located within the material brain centred in the head. This is the basic 'head doctrine' of modern science and there is considered to be no real 'I' within a human being.

THE HEART DOCTRINE

The heart doctrine is a unifying principle found within the esoteric teachings of the major religious teachings of Judaism, Christianity, Islam, Hinduism, Tibetan Buddhism, Egyptian and Native teachings, as well as in numerous other mystery teachings.

Eastern Sources

In a *Psychology Today* interview (1976), Guru Bawa, an Eastern wise man, made these rather startling comments about western psychology and the common misunderstanding of Self. According to the guru, psychologists are quite deluded about the origin of the mind (or consciousness):

> "I studied psychology once, and I became crazy," Bawa responded in a playful tone. "I lost all my powers. ... Psychologists don't know where the mind is. Some think it is in the brain. Others think it is in the genitals. Others think it is in the ass. But the mind is in the heart, and that is what psychologists do not know. Unless the heart opens, you will be driven crazy by the monkeys of the mind. [19]

This is a telling diagnosis of modern psychology and science. Certainly scientists are in a sad predicament if they do not know where the mind

---

[19] Guru Bawa, The Mind is in the Heart. (*Psychology Today*, Interview, April 1977).

is or where consciousness originates! Yet, from a mystical and spiritual perspective, this is precisely the case.

Guru Bawa describes some psychologists as thinking that the mind is in the brain-as in the modern head doctrine. Others relate it to the genitals- in reference to Freudian psychology with its focus on human sexuality; or 'in the ass' -in reference to the Kundalini, a primordial instinctual energy locked within the root chakra described in yoga psychology. However, Bawa insists: *"The mind is in the heart."* The deepest, most essential Mind and Self are established within the heart and more primary than what the yogis refer to as the *"monkeys of the mind."* In this viewpoint, mainstream psychology, philosophy and science alike are fundamentally mistaken about the nature of consciousness, mind and self. They are not *'Knowers of Self'* as described throughout the mystical literature.

Sri Chinmoy, another contemporary spiritual teacher, stresses the heart doctrine and also diagnoses human beings' *common ignorance* as to the true nature of self:

> He does not know himself precisely because he identifies himself with the ego and not with his real 'I.' What compels him to identify himself with this pseudo 'I'? It is Ignorance. And what tells him that the real 'I' is not and can never be the ego? It is his self-search. What he sees in the inmost recesses of his heart is his real 'I,' his God. [20/21]

Human beings lack true self-knowledge and are asleep to their deeper nature as spiritual beings. According to the mystics, we live in *ignorance* -identifying Self with the thoughts, feelings, desires and sensations which make up the contents of the mind and our personal daily life dramas. All the while, we do not know Self or "real I"-as related to the subtle mystical dimensions of the heart.

---

[20] Sri G. Chinmoy, *Yoga and the Spiritual Life*. (New York, Tower Publications, 1970.)

[21] The term 'ego' is usually taken to refer to our lesser self or personality, a part of the healthy development of a human being. However, sometimes the term Ego is used in the more archaic form, to refer to the true Self. A. Bailey capitalizes the term Ego when referring to the soul.

Ramana Maharshi, an Indian sage and mystic, similarly described the Self as related to the Heart Centre-deeper than the personal or ego level of the mind centred in the head:

> ... the final goal (of yoga, or life) may be described as the resolution of the mind in its source which is God, the Self; in that of technical yoga, it may be described as the dissolution of the mind in the Heart lotus. ... The mind and the breath spring from the same source. They arise in the heart, which is the centre of the self-luminous Self. ... Where the 'I' thought has vanished, there the true Self shines as 'I.' 'I' in the heart. ... The 'I,' the Self, alone is real. As there is no other consciousness to know it, it is consciousness. [22]

"I" or "Self" is identified most intimately with the spiritual and soul dimensions of the heart and is connected therein to God. The goal of yoga is the dissolution of the mind into its source-within the heart lotus or centre. The Self is "self-luminous" and "shining"-having an inherent light nature and this self-luminous Self is "consciousness itself." Consciousness is the light of Self.

Ramana Maharshi elaborates upon the mysteries of the heart. He explains how the Self emerges as a point source of light and consciousness associated with the true Heart centre and its influences circulate as light throughout the interior dimensions of a human being:

> The effulgent light of active-consciousness starts at a point and gives light to the entire body even as the sun does to the world. When that light spreads out in the body one gets the experiences in the body. The sages call the original point *'Hridayam'* (the Heart). ... The Individual permeates the entire body, with that light, becomes egocentric and thinks that he is the body and that the world is different from himself. ... The association of the Self with the body is called the *Granthi* (knot). ... When Atma (the Self) alone shines, within and without, and everywhere ... one is said to have severed the knot...[23]

---

[22] Ramana Maharshi, *The Sage of Arunacala*. (By Mahadevan, Allen & Unwin, London, 1977).90-1.

[23] K. Bhikshu, *Sri Ramana Gita (Dialogues of Maharshi)*, (India, Tiruvannamalai, 1966), 39-42.

The Self within the heart has inner connections to the universe, to spiritual realities and even to God. In the *Upanishads* of ancient India, the heart doctrine is elaborated most eloquently:

> Within the lotus of the heart he dwells, where, like the spokes of a wheel in its hub, the nerves meet. ... This Self, who understands all, who knows all, and whose glory is manifest in the universe, lives within the lotus of the heart, the bright throne of Brahman. ... Self-luminous is that Being, and formless. He dwells within all and without all. ... The Self exists in man, within the lotus of the heart, and is the master of his life and of his body. ... The knot of the heart, which is ignorance, is loosed, all doubts are dissolved .... *Mundaka Upanishad* [24]
>
> As large as the universe outside, even so large is the universe within the lotus of the heart. Within it are heaven and earth, the sun, the moon, the lightning, and all the stars. What is in the macrocosm is in this microcosm ... All things that exist ... are in the city of Brahman. *Chandogya Upanishad* [25]

Sacred religious texts from the world's religions associate states of illumined, spiritual and cosmic consciousness with the sacred Heart space. Such teachings in fact suggest that there is a deep holographic physics and metaphysics to the human heart and Self.

The *Bhagavad Gita* is a classic text of Indian spiritual knowledge described as *"the cream of the Vedas."* Lord Krishna, the Personality of the Godhead, elaborates upon the nature of the Self and the process of attaining self-knowledge. *"The Supreme Lord is situated in everyone's heart, O Arjuna, and is directing the wanderings of all living entities, who are seated as on a machine made of material energy."* [26] According to the Gita, both the Supreme Lord (the Supersoul or Paramatma) and the individual spirit soul (the jivatma) are associated with the heart: *"I am that Lord represented as the Supersoul, dwelling in the heart of every embodied being."*

---

[24] S. Prabhavananda & F. Manchester (Eds.), *The Upanishads:Breath of the Eternal.* (New York, New American Library, 1957), 45-6.

[25] Ibid., 74.

[26] A. Prabhupada, A. *Bhagavad-gita: As it is.* (Los Angeles, Ca., Bhaktivedanta Book Trust, 1972).

> Out of compassion for them, I, dwelling in their hearts, destroy with the shining lamp of knowledge the darkness born of ignorance. (10, 11)

> I am the Self, O conqueror of sleep, seated in the hearts of all creatures. I am the beginning, the middle and the end of all beings. (10, 20)

The Supersoul and the individual soul are compared to two birds sitting together on the branch of a tree. The individual soul is captivated by the fruits of the tree which represent material desires, while the Super Soul is a silent witness. To attain liberation, the individual spirit soul must overcome patterns of attachment to pleasurable experiences, desires and the fruits of action, and surrender to the larger Self of the Lord. Self-realization, or union with the Lord, comes through awakening to the eternal principle within the sacred temple of the heart.

Human consciousness originates from the jivatma, the individual spiritual soul embodied within the heart. According to this formulation, consciousness is the light of the spiritual soul as the jivatma is inherently self-illuminating: "... *as the sun alone illuminates all this universe, so does the living entity, one within the body, illuminate the entire body by consciousness.*"[27] Swami Prabhupada elaborates the meaning of this sacred text:

> As the sun is situated in one place, but is illuminating the whole universe, so a small particle of spirit soul, although situated in the heart of this body, is illuminating the whole body by consciousness. Thus consciousness is the proof of the presence of the soul, as sunshine or light is the proof of the presence of the sun. ... consciousness is not a production of the combination of matter. It is the symptom of the living entity. The consciousness of the living entity, although qualitatively one with the supreme consciousness, is not supreme because the consciousness of one particular body does not share that of another body. But the Supersoul, which is situated in all

---

[27] Ibid., 34.

> bodies as the friend of the individual soul, is conscious of all bodies. That is the difference between supreme consciousness and individual consciousness. [28]

A small particle of spirit soul (the spiritual spark) inhabits the material heart as the "sun" of the body. The spiritual soul is self-illuminating and its light is an expression of the infinite light of That Self, the Supersoul.

Swami Yogeshwaranand Saraswati in *Science of Soul: A treatise on Higher Yoga* (1987) provides one of the most comprehensive accounts of the nature of the soul and its relationship to the physical and subtle bodies. The jivatma is likened to *"an infinitesimal poppy seed,"* which has no form or colour. This atomic or indivisible entity is embodied in *"a hollow the size of a small thumb in the heart."* [29] Saraswati describes the *Bliss Sheath*:

> ... the golden sheath of the divine city ... which is a mass of light filled with bliss, has its abode in the subtle area of grape-sized hollow of this physical heart, the repository of blood. It is in the castle of this causal sheath that the immortal individual soul abides with its supreme protectos, all-powerful, omniscient, adorable father - God. The temple of a yogi is inside the heart alone. There ... the vision of Divinity ... the nectar of bliss ... the Bliss Sheath (or Anandamaya Kosha). [30]

The Bliss Sheath is the ensouled jivatma, the essential heart centre, also referred to as the causal body. Saraswati notes: *"... it is instinctually recognized that Jivatman denoted by the pure form of "I" has its abode in the heart, and in Samadhi there is direct realization of this."* [31] Within the Bliss Sheath, there are orbits of different principles which mediate between the divine atom, or jivatma, at the center, and the dimensions of the sheaths and bodies. Through yogic practices and austerities, consciousness can be freed from the outer sheaths and abide again in the bliss sheath-in its essential nature. As these processes of liberation occur, varied states of super-consciousness

---

[28] Ibid., 659-660.

[29] Swami Yogeshwaranand Saraswati, *Science of Soul: A treatise on Higher Yoga* (New Delhi, India, Yoga Niketan Trust, 1987), 36.

[30] Ibid., 37.

[31] Ibid., 69.

and realization (or *samadhis*) are experienced. There are subtle distinctions to be made between experiences of self, cosmic and divine realization, which can be attained through the awakening within the heart and the subsequent illumination of the higher centres. [32]

These teachings have practical application within self study, as is evident if we consider these profound comments provided by yogi and medical doctor Dr. R. Mishra:

> The physical heart and physical consciousness are related. In the same way, the spiritual heart and spiritual consciousness are related. ... Life and consciousness are byproducts of the heart. ... Biological heart and consciousness are physical in nature and they depend on the metaphysical heart and consciousness. In reality, consciousness is not created but manifested and this manifestation depends on the evolution of the nervous system ... and blood ... Your principle aim is to reach the spiritual heart and spiritual consciousness by means of the physical heart and physical consciousness. [33]

Whereas modern psychology and science have considered consciousness to be non-substantive, nothing in itself, the Dalai Lama and the mystical literature clearly equate consciousness with light. The Self is inherently self-illuminating. The Dalai Lama explains that consciousness is such an inner illumination which reflects the deeper Mind of Clear Light:

> Consciousness is defined as that which is luminous and knowing. It is luminous in the double sense that its nature is clear and that it illuminates, or reveals, like a lamp that dispels darkness so that objects may be seen. ... Consciousness is composed of moments, instead of cells, atoms, or particles. In this way consciousness and matter have different natures, and therefore, they have different substantive causes. [34]

---

[32] Following Descartes, the pineal gland is sometimes suggested as the seat for the soul. The light sensitive pineal gland has even been labelled as *'the heart of the brain'* and is said to anchor the thousand petaled lotus of the crown chakra. However, in yogic psychology the mind is regarded as the lunar orbit relative to the solar orbit of the heart.

[33] R. Mishra, *Fundamentals of Yoga*. (New York, Lancer Books, 1969), 139-40.

[34] Dalai Lama, *Advice on Dying: And living a better life* (New York, Atria Books, 2002), 129.

Consciousness is light which illuminates the objects of human experience — the material side of nature. The Dalai Lama notes: *"Matter cannot make consciousness."* [35]

Mid-eastern traditions point to the same teaching of the heart. The celebrated Sufi poet, Rumi depicts the plight of the lost souls searching for God and Self in the outer world:

> Cross and Christians, end to end, I examined. He was not on the Cross. I went to the Hindu temple, to the ancient pagoda. In none of them was there any sign. To the uplands of Herat I went, and to Kandahar, I looked. He was not on the heights or in the lowlands. ... I went to the Kaaba of Mecca. He was not there. ... I asked about him from Avicenna .... (finally) I looked into my own heart. In that, his place, I saw him. He was in no other place. [36]

Similarly, a poet of the heart and soul, Kahil Gibran, in *The Prophet* is asked by the people, to *"Speak to us of Self-Knowledge."* And the prophet answered, saying: *"Your hearts know in silence the secrets of the days and the nights. But your ears thirst for the sound of your heart's knowledge."* [37]

Mystical and esoteric teachings and practices can enable an individual to overcome the illusions, conditioning and limitations of *pseudo-I*--the sense of ego or I associated with the personality and mind centred within the head brain — and to realize the deeper dimensions of "I" within the heart. The realization of Self within the Heart is the basis for the mystical declaration *"I AM."*

---

[35] Dalai Lama, in R. Weber, *Dialogues with Scientists and Sages: The Search for Unity* (New York, Routledge & Kegan Paul, 1986), 236.

[36] Rumi, in I. Shah, *The Way of the Sufi* (London, Jonathan Cape, 1968), 105.

[37] Kahil Gibran, *The Prophet* (New York, Alfred Knopf, 1968), 54-55.

Western Sources

The heart doctrine is illustrated most simply in an Aboriginal tale about creation and the gods:

> One day ... the gods decided to create the universe. They created the stars, the sun and the moon. They created the seas, the mountains, the flowers, and the clouds. Then they created human beings. At the end, they created Truth.
>
> At this point, however, a problem arose: where should they hide Truth so that human beings would not find it right away? They wanted to prolong the adventure of the search.
>
> "Let's put Truth on top of the highest mountain," said one of the gods. "Certainly it will be hard to find it there."
>
> "Let's put it on the farthest star," said another.
>
> "Let's hide it in the darkest and deepest of abysses."
>
> "Let's conceal it on the secret side of the moon."
>
> At the end, the wisest and most ancient god said, "No, we will hide Truth inside the very heart of human beings. In this way they will look for it all over the Universe, without being aware of having it inside of themselves all the time. [38]

In Kabbalah, wisdom and understanding are associated with the Heart and truth is described in the Judaic tradition as *'under our noses'* the whole time. Scholar C. Kramer explains that *"... the heart is truly a wonder, for its creative action mirrors the original act of Creation."* [39] In terms of the creation of the universe, Kabbalah depicts the 'Zimzum' contraction as a process by which the infinite limits itself, or withdraws its limitless light from a volume of space to allow a finite being to emerge into existence. This creates a hollow or seeming void at the heart of being. Thus, within a human being, *"God is always extremely near, for God resides within one's heart - within one's "vacated space."* [40] The Heart is such a hollow Space within us, a form of *"nothingness*

---

[38] W. Mills, *Tone* Magazine. (Ottawa, Ontario, April, 1999).

[39] Chaim Kramer, *Anatomy of The Soul* (Jerusalem, Breslov Research Institute, 1998).

[40] Ibid., 218.

at the heart of being." Kramer explains: *"the passion of the heart is really an infinite desire for the Ein Sof."* [41]

The teachings of Kabbalah offer a complex mathematical and metaphysical model of the inner geometry of being and non-being, and the higher dimensional origins of consciousness within the sacred heart Space— within the *Sephiroth* of *Tipheret* in the *Tree of Life*. The microcosm of a human being is designed on the same basic principles of creation as embodied within the macrocosm of the Universe. Hence, key Kabbalist ideas concerning the creation of the universe provide then a valuable model for the emergence of human consciousness. In Judaic mysticism, the soul longs to experience the joy and revelations of God within the heart. Kramer notes: *"The power of joy is so intense that it can bring one to a revelation of Godliness within one's heart. …the Divine Presence corresponds to the joy of the heart. … One's burning desire for Torah and spirituality enables one to draw from the spirituality of the Supernal Heart (Binah).* [42]

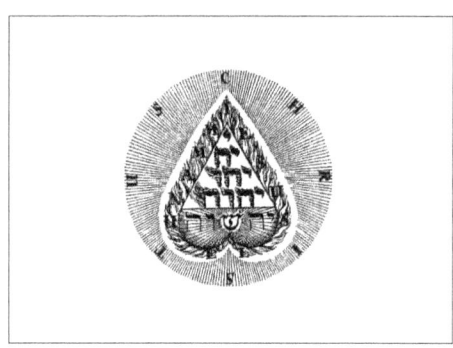

We are living Torahs with the Word and the laws of God written into our very being—in fact into the Heart. So then, there must be a form of higher dimensional physics and metaphysics to the heart. This figure from mystic Jacob Boehme depicts the Word, the four letter name of God, inscribed within the heart—although a spiritual heart of flames turned upwards relative to the material heart. [43]

Kabbalists maintain that there are such Divine source Emanations or Divine Sparks, as stars in space, points of supernal light related to the higher dimensional vacated Space of the heart! Such 'sparks of holiness' emerge from the primordial realm of *Adam Kadmon*.

---

[41] Ibid., 211.

[42] Ibid., 231-2.

[43] This illustration is from Manly Hall's *The Secret Teachings of All Ages: An encyclopedic outline of Masonic, Hermetic, Quabbalistic and Rosicrucian Symbolical Philosophy.* (Los Angeles, Philosophical Research Society, 1978)

A central mystical Christian teaching is that *"the kingdom of heaven is within"* and the state of Christ Consciousness involves the mystical awakening of the heart. This teaching is suggested within the *Old* and *New Testament* and numerous Christian writings, hymns and church doctrine. Matthew 5, 8, states: *"Blessed are the pure in heart: for they shall see God."* Generally, this teaching is not understood in its significance as a principle of psychology — as a science of the soul.

Early sects of the Gnostic Christians taught that to know oneself at the deepest level was simultaneously to know God or the Father as the source of the divine, spiritual and soul life within. The Gospels of the *Nag Hammadi Library*-manuscripts discovered in Egypt in 1945-provide a rich source of esoteric Christian teachings. In the *Gospel of Truth*, Christ encourages the disciples to gain the light which is within them, instead of living in outer darkness; and to *"proclaim the things that are in the heart of the Father in order to teach those who will receive teaching."* The roots of the Self are within the heart and the pleroma:

> ... you ... of interior knowledge ... Say, then, from the heart that you are the perfect day and in you dwells the light that does not fail. ... They are the ones who appear in truth since they exist in true and eternal life and speak of the light which is perfect and filled with the seed of the Father, and which is in his heart and in the pleroma, while his Spirit rejoices in it and glorifies the one in whom it existed.... [44]

Those of *"interior knowledge"* have realized their spiritual nature and know of the perfect light within the heart. The "seeds of the Father" are within the "pleroma" of the divine mother. The term pleroma, like that of the divine plenum, refers to the fullness of things, or the infinite potential latent within God as the En Soph.

The term *'the heart doctrine'* was used by H. P. Blavatsky in her classic *The Voice of the Silence* (1877), which depicts the plight of the soul and the process of spiritual attainment. Blavatsky notes that, *"The "Doctrine of the Eye" is for the crowd, the "Doctrine of the Heart," for the elect."* This suggests that the heart doctrine is a higher teaching than that which focuses upon

---

[44] J. Robinson (Ed.), *Nag Hammadi Library* (San Francisco, Harper & Row, 1981), 44 & 49.

the awakening of the third eye. Further, Blavatsky tells us that we must learn to separate *"Head-learning"* from *"Soul Wisdom"* and states that, *"'Great Sifter' is the name of the "Heart Doctrine"...."* If one so sifts through the esoteric literature, one can uncover this nugget of gold. In Blavatsky's *Secret Doctrine* (1888), one of the ancient *Stanzas of Dzyan* states: "THE SONS EXPAND AND CONTRACT THROUGH THEIR OWN SELVES AND HEARTS; THEY EMBRACE INFINITUDE. ... REFLECTING THE "SELF-EXISTING LORD" LIKE A MIRROR, EACH BECOMES IN TURN A WORLD." In the Stanzas, the term Son refers not only to any created Kosmos, but also to individual beings. Blavatsky regarded the heart as the centre of the original undifferentiated 'laya centre' and of buddhic consciousness.

In modern times, the American mystic Adi Da clearly embodies the heart doctrine:

> The true Self is Awake in your own heart. ... The region of the heart, which is the seat of the soul and the doorway to the true Self, is one of the primary areas of the body-mind traditionally inspected by mystical vision. ... The true center of the heart is intuitively felt.... The heart-root is prior to the physical and subtle structures of the body-mind. ... It is prior to all energies and forms in the Realm of Nature. [45]

The Self is prior to the physical and subtle dimensions of the heart. Adi Da explains that in the process of spiritual awakening, one transcends the death of the egoic psyche by *"awakening at the heart in the disposition that is prior to the heartbeat itself."* By this passage, the peripheral personality yields to the central consciousness of being!

Another enigma within modern science which has great significance from a mystical perspective concerns the manner in which the heart generates its own electrical impulses through the pacemaker—the SA Node, the AV node and the fibres of the Bundle of Hiss. Psychologist B. Brown once explained: *"The genesis of the heartbeat is as unknown as the genesis of man, and equally a miracle."* [46] Scientists have been unable to explain this phenomena from a

---

[45] Adi Da, *The Enlightenment of the Whole Body*. Dawn Horse Press, California, 1978, pp. 387-90.

[46] B. Brown, *New Mind, New Body: Biofeedback: New Directions for the Mind*. Bantam Books, Toronto, 1974, 227.

materialist perspective, whereas from an occult viewpoint, it is the presence of the jivatma, the living spiritual soul, which so enlivens the material heart. In this case, these material effects—the generation of the heartbeat—is due to metaphysical causes. Further, the distribution of consciousness through the body is related to the blood flow and the ensoulment of the living organism through the breath and the process of oxygenation. Consciousness is never simply centred up in the mind in the head, no matter what scientists may think. [47]

Concluding Remarks

Mystical teachings elaborate an alternative model of the higher dimensional origins of human consciousness and self. Whereas modern science presupposes that material processes within the brain produce consciousness and the experience of self, mystical perspectives describe consciousness as the light of Self and as emerging from *within-without* through some higher dimensional physics and metaphysics of the human heart. Mystical teachings further suggest profound possibilities for states of awakened consciousness, enlightenment, illumination and liberation—associated with the awakening of the heart and the subsequent illumination of higher centres.

These teachings provide an alternative viewpoint to those perspectives offered by so-called "exact science" -with its denial of spirit, soul and any transcendental or religious principle. If we speak off the tops of our heads, we can simply assume that the head-brain produces consciousness and mind, but if we penetrate to the heart of being, to the Heart of ourselves, might we indeed become *"Knowers of Self?"* From a mystical and spiritual perspective, modern psychology and philosophy are filled with head knowledge but lack the secret wisdom of the Self within the Heart. Consciousness and Self are substantive and should not simply be used as generic terms to identify the flow of thoughts, feelings and sensations that occur within subjective experience generated by the brain. There is something far deeper happening within a human being as concerns the origin and nature of consciousness. The Self exists in relationship to a hierarchy of interpenetrating world orders— metaphysical dimensions of spiritual and divine existence which underlie and sustain the realms of subtle and gross matter. These dynamics allow for afterlife existence and for

---

[47] In modern science, researchers map brain functions by monitoring blood flow to determine which parts of the brain are active during different cognitive tasks. Unfortunately, scientists do not consider that the blood flow might itself be related to the experience of consciousness.

complex relationships of the individual to the Sun, to the larger Universe and most importantly to spiritual and divine realities.

II
Zero Point Hypothesis

the Universe is contained in ovo in the first natural point.

*"material points without extension" are Leibnitz's Monads,
and at the same time the materials out of which the "Gods"
and other invisible powers clothe themselves in bodies…
such a point of transition must certainly possess special
and not readily discoverable properties.*

H. P. Blavatsky, *The Secret Doctrine*, 1888[48]

*the divine spark [is] buried deep in every soul. .
we must leave the physical world of matter far behind and rise to the
luminous world above to attain the divine principle of our superior soul. …
I … engraved the symbol of the knowledge of the Initiates:
a circle with a point in the center.
… all my life has been based on this symbol of the circle with its central point.
This center which is in us, we must find.*

Michael Aivanhov[49]

---

[48] Helena P. Blavatsky, *The Secret Doctrine*, Vol. I (Wheaton: Theosophical Publishing House, 1888), 118, 489, 628.

[49] O. Michael Aivanov, *Love and Sexuality*, Complete Works, Vol. 14 (France: Editions Prosveta, 1976), 73.

ABSTRACT

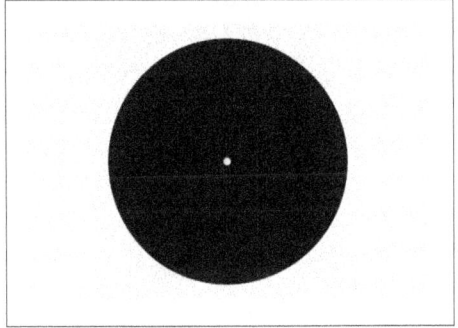

Varied mystical teachings depict the origin of consciousness as deriving from a zero point source or condition. Whether the Monads of Blavatsky, the divine sparks of the Gnostics and Kabbalists, the jivatma of yogic and Vedic teachings, or the "God spark" of Shirley MacLaine, the notion is that a human being does have a central "I" element, associated with the source of life and consciousness within the material body. This zero point "laya center" is associated with the human heart and is the means by which a higher dimensional metaphysics give rise to a lower dimensional physics. Zero point centers can be regarded as emanations or divine elements in higher dimensional space and/or as the portals between the spiritual and material realms. The essential life center or zero point element is inherently Self-illuminating and this light is that of consciousness. Modern physical views of universal creation illustrate such bizarre notions of zero point origins, although scientists do not conceive that human consciousness and being-existence might similarly have such zero point origins.[50]

---

[50] Pre-publication reviewers of this article had most valuable reservations concerning the tendency here to too simply equate ideas and teachings from different mystical traditions, when really there are subtle distinctions and emphasis which need to be more significantly examined. This is absolutely true and I agree with this sentiment whole heartedly. However, the point to be made is that such types of point source dynamics *are found* within varied traditions. The fact alone of isolating and identifying such a "zero point hypothesis" within different traditions is a starting point in exploring such mystery teachings. I, as author, am merely trying to isolate such profound concepts and draw similarities and comparisons. Similarly, although I draw relationships between the mystical traditions and modern physics and science, these also cannot be simply equated. Zero point dynamics and dimensions are multidimensional within both traditions, and I personally do not pretend to fully understand the mysteries of these things. Physicists themselves do not claim to fully understand these things either. We do firstly need a language in order to address these issues. Further, there are definitely aspects of such teachings within the mystical tradition beyond the concepts of modern science — particularly that 'living beings' have such point source origins. All the reviewers themselves acknowledged the value of this effort despite such reservations, which I myself similarly share

THE ZERO POINT HYPOTHESIS

The term *zero point* was used by mystic scholar Helena P. Blavatsky, founder of the Theosophical Society (1875) and author of *The Secret Doctrine* (1888). Blavatsky does not elaborate extensively upon zero point dynamics within *The Secret Doctrine* or elsewhere, but her few discussions are immensely valuable. The zero point teaching has been largely overlooked within modern theosophical studies.

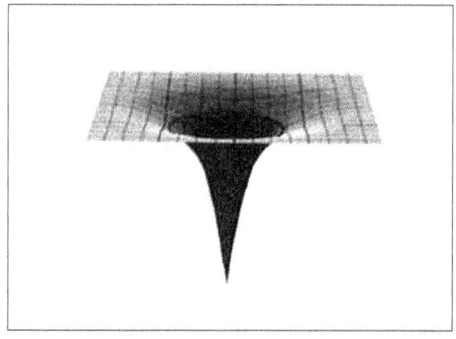

Figure 1 [51]

Volume I of *The Secret Doctrine*, *Cosmogenesis* deals with the origin of the universe and creation metaphysics. Blavatsky used the symbol of a point within a circle to represent the zero point origin of the cosmos — a point source of unfolding wherein the finite Kosmos emerged from the Infinite root principles at the beginning of time. The Kosmos expands within-without when the *Breath of the Father* is upon it and then eventually contracts without-within when the *Breath of the Mother* touches it. (See Figure 1) The Kosmos returns to a neutral zero point center at the end of time. Relative space-time worlds, or "Sons," emerge out of an underlying *Eternal Parent Space* and eventually return again to it. Cycles of the Seven Days and Nights of Brahma occur with Days of creation or *Manvantara*, alternating with Nights of Brahma — a period of Pralaya, or rest. Blavatsky depicted innumerable worlds over eons of time being created in cycles from such zero point sources or "laya centers."

Blavatsky uses various terms to depict these invisible points-labeling them also as *"layu centers"* and *"laya centers."* [52] The influences of divine or spiritual realms upon the physical realm emerge through these laya centers, which exist at or beyond the level of material differentiation.

---

[51] Figures 1, 2, 5, 7, 9, 10, 11 are in the public domain.

[52] *The Secret Doctrine* employs both terms, sometimes alone and sometimes together, but the meaning is the same. However, Layu is the term found in the original verses of the *Stanzas* or *Book of Dzyan* upon which much of *The Secret Doctrine* is based.

> ... the Laya condition, the point from which, or at which, the primordial substance begins to differentiate and thus gives birth to the universe and all in it.
>
> Laya does not mean any particular something or some plane or other, but denotes a state or condition. It is a Sanskrit term, conveying the idea of something in an undifferentiated and changeless state, a zero point wherein all differentiation ceases.
>
> ... from the "Zero-state" (or *layam*) it becomes active and passive, ... and, in consequence of this differentiation (the resultant of which is evolution and the subsequent Universe),--the "Son" is produced, the Son being that same Universe, or manifested Kosmos, till a new Mahapralaya.[53]

Not only did Blavatsky depict the point source origin of the universe, but she also described zero point laya centers as existent in all living beings—including ourselves. It is through zero point laya centers and dynamics that "the 'Gods' *and other invisible powers clothe themselves in bodies.*" Zero points are beyond the level of material differentiation:

> The chemist goes to the *laya* or zero-point of the plane of matter with which he deals, and then stops short. ... But the full Initiate *knows* that the ring "Pass-Not" is neither locality, nor can it be measured by distance, but that it exists in the absoluteness of infinity. In this "Infinity" ... there is neither height, breadth nor thickness, but all is fathomless profundity, reaching down from the physical to the "para-para-metaphysical." [54]

What Blavatsky describes as the *zero point* or the *Ring Pass Not* is similar to those levels of the Planckian units in physics, beyond which physical measurement becomes impossible.

---

[53] Helena P. Blavatsky, *Transactions of the Blavatsky Lodge*, (Los Angeles: Theosophy Company, 1889/1987), 5, 7, 38.

[54] Blavatsky, *The Secret Doctrine*, Vol. 1, 131.

However, zero point transitional states and dynamics might occur at varied levels within the Aethers of Space.[55]

Blavatsky gives this overview of the evolution and dissolution of the Cosmos:

> ... evolution ... may be thus formulated as an invariable law; a descent of Spirit into Matter, equivalent to an ascent in physical evolution; a re-ascent from the depths of materiality towards its *status quo ante*, with a corresponding dissipation of concrete form and substance up to the LAYA state, or what Science calls "the zero point," and beyond.[56]

The Secret Doctrine postulates the dissolution of the universe, or Son, into a Laya Center or neutral zero point center at the end of time.

When examined from a physical perspective, zero points are infinitely small and disappear from view. Zero points mark the transition between varied world orders within the hierarchies of creation. They are points at which something passes over from this world to THAT; where the physical dissolves back into the metaphysical or the material resolves back into the spiritual and divine. Zero points are rooted into higher dimensional Space. The actuality of human beings being based upon such a multidimensional physics of zero point dimensions allows for a much expanded view of human nature.

A century after the publication of *The Secret Doctrine*, theories in modern physics and cosmology now illustrate Blavatsky's seemingly bizarre concepts of the zero point origin of the Kosmos. In modern cosmology, the universe is described as emerging from *a singularity point*, 10^{-33} cm. in diameter at

---

[55] What might be regarded as a "point source" from one level of apprehension might constitute a *whole inner world* on another level of cosmic differentiation. A concrete example of this is a "fertilized ovum," which on one level appears visually as a point element, but which contains a whole inner world on another dimension of scale. The application of the zero point concept must be considered in a multi-dimensional way. The Ring Pass Not does not simply equate with the Planckian level of physics, which are simply the limits of perception from the vantage point of the lower ethers. The etheric level is far from the original impulse of the Monad as it starts its journey downwards through the seven planes. Helena P. Blavatsky, *Transactions of the Blavatsky Lodge*, (Los Angeles: Theosophy Company, 1889/1987), 5, 7, 38.

[56] Blavatsky, *The Secret Doctrine*, Vol. 1, 620.

the beginning of time, $10^{-45\text{th}}$ of a second. It emerged out of the quantum vacuum—a seeming void and plenum, a realm of hidden dimensions of being and non-being. Modern scientists consider that the universe emerged from such a singular point and it could ultimately return to such a singularity at the end of time, in what is referred to as the "big crunch" to contrast with the "big bang" creation event. *The Secret Doctrine* similarly described creation emerging from such a point source and eventually returning to such a state. However, in *The Secret Doctrine*, the zero point or laya center is not just there at the beginning and end of time, as the alpha and omega points, but instead exists throughout. It is the means by which the higher dimensional intelligences fashion and ensoul the material coverings or bodies.

Within the metaphysical teaching of Blavatsky's *The Secret Doctrine*, a Kosmos is labeled as a *"Son,"* as a *"wink of the Eye of Self-Existence"* and as a *"spark of eternity."* It is suggested that there are such zero point laya centers, elements and dynamics within all living beings.

A Monad is such a zero point source of light and life within self. Blavatsky wrote: *"... the Monad ... is not of this world or plane, and may be compared only to an indestructible star of divine light and fire, thrown down on to our Earth."* Just as the Macrocosm might have a first point of supernal *lux*, so does the Microcosm of a living breathing human being, in accord with the mystical axiom *"As above, so below."* Thus, there might theoretically at least be a "God spark" or divine element, or jivatma, within a living human being. This would constitute an "I" unlike any of those proposed by materialist scientists which are only the impermanent and illusory composites of molecules, cell or neurons in the brain. A zero point laya center within the heart would be an "I" for which there could be a whole inner higher dimensional physics and metaphysics.

The Secret Doctrine maintains that the universe is founded upon an original zero point and the laws of nature are based upon a further differentiation into *seven zero point centers*. Whether a Universe, a quantum or an individual divine spark, the laws of nature manifesting in the material worlds are due to Divine and spiritual forces and intelligences emerging within/without through seven dimensional zero point dynamics. Blavatsky describes seven minute *"holes dug in space"* as the means by which higher dimensional forces sculpt the void through the processes of creation. Blavatsky offers this explanation of the "Forces of Nature:"

> ... all the so-called Forces of Nature ... are *in esse*, i.e., in their ultimate constitution, the differentiated aspects of that Universal Motion. ... Fohat is said to produce "Seven Laya Centers" ... the GREAT LAW ... modifies its perpetual motion on seven invisible points within the area of the manifested Universe. *"The great Breath digs through Space seven holes into Laya to cause them to circumgyrate during Manvantara."* (Occult Catechism). We have said that Laya is what Science may call the Zero-point or line; the realm of absolute negativeness, or the one real absolute Force ... the neutral axis, not one of the many aspects, but its center. ... "Seven Neutral Centers," then are produced by Fohat .... [57]

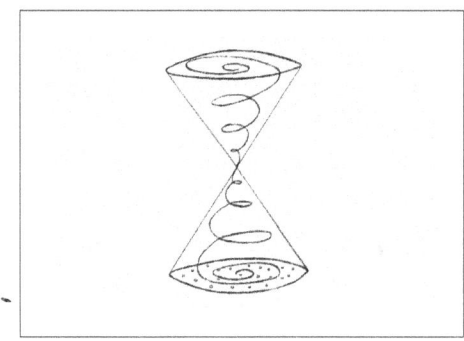

Figure 2

Blavatsky describes the great Breath or Law as *"digging holes in Space"* to channel intelligence and influences into the material realm. Thus, seven invisible zero point *holes dug in space* are established as a foundation for physical manifestation and the laws of nature. Any Cosmos, any Universe, any Monad (a divine or spiritual spark), any atom or quantum, is thus *"worked and guided from within outwards"* through the dynamics of such zero point centers.

A zero point can be regarded a "thing" in itself—and/or a condition or a place at which certain processes occur. A zero point can be considered as a "point particle" —like a monad in hyperspace, or as a portal or transitional point between dimensions. In fact, there could be multiple zero point transitions between dimensions and lives.

A *Stanza of Dzyan* from *The Secret Doctrine* (1888) reads: *"The Sons expand and contract through their own selves and hearts; they embrace infinitude. ... Each is a part of the web. Reflecting the 'Self-existing Lord' like a mirror, each becomes in turn a world."* [58/59]

---

[57] Ibid., 147-8.
[58] Ibid., 489.

The expansion and contraction of the Sons is through the zero point laya center associated with the heart and each individual in turn becomes a world. At the heart of the universe, a galaxy, the sun, a quantum and a human being are such zero point laya centers, whereby the Gods and other invisible powers clothe themselves in bodies. Thus, life and consciousness within a living being originates within/without out of higher space dimensions through the dynamics of a multidimensional heart.

Although the zero point is sometimes described as singular, at other times it is described as having a sevenfold differentiation. Like Fohat, it is One and Seven. Fohat is the messenger or agent of the seven spiritual intelligences above. He, and his seven sons, run *circular errands*, to convey the influences of Mind above to impress ideas upon matter below. This process proceeds through zero point dynamics, the *"holes dug in space."* Further, for Blavatsky, "real space," is the "Seven Skinned Eternal Parent Space," the ultimate Aether or Akasha.

The trinity of Intelligence, the cosmic electricity of Fohat and material nature are the spirit, soul and body of the Kosmos. It is through such mysterious zero point dynamics that the differentiation of a Cosmos, a quantum or Monad begins, and through which they are ensouled by Fohat.

Modern scientist, Paul Davies, described such a model of 11 dimensional theory in modern physics where 7 "compacted dimensions" are rolled up into elements at zero point levels. Davis explained, *"think of the extra dimensions as somehow inside the atom."*[60] Remarkably, Blavatsky explained exactly this type of peculiar inner dimensionality to "atoms," quanta, Monads and the Kosmos over a century ago. Accordingly, Blavatsky's model suggests that there is a complex metaphysics to reality at zero point levels.

---

[59] The *Stanzas of Dzyan* are described as *"the heart of the sacred books of Kiu-ti,"* once known only to Tibetan mystics. Blavatsky describes a *"very old Book"* originally recorded in Senzar—the *"sacred sacerdotal tongue"* and she maintains that the Stanzas originated from *"the words of the Divine Beings, who dictated it to the sons of Light, in Central Asia, at the very beginning of the 5th (our) race."* (p. xliii) certainly, these are the most unusual claims and the origin of the *Stanzas* seems largely lost in antiquity.

[60] Paul Davies, *Superforce: The Search for a Grand Unified Theory of Nature* (New York: Touchstone Books, 1984), 174.

> The "Imperishable Laya Centers" have a great importance, and their meaning must be fully understood if we would have a clear conception of the Archaic Cosmogony....[61]

The mystical conjunction of zero point divine sparks within the nothingness and seven hyperspace dimensions associated with the heart ultimately gives rise to human consciousness. The zero point divine spark is a quantum self—a point source of divine light and life and of spiritual consciousness. It is the source of the "I" that "I AM," the hidden Self pointed to by mystics and sages throughout the ages.

YOGIC SCIENCE OF THE SOUL

The *Mundaka Upanishad* compares individual spiritual souls to sparks which are thrown off from the fire of the supreme source and which eventually return to this underlying realm:

> As sparks innumerable fly upward from a blazing fire, so from the depths of the Imperishable arise all things. To the depths of the Imperishable they in turn descend.[62]

Swami Prabhupada explains that according to Vedic teachings both the Supersoul (the Paramatma) and the atomic individual soul (the jivatma) abide within the inner dimensions of the heart. A verse of the Gita reads: "... *the Supersoul accompany(s) the individual soul in all bodies....* " Prabhupada elaborates upon this distinction between the Supersoul and the individual soul:

> The Vedas declare, aham brahmasmi: "I am pure spirit soul." And as spirit souls we all have a relationship with the supreme spirit soul, Krishna, or God. The individual soul may be compared with a spark emanating from the fire of the Supreme Soul. Just as the spark and the fire are of the same quality, the individual

---

[61] Blavatsky, *The Secret Doctrine*, Vol. 1, 145.

[62] Swami Prabhavananda & F. Manchester, (Eds.) *The Upanishads: Breath of the Eternal* (New York: New American Library, 1957), 45.

> spirit soul is of the same spiritual quality as the Supreme Lord. Both share a spiritual nature of eternity, knowledge, and bliss.[63]

The atomic individual soul is a divine or spiritual spark emanating from the fire of the Supreme Soul. The individual life is thus an *apparently* discrete quantum emerging from a transcendental realm of infinite Being. Prabhupada writes:

> ... the soul is inconceivable by human experimental knowledge. The soul is consciousness and conscious ... The Supreme Soul is infinite, and the atomic soul is infinitesimal.
>
> Every living entity is only a spiritual spark.
>
> There are two kinds of souls-namely the minute particle soul (anu-atma) and the Supersoul (the vibhu-atma). ... Both the Supersoul (Paramatma) and the atomic soul (jivatma) are situated ... within the same heart of the living being ... the atomic soul, forgetful of his real nature ... requires to be enlightened....[64]

According to yoga philosophy, a human being has seven vital energy centers within the subtle (non-physical) anatomy. These centers are the *chakras*, a term implying wheels or vortices of energy. Of the seven chakras, the heart center is the fourth and central chakra with three above and three below. In an authoritative text on *Layayoga*, Shyam Sundar Goswami describes these:

> Each center consists of two parts-the center itself and a peripheral aspect. The center is an infinitesimal point which, from a material point of view, is zero. This point in the substratum is a power concentrated to its highest degree ... the peripheral aspect ... appears as circular radiant energy ... The *chakras* are subtler than atoms and particles. If an atom can contain a tremendous amount of energy, why should not a

---

[63] A. C. Bhaktivedanta Swami Prabhupada, *The Bhagavad Gita* (India: Bhaktivedanta Book Trust, 1972), 106, 209,100.

[64] Ibid., 123.

chakra, which is infinitely subtle, contain energy which is practically unlimited in quantity and capacity? [65]

The divine or spiritual spark, the jivatama, is a point source at the center of the heart chakra, from which differentiate seven such zero point centers, all quite consistent with Blavatsky's explanation.

In *Science of Soul: A Treatise on Higher Yoga*, Swami Saraswati, describes the nature of the spiritual soul within the orbits of the heart:

> The seat of the individual soul (is) in the heart..., which may be likened to an infinitesimal poppy seed. There is no form or color to the soul.
>
> In the innermost center of the orb of Chitta exists *Atman*, the self, like a living spark, radiant and beautiful.
>
> This luminous, gentle, diamond-like spark of the soul is enveloped by the apparel of Chitta which is snowy-white and radiantly luminous.
>
> … it is instinctually recognized that Jivatma denoted by the pure form of "I" has its abode in the heart, and in Samadhi there is direct realization of this.[66]

The spiritual spark, the jivatma abides within the "bliss sheath," a mass of unemergent light the size of a small grape.

Ramana Maharshi describes the Self as emerging as a point source of light and consciousness associated with the true Heart center:

> The effulgent light of active consciousness starts at a point and gives light to the entire body even as the sun does to the world. When that light spreads out in the body one gets the experiences in the body. The sages call the original point *"Hridayam"* (the Heart).[67]

---

[65] Goswami S. *Layayoga: An Advanced Method of Concentration* (London: Routledge and Kegan Paul, 1980), 144-5.

[66] Swami Yogeshwaranand Saraswati, *Science of Soul: A Treatise on Higher Yoga* (New Delhi: Yoga Niketan Trust, 1987), 22, 36, 69, 223.

[67] S. Krishna Bhikshu, Sri Ramana Gita: *Dialogues of Maharshi* (Tiruvannamalai, India: Arunachala Ashrama,1966), 42.

The jivatma is essentially an element at zero point levels beyond the level of physical differentiation, yet ultimately the essential point source of individual light consciousness and the life force within a living being.

DIVINE SPARKS OF KABBALAH

Kabbalists describe *three Realms of Negative Existence* as underlying and sustaining the worlds: *Ayin,* or Nothingness, *En Soph,* the Plenum or All, and *En Soph Aur,* the limitless light. These realms are associated with the numbers of 0, 00 and 000. Kabbalist, Z'ev ben Shimon Halevi states: *"the mystic knows that everything has its origin in Absolute Nothing and Absolute All..."* [68]

Kabbalists portray the creation of the universe as emerging from a supernal point of no-dimension out of a background in NEGATIVE EXISTENCE. This point is established within the first Sephira of Kether. The scientific theory of "vacuum genesis" is in fact quite consistent with the Kabbalist description of creation as emerging from within the three realms of Negative Existence—the *creation ex nihilo* of the mystics. Mystics and scientists both regard creation as emerging from point sources out of a seeming Nothingness.

Kabbalists further described the zero point origin of the universe well ahead of the modern scientists who imagine that they originated such a concept. In *Visions & Voices,* Jonathan Cott interviewed Rabbi Lawrence Kushner, whose writings explore the parallels between modern science and Jewish mysticism:

> *Jonathan Cott*: Cosmologists have speculated that at the first explosive moment of the birth of the universe, everything that exists-or ever will exist-was contained within a single spark of energy, smaller than an atom's nucleus and ruled by a single primordial law.
>
> *Rabbi Lawrence Kushner*: One dot—a point of light. Perhaps the fact that contemporary cosmologists talk about a dimen-

---

[68] Z'ev ben Shimon Halevi, *A Kabbalistic Universe* (New York: Weiser Books, 1977), 10.

sionless point of light from which all being sprang and that the Kabbalists long ago came up with precisely the same image (in the fourteenth century, Moses de Leon spoke of *"a hidden supernal point"* whose *"primal center is the innermost light, of a translucence, subtlety, and purity beyond comprehension"*) means that this awareness comes from something we all carry within us. We're walking Torahs ... if we could just shut up and listen to it.[69]

Kabbalists and Rabbis, as well as modern scientists, suggest the zero point origins of the universe – depicting it as originating from *"a dimensionless dot in the midst of the Absolute;"* [70] a "supernal point" or *"primal center."* However, the Kabbalists extends this notion to apply to ourselves – as we are living Torahs with the Word and the laws of God written into our very being – in fact into the Heart. So also, we might imagine a human being as having such zero point origins in a type of ultra-physics of consciousness and the heart.

Rabbi Chaim Kramer describes such "sparks of holiness" and their emergence from the primordial realm of *Adam Kadmon*:

> The consequences of Adam's fall can be compared to a beautiful and expensive piece of crystal that is dropped from a great height and shatters into thousands of tiny pieces which become scattered over a large area. Adam had contained within himself the souls of all mankind in a state of perfect unity. His fall shattered that holy unity into countless *"sparks of holiness"* which subsequently became dispersed throughout the entire world. It has since been man's mission, utilizing the spiritual inclinations incorporated within his system, to search for, find, purify and elevate these sparks, that they may return to their source. This will ... even improve upon, the vessel from which they originated – Adam. ... [71]

---

[69] Jonathan Cott, *Visions & Voices* (New York: Doubleday, 1987), 209.

[70] Halevi, *A Kabbalistic Universe*, 10.

[71] Chaim Kramer, *Anatomy of the Soul* (Jerusalem: Breslov Research Institute, 1998), 56.

Human beings have a remarkable nature according to Kabbalist teaching—as "sparks of holiness." "I" originates from within the deepest realms as an infinitesimal point source of Divine Will and Light Consciousness— "I" stands out and declares *"I AM."*

> *... every created being cries out the name I AM as it emerges from Kether, before plunging into the Cosmic Sea below.*[72]

Kabbalist teachings certainly support the zero point hypotheses and the notion that human beings have such a "primal center," as illustrated in this depiction of a multi-dimensional *Star of David* with its 7th central element: (See Figure below.)

Figure 3 [73]

Another creation process described by Kabbalists involves the withdrawal of the Infinite Light (the En Soph Aur) from around a central point—which creates an empty space or vacuum. This concept has application to understanding the mysteries of the vacated heart Space and the psychology of human consciousness.

Luria describes the Zimzum or Self-constriction:

> BEHOLD HE THEN RESTRICTED HIMSELF, IN THE MIDDLE POINT WHICH IS IN HIM, PRECISELY IN THE MIDDLE, HE RESTRICTED THE LIGHT. AND THE LIGHT WAS WITHDRAWN TO THE SIDES AROUND THE MIDDLE POINT. AND THERE HAVE REMAINED AN EMPTY SPACE, ATMOSPHERE, AND A VACUUM SURROUNDING THE EXACT MIDDLE POINT.[74]

---

[72] Halevi, *A Kabbalistic Universe*, 11.

[73] Mandala with permission from NgAng.

[74] Isaac Luria, *The Kabbalah: A Study of the Ten Luminous Emanations from Isaac Luria, with Two Commentaries by Yehuda L. Ashlag,* translated by Levi I. Krakovsky (Jerusalem: Research Center of Kabbalah, 1984).

God as the Creator withdrew the Limitless Light from that Space surrounding an exact middle point. This created a form of *"nothingness at the heart of Being."* It is of course quite logical that the Infinite Being would have to withdraw from a space in order to allow a finite being or Universe to come into existence. Without this self-contraction, everything is swallowed up in the Infinite.

Kramer explains the *"Torah of the Vacated Space,"* known in Hebrew as the *Challal HaPanuy*:

> Prior to the Creation, there was only God. ... Since God is everywhere, there was no "room" for the Creation to come into being, no *place* which could accommodate His Infinite Light. God thus restricted His Light away from a "center point," as it were, to create the Vacated Space. In this space would be created all the supernal Universes, and also the material world ... God contracted His Light, as it were, concealing Himself from man, making it seem to man's limited vision as if there is a vacuum, a place devoid of Godliness. This is the mystery of the Tzimtzum (Self-constriction).[75]

Kramer explains that the action of the Heart *"mirrors the original act of Creation"* and the Heart is such a hollow Space within us. Hence, Kramer explains: *"the passion of the heart is really an infinite desire for the Ein Sof."* Further, *"God is always extremely near, for God resides within one's heart—within one's 'vacated space.'"*[76] The Heart is such a hollow Space within us, a form of "nothingness at the heart of being."

The Kabbalist *Tree of Life* is a mystical symbol depicting the higher dimensional structures of existence. It is essentially a diagram of God: a diagram of the microcosm or macrocosm and the principles of design inherent to nature. All things in creation embody the sacred principles of the Laws of Three and Seven depicted in the *Tree of Life*, through different generations of causes and effects—all worked out from *within without*. The *Tree of Life* can be used as a model for mystical states and applied to the study of physics and metaphysics, as well as to any other area of inquiry.

---

[75] Ibid., 207.

[76] Ibid., 218.

The *Tree of Life* is composed of 10 Sephirot and the paths which link them. The term "Sephirot" refers to "numerations," "Lights" or "aspects" of God. (See Figure 4) The Sephirot are represented as spheres and are arranged on Three Pillars. An eleventh invisible Sephira, Da'at, is also part of Kabbalist teaching and is located between the supernal triad of Sephirot and the seven lesser Sephirot below.

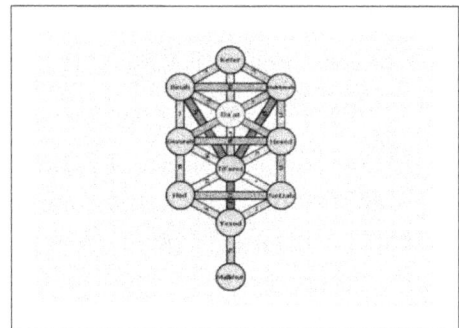

Figure 4

In the *Tree of Life*, the three superior Sephirot are within the *unmanifest supernal realm* and reflect the three-fold nature of Negative Existence. Ayin is embodied in the first Sephira, Kether, the Crown and portrayed as a dimensionless point. Chokhmah is the Divine Father, the active spiritual force and embodies the En Soph Aur—the Limitless Light. Binah is the Divine Mother and embodies En Soph, the plenum, the seven-fold Aether of Space -the roots of material nature. Binah is associated with the Heart.[77]

> When applied to the Act of Creation and to the Vacated Space, the Creation represents Chokhmah while the Vacated Space represents Binah. With Chokhmah alone, there would be no diversification within Creation. It is through the Vacated Space, corresponding to Binah, that the design of all the Universes comes into being.[78]

In the next illustration, the three realms of Negative Existence are suggested by the three overriding arches. Kether is the all-potential, Chokhmah the

---

[75] There are several Kabbalistic "schools" and this material derives from the Lurianic Kabbalah (Isaac Luria, 1533-72), the basis for modern Judaic Kabbalistic thought. The idea that Binah is associated with the heart is particular to the Lurianic idea of Adam Kadmon. In the Western Mystery Tradition, Binah is often associated with the right side of the face and the three supernal Sephiroth form the head of Adam Kadmon. The tradition that Binah also forms the heart is because the heart was at one time understood to be the location of thought, while the head was for rationalization and judgment (see Charles Ponce *Kabbalah: An introduction and illumination for the world today*, Wheaton, Il: Theosophical Publishing House, 1973, 136).

[78] Chaim Kramer, *The Anatomy of the Soul*, 210, 211.

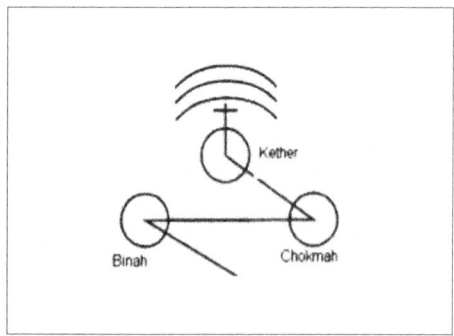

Figure 5

active creative force and Binah the structuring, containing force—all necessary before creation begins.

Chokhmah is assigned the attribute of Wisdom. In the Bible, it is written, *"In the hearts of the wise, I have placed wisdom."* (Exodus 31:6) God is said to have made all things with Chokhmah or Wisdom and these take form within the heart in Binah. The heart is *"the one that gives form to this thought."* (sic) Rebbe Nachman explains: *"For the heart is the 'tZuR of the worlds' (Isaiah 26: 4), meaning, tZayaR, the one that gives form to the Attributes."* The *vacated space of the heart* is a sevenfold hyperspace dimension underlying the sevenfold material realms within positive existence. The Mind of God illuminates the Vacated Space of the Heart, as Chokhmah and Binah, and the matrix of creation is set into motion through these metaphysical processes.

The conjunction of Kether, Chokhmah and Binah (the supernal Father and Mother) produces the Son, Da'at—the 11th invisible Sephira, also represented as a point within a circle. Kramer explains: *"Daat is the external manifestation of Keter, It is a quasi-sefirah that must be formed by the confluence of Chokhmah and Binah."* Further, *"Chokhmah is the male aspect that unites with Binah, the female aspect, to create Daat."*[79]

Da'at is the first external manifestation of the Supernal Triad into the worlds below the abyss. Kramer thus explains that: *"Daat itself went into exile"* and further, that an individual can *"redeem Daat from its exile."* The Point that stands out and emerges from the Supernal Triad is the "spark of holiness." Blavatsky similarly describes the three falling into four and initiating the pilgrimage of the Son.

Chokhmah is associated with Wisdom, Binah with Understanding and Da'at with Knowledge—including the Knowledge of God. Kramer explains in regards to Da'at: *"Man's goal must therefore be the pursuit of Daat, to build his personal sanctuary of spirituality, wherein Godliness can be revealed."*[80]

---

[79] Ibid., 181.

[80] Ibid., 180.

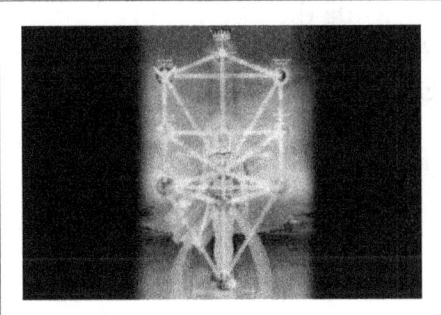

Figure 6 [81]

Da'at embodies Kether as one descends the central pillar of the Tree into the sphere of Tipheret—associated with the Heart. The central pillar of the *Tree of Life* represents the pillar of light, will and consciousness, relative to the side pillars of force and form, the masculine and feminine principles and their generations. (See Figure 6) The supernal triad manifests as Da'at and this is brought down into the Heart in Tipheret. The Self is thus established within the heart. Tipheret is associated with the Sun and with the attribute of beauty. Tipheret is the only Sephira directly connected to each of the three supernal Sephira and it is the seventh Sephira central to the other six lesser Sephirot.

The Sephirot on the central pillar (*Kether, Da'at* and *Tipheret*) represent possible higher levels of human consciousness and illumination, while the lesser *egoic* consciousness is centered over *Yesod* or *Malkuth*. Although Kether and Da'at are frequently represented as a point within the circle, as a symbol of I AM, this is not unsual for Tipheret.

However, the symbol of the Sun is of a point within a circle and I would argue that the spiritual Self within the heart can be similarly presented as a zero point source on a lower plane of existence, to contrast with the divine element within the world above.

According to Kabbalah, creation involves the *"descent of supernal light,"* the *kav* or Ray, from above into the hollow or vacuum created through the Zimzum or Tzimtzum contraction (and the withdrawal of the Infinite Light). This leads to the sequential unfoldment of the ten Sephirot within the *Tree of Life*. The Kabbalah also describes four world orders of *Emanation, Creation, Formation* and *Made*, which can be depicted on the Tree of Life, or as four *Trees of Life*, which overlap and descend from each other as one world order generates the next successive world order. (See Figure 7) The four worlds illustrated above represent the elements fire, air, water and

---

[81] Permission for this image was given by http://www.Crystalinks.com.

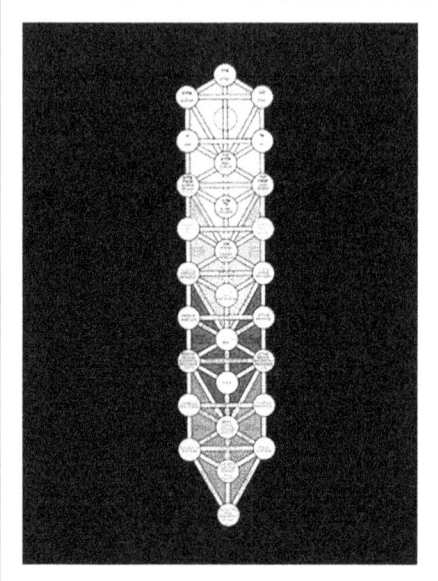

Figure 7 [82]

earth, while the fifth realm of *Adam Kadmon* is the realm of Unity within Negative Existence.

The Kabbalist model of the cosmos is most relevant to the study of a human being and the origins of consciousness and Self. Like the macrocosm, the microcosm or Self, originates as a point source of supernal light and is then conditioned by the three pillars of nature and embodied within seven different world orders. Further, a human being and the human heart have a physical nature in the *world made*, a psychical and soul nature in the *world of formation*, a spiritual nature in the *world of creation* and a divine nature in the *world of Emanation*. There is an entire inner physics and metaphysics of being, which serves to *clothe those material points without extension* in different interpenetrating bodies and dimensions.

This "God spark" or divine source emanation is brought down into a spiritual world, where in it is a "spiritual spark," then into a psychical (soul) world and embodied as the electromagnetic center within the physical heart. The presence of Self initiates the heartbeat and diffuses the light of consciousness and life energies through the processes of oxygenation and the blood, and through subtle matters to various levels of the body and psyche. The presence of the Self as a "self-illuminating element," the Sun of the body, serves to illuminate the psychological and psychic processes within the inner world.

The teachings of Kabbalah offer a complex mathematical and metaphysical model of the inner geometry of being and non-being, and the higher dimensional origins of consciousness within the sacred heart Space. The microcosm of a human being is designed on the same basic principles of

---

[82] Permission for this image was given by the Kabbalah Society: www.kabbalahsociety.org.

creation as embodied within the macrocosm of the Universe. Hence, key Kabbalist ideas concerning the creation of the universe provide a valuable model for the emergence of human consciousness.

The zero point teaching in Kabbalah is also represented in this illustration from Manly Hall's *Secret Teachings of All Ages*. (See Figure below) The diagram shows the En Soph (Limitless) concentrating/contracting through the four worlds (Atziluth, Briah, Yetzirah, Assiah) to a central point of manifestation.

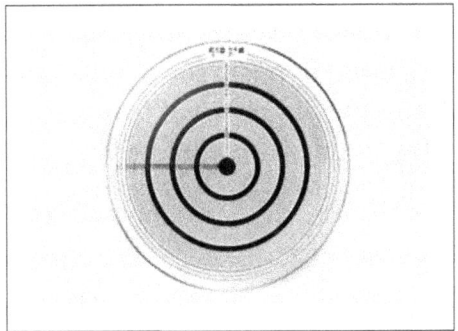

Figure 6 [83]

Kabbalist Lenora Leet depicts the nature of *Da'at*, the 11th invisible *Sephira* the Son born of the Supernal Triad, which crosses the abyss and declares "I Am." (See Figure above) The central point of Da'at is surrounded by the *"matrix of creation"* generated as the Ladder of Jacob unfolds. A multidimensional Star of David surrounds a central point and the "I" is embodied within the *"matrix of creation,"* as a spider in a web spun of spirit and matter. In essence, this might be considered to be the "God Particle" of the Kabbalists.[84]

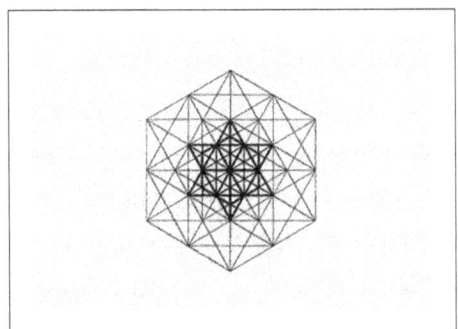

Figure 9

It embodies the Star of David pattern with a seventh central element, described by H.P. Blavatsky as *"the seventh key"* depicted in Theosophy by an ankh at the center of the *Star of David*.[85]

These ideas of the Kabbalists certainly suggest a profoundly

---

[83] http://www.prs.org/gallery-kabblh.htm.

[84] Leonora Leet's discussion of Sacred Geometry is far-reaching and complex. The more normal association of the Hexagram/Star of David on the Tree of Life places Tipheret at its center. The author would treat these two similarly, as Da'at is manifest through Tipheret.

[85] Leonora Leet, *The Secret Doctrine of the Kabbalah: Recovering the Key to Hebraic Sacred Science* (Rochester: Inner Traditions, 1999). Leet is not referencing Blavatsky's *S.D.* in this title.

alternative approach to the enigmas and mysteries of human consciousness and self existence.

FROM GNOSTICISM TO ADI DA

In explaining *Gnosticism*, Dean Edwards writes:

> The true nature of the Soul is as a divine spark, which originally issued forth from the fountainhead of God. ... The world is often seen as a training ground or prison for Soul as it seeks spiritual liberation, a return to its true home in the Pleroma or realms of pure spirit beyond the physical and psychic regions of matter, emotion and the mind. ... Soul refers to the spark of individualized spiritual essence that dwells within the consciousness or mind.[86]

The term gnosis derived from the Greek language means "to know." The Gnostics believe that the knowledge of God and of spiritual realities can be directly experienced. Thus "I" can be recalled, remembered or realized in its cosmic and divine nature.

Some mystical teachings emphasize the quantized nature of Space as the basis for individual consciousness. The Gnostic *Gospel of Truth* of the Nag Hammadi library depicts the "spaces" as "emanations," which exist within the underlying invisible source:

> ... the Father of the all was invisible, the one who is from himself, from whom all spaces come forth. ... All the spaces are his emanations. They have known that they came forth from him like children ... though truly within him, they do not know him. But the Father is perfect, knowing every space within him. ... all the emanations of the Father are pleromas, and the root of all his emanations is in the one who made them all grow up in himself. ... In time Unity will perfect the spaces. It is within Unity that each one will attain himself; from multiplicity into Unity.[87]

---

[86] Dean Edwards, *Gnosis-Overview*. Deane@netcom.com. (accessed December 7, 1996).

[87] James M. Robinson, *Nag Hammadi Library* (San Francisco: Harper & Row, 1981), 39-41, 47.

All individual spaces are thus rooted within the invisible pleroma and Unity, which sustains them as individual I's (eyes) of the One.

These spaces are "pleromas" as they emerge from the fullness of things (all possible potencies, in the En Soph). The zero point center is an emanation, a "quantum of original light" arising in association with a "quantum of space." The mystical conjunction of a zero-point source of original light within higher Space dimensions gives birth to individualized consciousness.

The Dalai Lama explains that to understand human consciousness, we have to distinguish between matter and consciousness. "Space particles" (space quanta) are the basis for matter, while the "mind of clear light" is the basis for consciousness:

> In Buddhism, there are levels of coarseness and subtlety of particles, and the most subtle of all particles would be the particles of space. These serve as the basis for all of the particles ... The particles of space remain forever. ... When you go back and back, researching what the substantial causes are, you will eventually get back to the particles of space. ... new worlds will form physically on the basis of the empty space-particles.[88]

> ... prior to its formation, any particular universe remains in the state of emptiness, where all its material elements exist in the form of potentiality as "space particles."[89]

According to the Dalai Lama, "... *new worlds will form physically on the basis of the empty space-particles.*" Conscious experience consists of this conjunction of the mind of clear light with a quantized space particle, again which might be considered as a zero point source.

In his autobiographic writings, Adi Da describes varied experiences of enlightenment and self-realization which occurred at different periods of his life. Adi Da describes an ultimate process of "Translation" or

---

[88] Renee Weber, *Dialogues with Scientists and Sages: The Search for Unity* (New York: Routledge & Kegan Paul, 1986), 235-6.

[89] H. H. Dalai Lama, *The Universe in a Single Atom: The Convergence of Science and Spirituality* (New York: Morgan Road Books, 2005), 89.

"Transition," whereby consciousness normally polarized around the ego identity or personality surrenders the position of Narcissus and experiences the prior condition of Self— related to the deepest Spaces of the Heart.

> In this Process of Translation, we pass as if through a point in space, at the root center of the heart. All awareness converges on that point in a kind of spiral or vortex. And that point is so small it is without dimensions, or any conceptions, or any objects. The independent self seems to dissolve in this narrow Passage. ... The Divine Translation is a matter of Transcendence of separate bodily, emotional, mental, astral, supermental, and egoic states of experience. It is a Transition through the infinitesimal space of the Heart.[90]

Adi Da states that: *"When the soul truly awakens, it breaks out of its atomic state in the heart and Radiates through and beyond the body-mind."*[91] The individual becomes diffused with the Radiance of Consciousness.

Adi Da describes how an individual awakened in the Heart can still move about and function in the world, although there is no sense of being identical with, or limited to, the mind and body:

> I am no-seeking in the Heart. ... The zero of the heart is expanded as the world. ... There is a constant observation of subject and object in any body, any functional sheath, any realm, or any experience that arises. Thus, I remain in the unqualified State. There is a constant Sensation of "Bright" Fullness permeating and surrounding all experiences, all realms, all bodies, all functional sheaths. It is my own "Bright" Fullness, which is radically non-separate. My own "Bright" Fullness includes all beings and all things. I am the Form of Space Itself, in which all bodies, all functional sheaths, all realms, and all experiences occur. It is inherently "Bright" Conscious-

---

[90] Adi Da. (Da Love Ananda, Bubba Free John, born Franklin Jones from Brooklyn, N.Y.). *The Enlightenment of the Whole Body* (Middletown, Dawn Horse Press, 1978), 83.

[91] Adi Da, *The Knee of Listening: The Early-life Ordeal and the Radical Spiritual Realization of the Divine World Teacher*, (Middletown: Dawn Horse Press, 1975), 103-4.

ness Itself, which Reality is even every being's Very Nature (or Ultimate, inherent, and inherently perfect, Condition) now and now and now. ... I awakened as perfect, absolute, awesome Love-Bliss, in which the body and the mind, and every functional sheath, boiled into a solder of undifferentiated Reality. It was the madness of Dissolution into most perfect Self Awareness.[92]

Adi Da describes the Divine Domain as Shining through *"an atomic window"* and becoming the illusory and narcissistic ego — as a knot or contraction out of the Infinite. Experiences of enlightenment involve glimpses of such inward zero point dynamics:

> ... the soul ... is a "seed" or "spark" of Radiance, and atom of Original Light ....
>
> ... body-mind arises within the soul, the atom, which is prior to space, time, size, shape, and all relations.
>
> ... all souls, or all living beings (human or otherwise), are points or atoms of the Original Light or Radiant Bright Consciousness of God.
>
> In that Process (of Re-cognition), the infinitely small space or door of the heart, the intuition of the atomic condition of the soul, is penetrated.[93]

Adi Da explains that the zero point is not in the body as such-because in reality, the mind/body and even the subtle mind/bodies are within or surrounding the zero point. All things exist within space secondary to the prior zero point condition.[94] Further, Adi Da describes *"all living things,"* human or otherwise as having such zero point origins.

---

[92] Ibid., 364.

[93] *Enlightenment of the Whole Body*, 476, 489, 492, 541.

[94] Adi Da explains that even mystical experiences of the Crown Chakra, the *Sahasrara,* resolve back into the point within the Heart. The Sahasrara is the lunar orbit, reflecting the light originating within the solar realm, the Bright within the Heart.

For Adi Da, there is a living awareness of these profound depths of Self. He states, *"I remain Aware of the Free point in the heart ... Everything only appears to me, and I remain as I am. There is no end to This."* [95]

SUFI SECRETS

Sufis suggest that humans are generally not awake to the inner life of the heart, as they are turned towards the external senses and dramas of life. The greatest treasure is to live fully within the life of the heart and thereby, increasingly within the life of the soul. Even the hosts of heaven visit the chambers of the Heart.

Robert Frager, by his Sufi name—Sheikh Ragip, is an American psychologist and Sufi teacher. Frager describes essential Sufi practices and teachings:

> The secret of secrets is the divine spark within each of us. Remembrance is remembering that which we already know. It is to get in touch with that divine spark that God has placed within each human being. In the Koran it says that God breathed from the divine soul into Adam; another way of translating that would be that God placed a divine spark into every human being. And that divine spark is the secret of secrets. My master put it this way: That spark in us could set the whole universe on fire. It's greater than the universe itself because it's a spark of what is infinite. And it's within every one of us. Who we are is far more than who we think we are.[96]

A divine spark is a zero point source emanating out of the infinite realm within. This spark is beyond the level of physical differentiation in terms of the Planckian units of physics, beyond which we cannot measure. A divine spark does not "have extension," as judged from the external viewpoint. Recall Blavatsky described *"material points without extension"* as the basis upon which the Gods and other invisible powers clothe themselves in bodies. The divine spark exists always at the center of our being at zero

---

[95] Ibid., 408.

[96] Robert Frager & J. Fadiman, *Essential Sufism* (New Jersey: Castle Books, 1997), 213.

point levels, and through the heart, the breath and blood, consciousness and life are infused into a living, breathing human being. Remembrance is recalling and living within this inner experience which has strangely been forgotten.

RELATIONSHIPS TO SCIENCE

Scientists now consider that the universe itself arose from a singularity condition at Planckian lengths and such possibilities are also considered for galaxies and galactic clusters. On a lower order of scale, one might consider the human being to have grown from a zero point source—a fertilized ovum, a barely visible point element to human perception. Somehow, the forces inherent to this fertilized ovum unfold from within without to form an infant, which is certainly not constructed or made from without. Of course, a scientist would say, but a fertilized ovum has a whole inner world to it, even though it may appear as an unextended point. So also, this is true of the zero points of occultism.

Mystic philosopher Peter D. Ouspensky explained such a notion:

> The zero-dimension or the point is a *limit*. This means that we see something as a point, but we do not know what is concealed behind this point. It may actually be a point, that is, a body having no dimensions and it may also be a whole world, but a world so far removed from us or so small that it appears to us a point... seven cosmoses related to one another in the ratio of zero to infinity.[97]

The term zero point can be used in varied manners in reference to different domains of science, from the singularities of creation, to the growth of living beings and to the superstring and membrane structures thought to exist at Planckian levels in modern physics.

The most advanced models of modern physics actually propose that at zero point levels, material elements have varied extension into seven hidden compacted dimensions. The four large dimensions of space-time are

---

[97] Peter D. Ouspensky, *In Search of the Miraculous*: Fragments of an Unknown Teaching (Mew York: Harcourt, 1949), 209.

founded upon a seven dimensional hyperspace and a seven dimensional "space" is described as existent at every point. Popular texts on physics depict such a Calabi Yau space as shown here, which is really not so dissimilar to the "Da'at" zero point structure depicted by Kabbalist with their God Particle.

Figure 10

The most advanced M-theory posits eleven dimensions—with a seven dimensional hyperspace existing at every point underlying the four large space-time dimensions of the everyday world. (See below)

In *Galileo's Finger: The Ten Great Ideas of Science*, Dr. Peter Atkins writes:

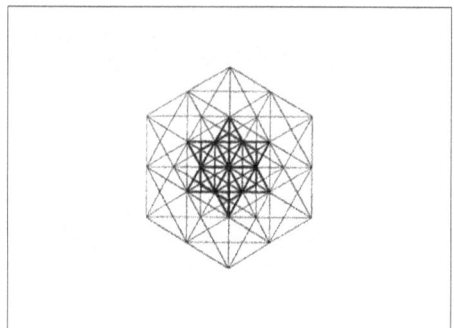

Figure 11

...string theory is all about strings vibrating in ten dimensions of space and one of time. ... In actuality, there are seven dimensions compactified in this way at each point, with the strings somehow wrapped round them, like a rubber band wrapped round a pipe. The compactified dimensions are thought to adopt a

> special shape at each point ... called *Calabi-Yau spaces* ... Shapes like these-in seven dimensions-are the hosepipes of string theory, for the strings wind round them and through their holes.[98]

Closed strings can loop around the Calabi-Yau space many times, while not be extended at all within the ordinary directions of space. Atkin says: *"Think of a structure like this (but in more dimensions) as attached to every point in space."*

---

[98] Peter Atkins, *Galileo's Finger: The Ten Great Ideas of Science* (New York: Oxford University Press, 2003), 197-9.

The latest version of string theory is called M-theory. The "M" is related to "membrane," although Atkins suggests that it might be also in reference to *"the mother of all theories,"* or to *"matrix."* Physicist and String Theorist, Brian Greene suggests that it might be related to *"mysterious."* Regardless, M-theory describes higher dimensional "membranes" or matrices -instead of one-dimensional strings—wrapped up in these hyperspaces.

The Calabi-Yau spaces or strings vibrate through all of the hidden dimensions and the manner in which these extra dimensions are twisted up and curled back upon each other determines the possible resonant vibration patterns. Hence, scientists are especially interested in exploring *"the dimensionality of the holes in these spaces ... through which the strings are threaded."* [99]

Calabi-Yau spaces contain a variety of *"multi-dimensional holes"* and different families of particles are a reflection of the *"number of holes in the geometrical shape comprising the extra dimensions."* [100] Atkins notes, cryptically, that somehow *"the number three is emerging as possibly significant,"* as there are three primary families of elementary particles, each of which exists at three distinct energetic levels (three generations). Perhaps the number three is inherent to the geometry of the world—as is the number seven!

Furthermore, if a string is wound around a compact dimension, it acquires an electrical charge. Each turn of the string gives a unit of charge, and these charges are positive or negative according to the directions of the turns. Such entities might be viewed as-a ball of electric charges, although it might appear from a four dimensional perspective, as electrically neutral, like a laya center.

The most recent holographic model in physics provides for an even more complex dynamics at zero point levels, postulating the existence of micro black hole information processors in higher dimensions of anti-de-Sitter space. The information processing activities of these mini black holes are rendered equivalent to the string and M-theories, and quantum field

---

[99] Atkins, *Galileo's Finger*, 199.

[100] Brian Greene, *The Elegant Universe: Superstrings, Hidden Dimensions, and the Quest for the Ultimate Theory* (New York: Norton & Co, 1999), 217.

theories, upon different levels of holographic shells. These emerging notions are too complex to elaborate fully here, but again provide a basis upon which to understand *The Secret Doctrine* about *"seven holes dug in space,"* as the means by which an informational world of Mind, is impressed upon successive layers of Space, or the Akasha.[101]

Remarkably, Blavatsky explained exactly such a peculiar inner dimensionality to "atoms," quanta, Monads and the Kosmos over a century ago. There is a complex metaphysics to reality at zero point levels. As Blavatsky explains, *"God 'geometrizes!"* and all living cosmoses differentiate from apparent point sources.

CONCLUDING REMARKS

Occultists have anticipated modern views in physics of vacuum genesis and of creation from singularities by centuries, although their cosmic insights were far beyond the science or physics of their day. The zero point hypothesis is relevant, however, not only to the birth of the universe, but also, according to occultists, to the birth of every living being and the issue of the origin of consciousness. Life comes from life and it is through zero point dynamics, that processes within higher dimensions infuse life and consciousness into the material form. God and other invisible powers "clothe themselves" in bodies based upon such higher dimensional processes.

One must wonder if it is any more inconceivable to imagine that a human being has such a zero point I, or quantum self, than it is to accept the discovery of modern physicists and cosmologists that indeed the universe did! Of course, the scientists imagine that there are the alpha and omega points of creations, but they do not seem to consider that such a zero point laya centers might be existent throughout a cycle of creation, evolution and dissolution.

The subjects of zero points and the meanings of this term are very complex

---

[101] These issues are explored in depth in Christopher Holmes' *God, Science & The Secret Doctrine: The Zeropoint Metaphysics and Holographic Space of H. P. Blavatsky* (Kemptville, Ontario: Zero Point Publications, 2010.)

and subtle. We have considered it to refer to elements beyond the level of physical differentiation existent in hyperspace dimensions, and/or as representing "portals" or "holes dug in space" through which higher dimensional processes sustain material processes within the worlds below. [102 / 103]

III
Towards a Holographic Metaphysics of the Human Heart

I cognized the center of the empyrean as a point of intuitive perception in my heart. Irradiating splendor issued from my nucleus to every part of the universal structure.

- **Yogananda**[104] -

In some sense man is a microcosm of the universe; therefore, what man is, is a clue to the universe. We are enfolded in the universe.

- **Physicist David Bohm**[105] -

---

[102] Such zero-point concepts might also be applied within other contexts — for example, considering cycles of humanity, time and history, as in Gregg Braden's popular *Awakening to Zero Point*. However, Braden does not consider that human beings, or self-existence, might have such zero point origins.

[103] Dr. Leon Maurer, a chemical engineer, specializing in atomic energy, modern physics and material science, and Dr. J. Dea, a physicist who has written *Space, Time, & Matter: Modern Views Vs the Secret Doctrine* are two Theosophists to have explored such interfaces between Blavatsky's zero point concepts and modern ideas in physics.

[103] Paramahansa. Yogananda, *Autobiography of a Yogi* (Los Angeles: Self Realization FellowShip, 1988), 46.

[104] David Bohm, *Creativity: The Signature of Nature,* interview in Rene Weber, *Dialogues with Scientists and Sages: The search for unity* (New York: Routledge & Kegan Paul, 1986).

THE SONS EXPAND AND CONTRACT THROUGH THEIR OWN
SELVES AND HEARTS; THEY EMBRACE INFINITUDE. ...
EACH IS PART OF THE WEB.
REFLECTING THE "SELF-EXISTING LORD" LIKE A MIRROR,
EACH BECOMES IN TURN A WORLD.

Stanza of Dzyan, from Blavatsky, *The Secret Doctrine*, 1888[105]

ABSTRACT

If there is truth to the possibilities of life after life, psychical phenomena, experiences of other worlds, disembodied mind, spirits and souls, and so on, then a fundamental revision is required in the modern understanding of the nature of human consciousness and the dimensionality of existence. A human being is something completely different from what is currently imagined in those modern psychological and scientific theories which regard humans as simply biological and material animals evolved through happenstance and random processes, and who lack any soul or spiritual nature. The holographic paradigm emerged in modern psychology and science in the 1980s, based upon the work of neuroscientist Karl Pribram and physicist David Bohm and provided a basis for exploring hidden dimensions of consciousness, space and time. Unfortunately, there were fundamental errors made in the approach. Esoteric and mystical studies suggest that the human holography is based not upon neurological processes in the brain, as largely assumed by modern theorists, but rather, upon the physics and metaphysics of a zero point element or center established within the multi-dimensional Aether of the heart Space. Yogananda's account of cosmic consciousness is used to illustrate an archaic mystical claim concerning the holographic dimensions to the human heart, and then concepts from modern physics and *The Secret Doctrine* of Helena Blavatsky are used in order to elaborate a holographic

---

[105] Helena P. Blavatsky, *The Secret Doctrine* (Passadena: Theosophical Society, 1988), 27.

model of consciousness and the human heart.

ESOTERIC DIMENSIONS OF SELF

One of the most unusual dimensions ascribed to Self or "I" is that of an infinitely small source at zero point levels. An invisible and indivisible sub-atomic element, a divine element or God spark, exists within the sacred heart space. In the terminology of modern physics, the Self is a quantum, a particle/wave or element existing beyond the atomic level of material organization. The divine spark can be regarded as a "quantum of consciousness" or a "quantum Self." Alternatively, it can be conceived of as a singularity condition, a first point source of supernal *lux*, minute with no extension in external space/time. This zero point element does not exist within external four dimensional space as such, but underlies this while established within a seven dimensional hyperspace. Modern scientists hypothesize that the vast universe emerged from such an infinitely small singularity at the beginning of time, out of the apparent nothingness of the quantum vacuum, now considered as a seven dimensional hyperspace. The singularities and hyperspace of modern physics bear a profound relationship to the divine sparks described by mystics as emanating out of the mystical void and plenum, the *seven skins of the Mother Deep*, as described by Blavatsky. At the singularity point, the finite merges into the infinite, as the individual Self merges with That Self.[106]

Swami Yogeshwaranand Saraswati notes: "... it is instinctually recognized that *Jivatman denoted by the pure form of 'I' has its abode in the heart, and in Samadhi there is direct realization of this.*"[107] Both the Jivatma (the Individual Self) that is subtle and minute, and Ishwara (or Paramatman, the Supreme Self) the greatest of all, dwell within the cave of the heart. The jivatma is likened to "an infinitesimal poppy seed," which has no form or color. This atomic or indivisible entity is embodied *within* the Bliss Sheath, itself a "mass of light filled with bliss."

A first mystical dimension ascribed to the Self involves such descriptions

---

[106] These concepts have been previously elaborated through parts 1 and 2 of this series.

[107] Swami Yogeshwaranand Saraswati, *Science of Soul: A treatise on Higher Yoga* (New Delhi: Yoga Niketan Trust, 1987), 69, 36.

of a spiritual or divine spark as the smallest of elements. Another mystical dimension ascribed to Self is that of the universe. An ancient Vedic saying declares: *"Thou art that,"* meaning you are the world. As a microcosm of the macrocosm, the individual self, in blending with the larger SELF, reflects or contains all things within Self. The individual spirit soul is a seed or atom of the Supreme Supersoul and can experience the deeper realities and the larger structures of the universe. In this way, one might *know thy Self, the universe and the Gods*, as suggested by an ancient Greek axiom. Various Upanishads suggest this holographic possibility of the heart as being a microcosm of the larger macrocosm:

> Self-luminous is Brahman (God), ever present in the hearts of all. ... In him exists all that moves and breathes. In him exists all that is. ... This Self, who understands all, who knows all, and whose glory is manifest in the universe, lives within the lotus of the heart, the bright throne of Brahman.[108]

> As large as the universe outside, even so large is the universe within the lotus of the heart. Within it are heaven and earth, the sun, the moon, the lightening, and all the stars. What is in the macrocosm is in this microcosm ... All things that exist ... are in the city of Brahman.[109]

These are the most paradoxical and unusual claims. How could the "heart" contain the universe within itself and could consciousness somehow expand into such subtle realms of the inner cosmos? This ancient mystical claim illustrates the idea of a part embodying the whole as within the modern holographic paradigm. Similarly, a point source element within the Heart Space might unfold into the larger universe.

---

[108] Swami Nikhilanda, *The Upanishads*, (New York, Harper & Row Publishers: 1963), 161.

[109] Swami Prabhavananda & F. Manchester (Eds.) *The Upanishads: Breath of the Eternal* (New York: New American Library, 1957.)

YOGANANDA'S EXPERIENCE OF COSMIC CONSCIOUSNESS

There are reports within the mystical literature of individual experiences which illustrate these paradoxical ideas about the spirit soul being a microcosm of the macrocosm. Paramahansa Yogananda, a twentieth century Indian saint and master of kriya yoga, in his classic work *Autobiography of a Yogi*, provides an extraordinary account of the fantastic possibilities inherent to Self. Yogananda describes his experience of "cosmic consciousness" as initiated by his Master striking him gently over the heart—to awaken it. Yogananda receives grace from his Master in order to *"fulfill his heart's desire."* He then experiences these extraordinary states of enlightenment and cosmic consciousness:

> My body became immovably rooted; breath was drawn out of my lungs as if by some huge magnet. Soul and mind instantly lost their physical bondage and streamed out like a fluid piercing light from my every pore. The flesh was as though dead; yet in my intense awareness I knew that never before had I been fully alive. My sense of identity was no longer narrowly confined to a body but embraced the circumambient atoms. People on distant streets seemed to be moving gently over my own remote periphery. The roots of plants and trees appeared through a dim transparency of the soil; I discerned the inward flow of their sap.
>
> The whole vicinity lay bare before me. My ordinary frontal vision was now changed to a vast spherical sight, simultaneously all-perceptive. Through the back of my head I saw men strolling far down Rai Ghat Lane, and noticed also a white cow that was leisurely approaching. ... After she had passed behind the brick wall of the courtyard, I saw her clearly still.

It is instructive to review Yogananda's experiences in order to have a clearer account. Yogananda firstly feels his soul and mind stream out of his body *like light*, so that his awareness is interpenetrating the entire volume of space around his body and the ashram. He senses the inner activity of the plants, the soil and the ashram, while experiencing a *"vast spherical sight, simultaneously all-perceptive."* This description is of a level of *samadhi*, wherein consciousness interpenetrates material nature and larger volume of space/time.

> All objects within my panoramic gaze trembled and vibrated like quick motion pictures. My body, Master's, the pillared courtyard, the furniture and floor, the trees and sunshine, occasionally became violently agitated, until all melted into a luminescent sea; even as sugar crystals, thrown into a glass of water, dissolve after being shaken. The unifying light alternated with materializations of form, the metamorphoses revealing the law of cause and effect in creation.

Yogananda experiences the objects and scene surrounding him melting into a luminescent sea, with materializations of forms alternating with experiences of the unifying light. He experiences the inner dimensions of things as they crystallize out of an underlying realm of light into material forms and then dissolve back into the underlying light realm. Yogananda has united the light within himself with the unifying light of Brahman, which he describes as *"the structural essence of creation."* In doing so, he witnesses the cosmic dance of the involution and evolution of elements within an infinite Sea of Light.

> An oceanic joy broke upon calm endless shores of my soul. The Spirit of God, I realized, is exhaustless Bliss; His body is countless tissues of light. A swelling glory within me began to envelop towns, continents, the earth, solar and stellar systems, tenuous nebulae, and floating universes. The entire cosmos, gently luminous, like a city seen afar at night, glimmered within the infinitude of my being. ...

> The divine dispersion of rays poured from an Eternal Source, blazing into galaxies, transfigured with ineffable auras. Again and again I saw the creative beams condense into constellations, then resolve into sheets of transparent flame. By rhythmic reversion, sextillion worlds passed into diaphanous luster, then fire became firmament.

Yogananda's awareness then enveloped larger and larger realms passing from towns, to continents, the earth, the solar system, the galaxy and floating universes! Creation is revealed to involve the *"dispersion of rays poured from an Eternal source,"* which condenses or crystallizes into galaxies and constellations, which again resolve back into sheets of transparent flame. As before, Yogananda experiences the process of inward creation and dissolution, although this time at the level of the universe.

> I cognized the center of the empyrean as a point of intuitive perception in my heart. Irradiating splendor issued from my nucleus to every part of the universal structure. ...
>
> Suddenly the breath returned to my lungs. With a disappointment almost unbearable, I realized that my infinite immensity was lost. Once more I was limited to the humiliating cage of a body, not easily accommodative to the Spirit. Like a prodigal child, I had run away from my macrocosm home and had imprisoned myself in a narrow microcosm...
>
> "It is the Spirit of God that actively sustains every form and force in the universe; yet He is transcendental and aloof in the blissful uncreated void beyond the worlds of vibratory phenomenon," Master explained.[110]

Figure 12

Finally, Yogananda cognized the *"center of the empyrean."* The term empyrean from ancient and medieval cosmology refers to the highest seventh heavenly sphere consisting of fire and light. The center of the empyrean and of the universe was *"a point of intuitive perception in his heart"*! From this point or nucleus, Yogananda experienced an *"irradiating splendor"* issuing to every part of the universal structure. Somehow, the universe as it were, concentrates itself into a point.

---

[110] Yogananda, *Autobiography of a Yogi*, 45.

Yogananda offers an awe-inspiring glimpse into the hidden dimensions of consciousness, life and the universe. Figure 1 illustrates this idea of the heart embodying the cosmos.[111] If this is an objectively valid account of an awakening of consciousness within the heart and its expansion into the dimensions of the universe, then somehow there is something fundamentally mistaken with the entire approach to consciousness found within the mainstream of western psychology, science, cosmology and education.

Yogananda's experiences illustrate the most unusual dimensions ascribed to the spiritual soul or divine spark—that it is a point source of *"omnipresent Spirit"* emerging from the unifying Light and which is interconnected to the Whole. Yogananda's experience illustrates the statements of the Chandogya Upanishad: *"As large as the universe outside is the universe within the lotus of the heart. ... All things that exist... are in the city of Brahman."*[112]

Yogananda explains the principles behind this cosmic experience, the *"law of miracles:"*

> The consciousness of a perfected yogi is effortlessly identified not with a narrow body but with the universal structure. ... He who knows himself as the omnipresent Spirit is subject no longer to the rigidities of a body in time and space. The imprisoning "rings-pass-not" have yielded to the solvent: *I am He*.... "If therefore thine eye be single, thy whole body shall be *full of light*." (Matthew 6:22) ... the liberating spiritual eye has enabled the yogi to destroy all delusions concerning matter and its gravitational weight; he sees the universe as the Lord created it: an essentially undifferentiated mass of light.
>
> *The law of miracles is operable by any man who has realized that the essence of creation is light.* A master is able to employ his divine knowledge of light phenomena ... a yogi rearranges the light atoms of the universe ... The colorful universal drama is ... issuing from the single white light of a Cosmic Source. ...

---

[111] Artist: Anita J. Mitra by permission.

[112] Nikhilanda, The Upanishads, 279.

> "My sons are children of light; they will not sleep forever in delusion."... The so-called miraculous powers of a great master are a natural accompaniment to his exact understanding of subtle laws that operate in the inner cosmos of consciousness.[113]

The mystical heart doctrine provides an intriguing holographic model of the Self (and Super Self). The Self is a point source of coherent light consciousness emanating from a realm of Eternal Light, higher dimensional Space and the uncreated Void. A point of intuitive perception within the heart can thus be related to the larger dimensions of the macrocosmic universe!

Mystical teachings suggest that light has a deep, hidden, supernal nature, unrecognized within science. When Yogananda's consciousness expands to embrace the universe, it does so at speeds greater than the speed of light! It must as the universe is billions of light years across and yet his experience lasts only minutes. However, Yogananda consciousness is not really travelling anywhere, as the whole universe is embodied within the point of intuitive perception within his heart. The usual notions of time and space simply do not apply within the subtle implicate and super-implicate orders of a holographic universe, wherein information about the whole is present everywhere instantaneously in omnipresent Spirit. The universe within is as vast as the universe without.

THE EMERGENCE OF THE HOLOGRAPHIC PARADIGM

> The brain is a hologram perceiving and participating in a holographic universe. ... the new science demands spirit; at least, it makes ample room for spirit. Either way, modern science is no longer *denying* spirit.[114]

In *The Doors of Perception*, Aldous Huxley described the possible relationship of individual mind to "Mind at Large:"

---

[113] Yogananda, *Autobiography of a Yogi*, 315- 321.

[114] Ken Wilber, (Ed.) *The Holographic Paradigm and other Paradoxes* (Boulder, Shambhala, 1982).

> ... each one of us is potentially Mind at Large. But insofar as
> we are animals our business at all costs is to survive. To make
> biological survival possible, Mind at Large has to be funnelled
> through the reducing valve of the brain and nervous system.
> What comes out at the other end is a measly trickle of the
> kind of consciousness, which will help us to stay alive on the
> surface of this particular planet. ... The various "other worlds"
> with which human beings erratically make contact are so
> many elements in the totality of awareness belonging to Mind
> at Large.[115]

Several philosophers have speculated upon this idea that the human brain acts as a reducing valve for *Mind at Large*.

The holographic paradigm emerged in modern psychology in the 1980s when Karl Pribram, a distinguished neuroscientist, applied the principles of holography to the functioning of consciousness, the brain and mind. The holographic paradigm derived from Pribram in conjunction with the ideas of physicist David Bohm. Essentially, the mind/brain is taken to exist in relationship to an underlying *"frequency domain,"* which consists of hidden dimensions containing information. The mind/brain then acts as a lens or filter which focuses one particular space/time reality out of the underlying Mind at Large.

The principles of holography, a form of lens-less photography, were outlined in 1947 by Dennis Gabor. Holographs yield remarkable three-dimensional images of objects by using no lens, which contrasts with the usual flat two-dimensional photographs produced through the use of a lens. The creation of a holograph requires a source of coherent light derived from a point source, usually provided by a laser, as illustrated in Figure 13.[116] In holographic photography, the coherent light beam is split into two beams by a partially coated mirror. The *reference beam* impinges directly upon a holographic plate; while the *object beam* reflects off an object before impinging on the plate. The two light beams interact on the holographic plate to produce a wave interference pattern (determined by the phase shifts of the interacting waves and their mutual enhancement or reductive effects).

---

[115] Aldous Huxley, *The Doors of Perception*, (New York: Harper & Row, 1954).

[116] Graphic by Željka Županić, with permission.

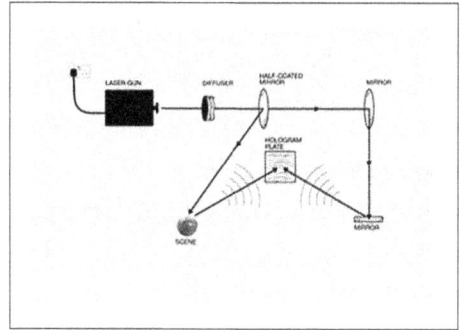

Figure 13

To visual inspection, a holographic plate bears no resemblance to the object "*holographed*" until the plate is again illuminated by a coherent light source. In this event, a three dimensional image of the object is projected out from the holographic plate into space. In the reconstruction of the image, the interference pattern stored on the plate acts as a grating to bend the light by diffraction to re-establish the image. A holographic image produced with modern technology can be so similar to the original that it is impossible to tell the two apart. The projected *virtual image* can be viewed from various angles and appears quite substantial and three dimensional-apparently real like our apparently real world.

The most unusual property of a holograph is that any portion of the holographic plate illuminated by a light source will recreate an image of the "whole" object: The term holography means literally *"to write the whole."* Whereas a camera has a lens which focuses the light from an outside source to establish a point-to-point correspondence between any part of the scene photographed and a portion of the recording film; by contrast in holography, no lens is used and so light from the whole of the object impacts upon every point on the holographic film. The whole is thus *implicated* in any part, enfolded into each point. This unusual property of holographs suggests mechanisms for mystical states and knowledge, where the microcosm (the individual) embodies at some deep level the macrocosm (the larger world), or as an individual mind might implicate Mind at Large.

This unusual property of holographs led Pribram, to apply this model to the study of the brain/mind. Initially, Pribram was attempting to explain why "memory engrams," the supposed site and substance of memory, did not appear to be localized within the brain. The traditional mechanistic model of memory predicted that memories are established by specific microcircuits or cell assembles (an atomistic approach) localized in particular areas of the brain. However, experimental evidence demonstrated that learning and memory were maintained in laboratory animals despite the removal or destruction of large brain areas. The expected one-to-one correspondence between brain sites and particular memories did not seem to exist. This fact has historically posed a fundamental enigma in the study of the brain: how and where are memories stored?

In *Languages of the Brain* (1971), Pribram explained how various psychological processes could be based on holographic principles. The neuro-circuitry of the brain with its own standing wave patterns could serve as a referent beam and interact with environmental stimuli (other wave patterns) to produce complex wave interference patterns spread over areas of the brain. Neurological processes store the resultant wave interference patterns holographically over both small and large volumes of the brain, with different interaction patterns superimposed upon one another. This could explain why attempts to isolate particular memory engrams have been unsuccessful. A holographic model of memory and the brain would allow for the storage of immense amounts of information. Scientists have developed ways of taking "multiple holograms" which can record billions of bits of information within a cubic centimeter of a thick holographic plate. In multiple holograms, successive wave fronts are superimposed in infinitesimal layers upon each other by varying the angles of the projecting light beams. Layers of neurons provide the *holographic film* necessary to record successive interacting wave patterns. This would be a highly efficient way to encode, analyze and synthesize immense amounts of information.

On one level, Pribram suggests that the whole brain might operate holographically, while at another level, this holograph would be composed of innumerable small *"patch holograms."*

> The holograms within the visual system are patch holograms. The total image is composed much as it is in an insect's eye that has hundreds of little lenses instead of one big lens. ... In each patch, the activity of the cells creates a wave front; I believe that the interaction of these wave fronts is what you experience. You get the total picture all woven together as a unified piece by the time you experience it.[117]

An essential feature of Pribram's model was the proposal that the same mathematics used by Gabor to develop holography (Fourier transforms)

---

[117] Karl Pribram, *Psychology Today* Interview February 1979), 80.

are used within the brain to process and analyze sensory, perceptual, imaging and memory data. Fourier transforms provide methods of breaking any complex wave interference pattern into its component frequencies. Laboratory data confirmed Pribram's prediction: in effect, the brain/mind performs mathematical Fourier transforms on wave patterns established in the neuro-circuitry of the brain. This was a radically different perspective on the functioning of the brain and mind.

Although Pribram regards the brain as operating holographically, he does not believe that there is any *"laser beam in the brain"* — that is, any source of coherent *inner light*, equivalent to the point source of laser light used to produce an actual holograph. In an *Omni* interview, Pribram was asked about this:

> Omni: I'm a little puzzled by one thing. When I first read about the holographic brain, I thought of it as a metaphor. Then I began to think you meant it as an actual model. Which is correct?
>
> Pribram: Both. First it was a metaphor. Then ... a model developed, because the mathematics fitted the data gathered in several laboratories around the world. *There are no laser beams in the brain.* I'm simply saying that the brain performs certain operations, which can be described by Gabor's mathematics, to code, decode, and recode sensory input.[118]

Despite its revolutionary account of the dynamics of the brain, Dr. Pribram's theory remained in essence an *"under the hat theory"* of holographic mind. He assumed that the holographs are produced by the brain's physiological mechanisms and processes, and further, he did not consider there to be *an inner source of light* to illuminate the holographs of human experience. There is no laser beam, no coherent light source within the inner world. Further, the heart is not recognized as the source of any "standing wave patterns" or as the main source of electromagnetic influence within the human being. Instead, Dr. Pribram assumes that the brain

---

[118] Karl Pribram, *Holographic Brain*, in *The Omni Interviews*, (Ed.) P. Weintraub (New York: Ticknor & Fields, 1982), 33-34.

produces consciousness and the holographs are within the head where the mind is assumed to be.

However, it was the combination of Pribram's model of the holographic mind/brain with David Bohm's model of *wholeness and the implicate order* which created the basis for holographic paradigm. We will explore the more detailed physical theories of Bohm currently. Most importantly, Bohm suggested that there are incredible amounts of information present within the frequency domain which the mind/brain can access—because *"the entire Universe ... (is) ... a single undivided whole."* The holographic theory and Bohm's model suggest that a human being is a microcosm of the macrocosm rooted into interior dimensions of being and the plenum, and connected to the larger universe! Paranormal researcher, Stanislov Grof noted: *"If this (holographic paradigm) is true, then we each hold the potential for having direct and immediate experiential access to virtually every aspect of the universe...."*[119] Certainly, a holographic universe provides an unimaginable playground for a similarly holographic mind, consciousness and Self.

If the whole of the universe is implicated in any (apparently) localized region (or point) in space/time, then the brain/mind could potentially have unlimited access to this underlying storehouse of information in the implicate orders—the *Mind at Large*. Pribram viewed the brain as mathematically extracting information out of the underlying frequency domain. Now it seemed that this frequency domain could indeed contain vast amounts of the information potentially available for analysis by the mind and brain. Dr. Pribram described the possibilities of a holographic mind/brain in a holographic universe:

> ... if you penetrate through and look at the universe with a nonlens system (holographically), you arrive at a different view, a different reality ... that can explain things that have hitherto remained inexplicable scientifically. ... the mystical experiences people have described for millennia begin to make some scientific sense. They bespeak the possibility of tapping into that order of reality that is behind the world of appearances. ... I wonder if somehow (the mystics) haven't hit

---

[119] Stansilov Grof, *The Holotropic Mind; The three levels of human consciousness and how they shape our lives.* (San Francisco: Harper, 1993).

> upon a mechanism that lets them tap into the implicate order. ... In terms of holographic theory, all those events (paranormal and transcendental states) are plausible if the brain can somehow abrogate its ordinary constraints and gain access to the implicate order.
>
> ... Leibnitz talked about "monads," and ... (an) indivisible entity that is the basic unit of the universe and a microcosm of it. God, said Leibnitz, was a monad. ... In a monadic organization, the part contains the whole-as in a hologram. "Man was made in the image of God." Spiritual insights fit the descriptions of this domain. They are perfectly plausible by the invention of the hologram. [120]

Unfortunately, although Pribram speaks of Leibnitz's Monads, he does not consider such an idea seriously in his own holographic theorizing, to argue that an individual might have such a zero point Monadic essence or some inner point source of supernal light to illuminate the inner holographic world. Instead, he maintains a view of the brain as the site of his holographic model with no light of its own.

Pribram contrasted two fundamentally different assumptions *"about the brain."* The first traditional materialist viewpoint regards the brain as organizing input from the physical world and constructing mental properties. Scientists assumed that mental properties are derived from physical processes. The second viewpoint is that: *"Mental properties are the pervasive organizing principles of the universe, which includes the brain."* Many influential physicists and mathematicians have subscribed to the second viewpoint. Sir James Jeans, a prominent physicist of the early part of the twentieth century, famously asserted that the more we penetrate into the nature of matter, the more it appears as *"a great thought, rather than as a vast machine."*

A critical idea linking the holographic theory of consciousness to holographic views of the world is that the mind is *isomorphic* to the world. Isomorphism suggests *"a one-to-one correspondence between the form (morphology) of the world around us and the form in the brain representing that*

---

[120] Karl Pribram, *What the Fuss is all About*, in. Ken Wilber (Ed.) *The Holographic Paradigm and other Paradoxes*, (Boulder: Shambahala, 1982), 33-4.

world." In this case, mind is not simply an emergent property of the brain's material organization, but instead it *"reflects the basic organization of the Universe (including the organism's brain)."*[121] Similarly, Bohm explains:

> The mind may have a structure similar to the universe. ... The particular forms which appear in the mind may be analogous to the particles, and getting to the ground of the mind might be felt as light. ... (a) free, penetrating movement of the whole.[122]

Thus, a human might be a microcosm of the macrocosm, having an inner form which isomorphically corresponds to the inner structures of the universe. This isomorphic concept is illustrated by the point source origins of both the Cosmos and human self-existence.

The holographic paradigm attracted wide interest within the New Age movement and among those interested in the personal and scientific issues of consciousness. Shirley MacLaine gave this popular account of the emerging paradigm of wholeness:

> ... the seeds of all things, ourselves included, were present at the birth of creation, and every scrap of matter and energy and blood and bones and thought present in the cosmos today could be traced back to the origins of the universe from one small subatomic particle of light. That makes us each sparks of the same light. It also makes each of us a hologram of the entire event. The energies that fragmented and separated and multiplied as the young universe expanded and cooled continue to operate in the beating of our hearts and the movement of our bodies, as well as in the alignment and behavior of the stars. We and they—all things and everything are a connected whole. That is the meaning of "We are all one." The evolution of the Universe then is continuing not only around us but within us. Our thoughts, our dreams, and

---

[121] Ibid., 33.

[122] Bohm, *Creativity: the Signature of Nature*, 48-49.

> our awareness are part of that universe, the physical and the spiritual inextricably bound together.[123]

Bohm's theory, the holographic paradigm and quantum theory (with its non-local effects and quantum interconnectedness) collectively paint a picture of the ultimate interconnectedness of things. Everything did originate from a singularity or zero point state, out of a state of perfect symmetry as an original point source of light. Further, quantum theory suggests that all quanta are ultimately interrelated in higher dimensional spaces, the active information fields, zero point fields or the frequency domain of holographic theory.

Unfortunately, the holographic paradigm has lacked *key elements* — which meant that the full implications and applications of this model have not been substantiated as a model of consciousness. In this regard, Pribram's comment — *"There are no laser beams in the brain"* — is most telling. Firstly, it indicates that the idea of a laser beam or of a "point source of coherent light" to light the inner world is not seriously considered. Further, consciousness needs to be considered as light itself. Further, his comments indicate that scientists have primarily looked for such holographic dynamics within *"the brain"* Once again, we encounter the limits of *the head doctrine* and the neglect of mystical, spiritual and occult views concerning the deepest levels of Self and the higher dimensional physics and metaphysics of the Heart.

In 2003, the *Scientific American* published an issue with the question "Are you a *Hologram?*" on the front cover. The illustration is of a bubble like sphere surrounding a brain and head. This illustrates the assumptions of the modern psychology and science, that the head would be the basis for the human holographic system. Of course, the mind may function in terms of holographic principles, but it certainly is not the only basis of our experience of life.[124] From an occult perspective, the holographic paradigm needs to include the whole human being as a quantum system of electromagnetic influences centered upon the higher dimensional physics and metaphysics of the heart. A *point source of supernal light* is established within the higher dimensional Aether of the heart space. The addition of

---

[123] Shirley MacLaine *Going Within* (New York, New York: Random House, 1989), 259.

[124] Recall from part II of this series, that each chakra can be regarded as having a zero point center, as there are seven fundamental differentiations of the original zero point, and each of these would work on holographic principles as portions of the larger whole.

such elements to a holographic model would provide a source of coherent light, even of *divine lux*, to illuminate the holograms of our lives.

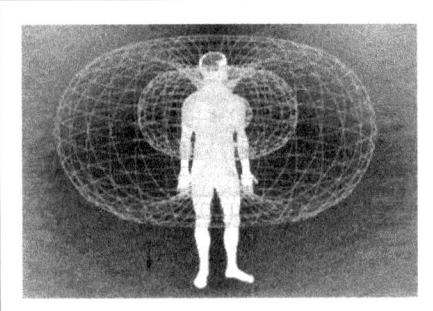

Figure 14

Figure 14 from the *Heart/Math Institute* is a more apt depiction of the human holograph. In *The Heart's Code*, psychologist Paul Pearsall maintains that, energetically speaking, the heart rather than the brain is clearly the center of the psychological universe:

> The heart's EMF (electro-magnetic field) is five thousand times more powerful than the electromagnetic field created by the brain and, in addition to its immense power, has subtle, non-local effects that travel within these forms of energy. ... the heart generates over fifty thousand femtoteslas (a measure of EMF) compared to less than ten femtoteslas recorded from the brain.[125]

Ervin Laszlo[126] provides valuable and more contemporary commentary on the possible holographic nature of a human being. Laszlo describes us as living within the information fields of the ether or *Akasha*, and memory is regarded as inherent within all structures within the Akasha based upon interfering vacuum vortices. He states: "the Akashic Field (is) a cosmic holofield ...."[127] Laszlo's answer to the neurological issues of where and how memories are stored is that "... long-term memory is not stored within the brain: it is extra-somatic." (p. 57) Memories are available within the zero point fields and the Akasha and there are no discrete memory engrams within the brain.

Laszlo reports a curious case study which illustrates the potential information latent within the Akasha. He describes the talents of an *idiot savant*, an individual who is supposed to be below normal functioning in

---

[125] Paul Pearsall, *The Heart's Code: Tapping the Wisdom and Power of Our Heart Energy* (New York: Broadway Books, 1998),55.

[126] Founder of systems philosophy and general evolution theory.

[127] Ervin Laszlo, *Science and the Reenchantment of Nature*, (Rochester: Inner Traditions, 2006), 35.

intelligence and adjustment, but who can speak seven languages, compute cube roots as fast as a calculator and recall the constant *pi* to 22,514 decimal places! There is no known mechanism within a materialist and reductionist viewpoint to explain such unusual talents, clearly not the result of education or the usual faculties of mind. Such case studies suggest that individuals can tap information fields latent within space or the Akasha itself. Laszlo notes: "… the vacuum is … the seat of the *consciousness that infuses my body and brain the same as the rest of the universe* …. " Laszlo describes the experiences of seekers and mystics which illustrate his basic concepts:

> The field of cosmic consciousness they experience is a cosmic emptiness—a void. Yet, paradoxically, it is also an essential fullness. … it contains all of existence in potential. The void they experience is fullness; the vacuum is a plenum. It is the ultimate source of existence, the cradle of all being.[128]

Laszlo considers that human beings can so experience within various levels of the aether as described for centuries throughout the mystical literature: Interfering vacuum-vortices are nature's holograms and the Akashic Field (is) a cosmic holofield.

DAVID BOHM ON WHOLENESS AND THE IMPLICATE ORDERS

> Ultimately, the entire universe (with all its 'particles,' including those constituting human beings, their laboratories, observing instruments, etc.) has to be understood as a single undivided whole, in which analysis into separately and independently existent parts has no fundamental status.[129]

David Bohm was an associate of Albert Einstein and author of the acclaimed *Wholeness and the Implicate Order* (1980). One of the world's foremost theoretical physicists, Bohm published classic works on quantum and relativity theory and was an important contributor to the debate

---

[128] Ibid., 88-89.

[129] David Bohm, Wholeness and the Implicate Order (London: Ark Paperbacks, 1980), 174.

concerning *hidden variables* in quantum theory. Because of his eminence as a physicist, Bohm was in the privileged position of being able to espouse his radical theoretical model—one that postulated the undivided wholeness of reality. Bohm's ideas generated widespread interest not only amongst scientists but also within philosophical, religious and New Age circles.

Bohm's model arose from his attempt to reconcile relativity and quantum theory while accounting for non-local effects and other quantum paradoxes. He distinguished between the outward, manifest physical reality—the *"explicate order"* and an underlying un-manifest realm—the *"implicate order."* Within Bohm's framework, all manifest phenomena of the explicate order (the manifest physical world) must be understood as particular cases of the unfolding of a more general set of implicate orders (the unmanifest underlying realm). The fundamental relationships are between the implicated structures, which interpenetrate each other throughout the whole of space and time. The explicate order flows out of the laws and processes of a multi-dimensional implicate order—as apparent differentiations of an undivided whole! Bohm explains:

> ... the central underlying theme (is) the unbroken wholeness of the totality of existence as an undivided flowing movement without borders. ... in the implicate order the totality of existence is enfolded within each region of space (and time). So, whatever part, element, or aspect we may abstract in thought, this still enfolds the whole and is therefore intrinsically related to the totality from which it has been abstracted. Thus, wholeness permeates all that is being discussed, from the very outset.[130]

Bohm's basic thesis is that even the whole of the Universe is implicated within any point. Such a view is remarkable—a profound revision of centuries of fragmentary little-bit scientific thought. Manifest reality is but a shadow of the deeper underlying realities.

Bohm emphasized that a quantum is a real particle plus a real wave, but it is linked to a new field composed of the *pilot wave* which guides the

---

[130] Ibid., 172.

[131] Nick Herbert, *Reality: Beyond the New Physics* (New York: Anchor Books, 1987).

movement of the particle.[131] Bohm viewed the electron or quantum as an ordinary particle but it is guided by a very non-ordinary wave. The "pilot wave" is instantaneously affected whenever a change occurs within the whole environment and it communicates this change to the particle altering its position and momentum. Thus, Bohm put forth a non-local causal model accepting the implications of quantum theory's baffling holism and non-local effects.

Bohm uses various analogies to explain his non-ordinary waves—the *pilot waves* that carry the *quantum potential*. These pilot waves carry *information* rather than energy or mass and serve to guide the particle. The quantum potential is the information content. Thus, we have a triad of *matter, energy and information*—in contrast with the traditional matter-energy duality:

> By way of illustration, think of a ship that sails on automatic pilot, guided by radio waves. The overall effect of the radio waves is independent of their strength and depends only on their form. The essential point is that the ship moves with its own energy but that the *information* within the radio waves is taken up and used to direct the much greater energy of the ship. In the causal interpretation, the electron moves under its own energy, but the information in the *form* of the quantum wave directs the energy of the electron.[132]

The external direction of the matter of the ship is determined by the energy expenditure of the engines informed by information content within the quantum potential. The quantum potential or pilot wave embodies *"active information"* with little (if any) energy. The equation for the quantum potential is highly unusual in that its strength is independent of distance and not limited by the speed of light. Instead, it is instantaneously present throughout the field. Bohm explains the profound implications of this view:

> The quantum field contains information about the whole environment and about the whole past, which regulates the present activity of the electron in much the same way that information about the whole past and our whole environment regulates our own activity as human beings, through

---

[132] David Bohm & F. David Peat, *Science, Order and Relativity* (Toronto: Bantam Books, 1987), 90.

> consciousness. ... what is going on in the full depth of that one moment of time contains information about all of it. ... In non-manifest reality, it's all interpenetrating, interconnected, one.[133]

Bohm takes quantum interconnectedness to the extreme by suggesting that any particular quanta (element, particle) is ultimately interconnected through the implicate and super-implicate orders to the whole of the universe! Certainly, such a concept of the universe as an undivided whole provided an ideal physics for a holographic model of consciousness and the mind. Bohm hypothesizes:

> ... a super-information field of the whole universe, a super-implicate order which organizes the first level (of the implicate orders) into various structures and is capable of tremendous development of structure. The point about the super-implicate order is that if we take the holographic theory, though we have an implicate order, nothing organizes it. It is what's called "linear" ... but it does not have an intrinsic capacity to unfold an order. The super-implicate order, which is the so-called higher field ... makes the implicate order non-linear and organizes it into relatively stable forms with complex structures.[134]

According to this scheme, the physical world is the external manifestation of multidimensional hidden dimensions. Reality as it appears to our senses—the everyday world of matter and energy in time and space-is essentially a holographic image projected out of vast interconnected hidden dimensions.

The implicate orders underlie the explicate orders and material reality in a sense *unfolds* from WITHIN/WITHOUT.

> ... a new notion of order is involved here, which we called the *implicate order* (from a Latin root meaning "to enfold" or 'to fold inward'). In terms of the implicate order one may say that everything is enfolded into everything. This contrasts with the *explicate order* now dominant in physics in which things are *un-folded* in the sense that each thing lies only in its own particular

---

[133] Rene Weber, *Dialogues with Scientists and Sages* (London: Routledge, Kegan & Paul, 1986), 39, 41.
[134] Ibid., 33.

> region of space (and time) and outside the regions belonging to other things.[135]

Bohm's model of the implicate orders suggest that there is indeed a more fundamental hidden reality, worlds beyond the level of the quanta and material organization. Since all things are interconnected in informational fields that inform material/energetic processes, then there must be inner dimensions of being capable of responding to this active information, some kind of receiver or resonator system. Bohm uses a radio analogy to explain this. The radio wave carries information or a signal which might be considered to be potentially available everywhere. However, for this potential information to have an active informational influence there has to be a radio set with electrical energy capable of responding to this information field. In this case, we might hear singing (molecular sound vibration) propagated from a radio. We require the material harmonic resonator (the radio set), the information and the energy (electrical power) to manifest within the explicate order (sound). This analogy with a radio set has startling implications for the necessity of other deep levels of reality. Bohm and Peat note:

The quantum wave carries "information" and is therefore *potentially* active everywhere, but it is *actually* active only when and where this energy enters into the energy of a particle. But this implies that an electron, or any other elementary particle, has a complex and subtle inner structure that is at least comparable with that of a radio. Clearly this notion goes against the whole tradition of modern physics, which assumes that as matter is analyzed into smaller and smaller parts, its behavior grows more elementary. By contrast, the causal interpretation suggests that nature may be far more subtle and strange than was previously thought.

But this inner complexity of elementary matter is not as implausible as it may appear at first sight. For example, a large crowd of people can be treated by statistical laws, whereas individually their behavior is immensely subtler and more complex. Similarly, large masses of matter reduce to simple Newtonian behavior whereas atoms and molecules have a more complex inner structure. And what of the sub-atomic particles themselves? It is interesting to note that between the shortest distance now measurable

---

[135] Ibid., 177.

in physics (10^{-16} cm) and the shortest distance in which current notions of space/time probably have meaning, (10^{-33} cm), there is a vast range of scale in which an immense amount of yet undiscovered structure could be contained. Indeed this range is roughly equal to that which exists between our own size and that of the elementary particles.[136]

It seems that the world within is potentially as complex as the world without. Only such inner dimensions of being could allow for a quantum to be responsive to the active information of the quantum potential containing information about the larger whole. Bohm predicted new levels of complexity as suggested now in the 21st century within superstring and M-theories, and by the holographic paradigm. The seven dimensional Calabi Yau Spaces of the physicists, considered to be existent at every point within four dimensional space/time, along with multidimensional *"branes,"* extended within hyperspace dimensions, certainly fulfill Bohm's predictions of there being additional levels of inner complexity. Such elements and dynamics could provide resonator systems with structures far more complex than those of a radio.

Bohm came to regard so-called *empty space* as full of an incredible range of energies and potentials:

> What is implied by this proposal is that what we call empty space contains an immense background of energy ... space ... is *full* rather than empty. ... the plenum ... the ground for the existence of everything, including ourselves. The things that appear to our senses are derivative forms and their true meaning can be seen only when we consider the plenum, in which they are generated and sustained, and into which they must ultimately vanish.[137]

All of creation is folded out of an immense underlying realm of the plenum and of Undivided Wholeness-as tiny ripples on a vast Sea. Bohm's model suggests that ultimately, any quantum exists in relationship to information about the whole, even the past: *"... what is going on in the full depth of that one*

---

[136] Bohm & Peat, 93-4.

[137] Bohm, *Wholeness and the Implicate Order*, 191-2.

moment of time contains information about all of it. ... In non-manifest reality it's all interpenetrating, interconnected, one. "[138]

Summing up, Bohm suggests a progression from the explicate order of manifest existence to multi-dimensional implicate and super-implicate orders—all of which are part of an immense sea of information/energy sensed as empty space. The space *without* (the *explicate order*) is unfolded from the space *within* (the *implicate order* and plenum). Bohm suggests that there might be various extensions of the implicate order beyond the critical limit of 10^{-33} cm. into *"unknown depths of inwardness."* Certainly, Bohm's ideas suggest the existence of rich playground for a holographic mind, heart or human being.

BLAVATSKY'S HOLOGRAPHIC SPACE AND ZERO POINT DYNAMICS

Blavatsky articulated a holographic model of creation—of physics and metaphysics, a century before science arrived at such concepts and possibilities. However, *The Secret Doctrine* suggested a more differentiated view of holographic dynamics than even that of contemporary science. Further, it applies the same perspective to understanding ourselves as holographic beings—microcosms of the macrocosm.

Blavatsky states: "The first and Fundamental dogma of Occultism is Universal Unity (or Homogeneity)...."[139] A holographic view is thus implicit in Occultism which generally espouses the unity and interrelatedness of creation. Further, Blavatsky notes:

> There is but one indivisible and absolute Omniscience and Intelligence in the Universe, and this thrills throughout every atom and infinitesimal point of the whole finite Kosmos which hath no bounds, and which people call SPACE, considered independently of anything in it.[140]

---

[138] David Bohm, in Weber (1986), 41.

[139] Helena Blavatsky, *The Secret Doctrine: The Syntheses of Science, Religion and Philosophy* (Pasadena: Theosophical University Press, California, 1888), 58.

[140] Ibid., 277.

This certainly suggests that there are vast informational and zero point fields within the very fabric of space. Blavatsky states that there is a correlation of all forces within real space or the plenum.

For Blavatsky, the seemingly solid material world is illusory, an outgrowth of causes at zero point levels wherein the forces of nature emerge within without from higher dimensional realms. In her view, the external space/time complex is quite illusory and there are many worlds interpenetrating and sustaining our own space! Blavatsky provides this remarkable passage discussing the presence of other worlds within the same Space as ourselves:

> *The Secret Doctrine* — postulating that conditioned or limited space (location) has no real being except in this world of illusion, or, in other words, in our perceptive faculties — teaches that every one of the higher, as of the lower worlds, is interblended with our own objective world; that millions of things and beings are, in point of localization, around and *in* us, as we are around, with, and in them; it is not metaphysical figure of speech, but a sober fact in Nature, however incomprehensible to our senses.
>
> ... the Occultist does not locate *these spheres* either *outside* or *inside* our Earth, as the theologians and the poets do; for their location is nowhere in the space *known* to, and conceived by, the profane. They are, as it were, blended with our world — inter-penetrating it and interpenetrated by it.
>
> .... Although as invisible as if they were millions of miles beyond our solar system, they are yet with us, near us, *within* our own world, as objective and material to their respective inhabitants as ours is to us. ... The inhabitants of these (worlds) ... may be, for all we know, or feel, passing *through* and *around* us as if through empty space, their very habitations and countries being interblended with ours, though not disturbing our vision, because we have not yet the faculties necessary for discerning them.

> ... such invisible worlds do exist. Inhabited as thickly as our own is, they are scattered throughout apparent Space in immense number; some far more material than our own world, others gradually etherealizing until they become formless and are as "Breaths." That our physical eye does not see them, is no reason to disbelieve in them; physicists can see neither their ether, atoms, nor "modes of motion," or Forces. Yet they accept and teach them.[141]

This is a remarkable conception of the nature of Space—compatible with holographic and quantum information theory in modern physics. Space is not empty. Ordinary four-dimensional space/time is an outward projection from within higher dimensions of real Space. Further, there are all kinds of other intelligences, worlds, dimensions and beings within the same space as us, although invisible to our perceptive faculties. This is analogous to how a scientist can produce multiple holographic images on a holographic plate by shifting the angle of the projecting light sources.

Blavatsky has provided a remarkable description of a holographic universe wherein a whole hierarchy of intelligences is implicated within any element—any living Kosmos.[142] Further, she describes how such a higher dimensional metaphysics produces a lower four dimensional physics as well as a law conformable cosmic order. She notes in regards to the abstruse and abstract teachings of *The Secret Doctrine*:

> These abstractions become more and more concrete as they approach our plane of existence, until they phenomenalise in the form of the material Universe, by process of conversion of metaphysics into physics, analogous to that by which steam can be condensed into water, and the water frozen into ice. (p. 45)

Apparent material realities are projected out of the holographic dynamics of higher dimensional Space, illusory manifestations of nominal realms which underlie and sustain them. Material realities veil the true nature of Deity.

---

[141] Ibid., 604-6.

[142] I use the term "Kosmos" when referring to Blavatsky as this is the more archaic spelling she uses, while otherwise using the more familiar and modern "Cosmos."

A human being in the material body is a quantum system based primarily upon the electrodynamics of the heart. The heart functions essentially as a quantum computer (with micro black hole information processors[143]) and exists within quantized information and zero point fields; ultimately, within an Omniscience which *"thrills throughout every atom and infinitesimal point of the whole finite Cosmos."* Human consciousness emerges through the dimensions of the Heart as the living entity is expanding and withdraws back into the heart at moments of death when it is contracting. Blavatsky explains that the "Sons" or the *"Winks in the Eye of Self-Existence"* do so expand and contract through their own Selves and Hearts.

Blavatsky's occult and mystical views of the zero point origin of human consciousness and of the Kosmos, and her metaphysical model of the laws of nature operating through zero point dynamics provide profound insights into modern scientific theories. Cosmoses emerge from zero point sources out of a seven dimensional mystical void/plenum of the Eternal Parent Space, wherein the Ceaseless Eternal Breath modifies its motion on seven invisible points. All of these dynamics can be considered in relation to the newest ideas in modern physics and could bear upon understanding the multidimensional holographic nature of a human being. These concepts provide the basis for a holographic model of human existence, not based upon neuro-networks in the brain but upon a physics and metaphysics of the heart and its zero point dynamics, and an original point source of *lux*.

Most modern neuroscientists and psychologists consider humans as only a *collection of neurons, molecules and particles*. None has been able to discover a human "I." Of course, it is hard to know how one might discover a form of 'nothingness at the heart of being' or a Monad established in hyperspace beyond Planckian depths! The newest theory in modern psychology and neuro-science is that a particular portion of the prefrontal cortex is the site where the experience of the social self arises. However, from a mystical perspective, these huge errors have arisen because the scientists search for self primarily with the brain instead of awakening to Self within the lotus of the Heart. Blavatsky explains: *"The Mind is the Great Slayer of the Real"*

---

[143] These bizarre concepts will be elaborated within the concluding article of this series and concerns the seven "holes dug in Space" described by Blavatsky as the foundations of the Kosmos, as elaborated in part II of this series.

and further, she directs the Initiate to *"slay the slayer."* The Sons expand and contract through the higher dimensions of the human heart—as winks in the eye of self-existence.

CONCLUDING REMARKS

A holographic model of creation is inherent to mystical and occult views which suggest the ultimate unity and interrelatedness of existence, and further, that a human being embodies the cosmos and can even have direct experience of this-as depicted by Yogananda. The holographic paradigm within modern psychology explored these concepts but tended to assume that the holographic principle applied exclusively to the mind and that there is no coherent light source within a human being. An occult perspective provides an alternative view of human beings as having some type of zero point element, a first point of supernal lux, deriving from within a higher dimensional Heart Space, which allows for the illumination of the inner cosmos. It is the conjunction of the self-illuminating zero point element within higher seven dimensional space that lies behind the creation of the human holographic experience originating out of the depths of the Heart.[144]

---

[144] A concluding section of this article series will explore the more complex notions of holography to emerge in 21st century physics; dealing with black hole information processsors in alternate space dimensions and the relationship of such concepts to Blavatsky's notion of "seven holes dug in space."

IV
An Alternate Model of the Higher Dimensional Structure of Human Existence

... "material points without extension" are Leibnitz's monads, and at the same time the materials out of which the 'Gods' and other invisible powers clothe themselves in bodies...."

"Whence the substance that clothes them — the apparent organism they evolve around their centres?"

- H. P. Blavatsky, 1888 [145] -

THE SWIFT AND RADIANT ONE PRODUCES THE SEVEN LAYA CENTRES ... AND SEATS THE UNIVERSE ON THESE ETERNAL FOUNDATIONS.

- (*Stanzas of Dzyan*, VI 2) [146] -

"... the heart is truly a wonder, for its creative action mirrors the original act of Creation."

- C. Kramer, Kabbalist [147] -

---

[145] Blavatsky, H. *The Secret Doctrine: The syntheses of science, religion and philosophy*. (Theosophical University Press, Pasadena California, 1888), 489 & 632.

[146] Capitals are used when quoting from the Stanzas, as this practice is used within the *S.D.*.

[147] C. Kramer, *Anatomy of the Soul*, (Breslov Research Institute, Jerusalem, 1998).

ABSTRACT

An alternate model of the higher dimensional structure of human existence is proposed based upon the archaic teachings of H. Blavatsky, *The Secret Doctrine* and the *Stanzas of Dzyan* and synthesized with emerging ideas in physics concerning the information-processing and holographic paradigm. Specifically, it is proposed that *the living entity* within a human being is a monadic essence which exists within a sevenfold hyperspace dimension — or Parent Space. This monad, or God Spark, has seven interior *'holes dug in space'* and these have inherent spin properties as manifestation of the *Ceaseless Breath* and its circumgyrating motion. These spin properties manifest as 'spin energy' or 'spinergy' and act upon the sevenfold Aether of Space to precipitate varied matters upon successive planes of being— hence to clothe the divine source emanation within spiritual, psychical and material bodies. The Sons or 'winks in the Eye of Self-Existence,' which we are, expand and contract through their own Hearts and Self within such a higher dimensional universe of unspeakable subtlety and beauty. Ultimately, every man and woman is a Star, a point source light emanation existing within higher dimensional space.[148] Seven *holes dug in space* serve as mini-white/black hole information processors and are the basis for such a higher dimensional magic and existence, weaving webs through spirit and matter. This is a theoretical attempt to synthesize ancient mystical axioms with emerging concepts in holographic physics.[149]

---

[148] A. Crowley states that the first principle of *magick* is that: *"Every man and every woman is a star."* In a similar vein, S. MacLaine comments that *"we each contain and hold the God-spark within us."* (*Going Within*, 1989, p. 108) To suggest that an individual *is a Star* is to reference such a divine source emanation or God-spark within.

[149] This article is the concluding section of a four part series. To some extent, it presupposes reader familiarity with concepts previously introduced: including the argument that human consciousness and the I-experience originate out of the depths of the heart; that living beings have dynamic 'zero point' centres rooted into the grounds of Being/Non-Being; and that there is reason to explore the possibility of a higher dimensional holographic metaphysics to the heart, as the possible basis for states of Samadhi and Cosmic Consciousness. This concluding article is the most speculative in nature, proposing a higher dimensional model of human existence based on archaic elements from *The Secret Doctrine* and emerging concepts in holographic physics.

COSMIC EVOLUTION

Book I of H. Blavatsky's *The Secret Doctrine* (1888), *Cosmogenesis*, deals with the "genesis" of the "cosmos" -the origin and creation of the universe. *Cosmogenesis* outlines the laws of cosmology, physics and metaphysics from an esoteric and occult perspective based upon Stanzas from the *Book of Dzyan*, an ancient poetic text of Tibetan origin which apart from Blavatsky's writings seems largely unknown to modern scholarship.[150] The *Stanzas of Dzyan* are referred to as *"the heart of the sacred books of Kiu-ti,"* once known only to Tibetan mystics. Blavatsky describes a *"very old Book"* originally recorded in Senzar — the *"sacred sacerdotal tongue"* and derived from *"the words of the Divine Beings, who dictated it to the sons of Light, in Central Asia, at the very beginning of the 5th (our) race."*[151] Certainly, these are unusual claims and the origin of the Stanzas seems largely lost in antiquity. Blavatsky explains that the *Stanzas of Dzyan* provide an *"abstract algebraic formula of ... Evolution,"* which can be applied to *"all evolution."* There are *"seven terms of this abstract formula, related to the seven great stages of the evolutionary process, as described in the Puranas as the "Seven Creations," and in the Bible as the "Days" of Creation."*

Within *The Secret Doctrine*, the Universe is claimed to have emerged from a zero point or singularity condition, out of a seeming void and plenum — a seven dimensional hyperspace or *'Eternal Parent Space'* with an underlying fundamental holomovement or *'Eternal Ceaseless Breath.'* These primordial Mother and Father principles are the basis for the material and spiritual worlds. A Kosmos grows from a zero point source within-without to become a world and will eventually contract without-within back to a final zero point — to return into the sevenfold hyperspace of the Divine Mother. Blavatsky, in the 19th century, regarded our Kosmos as simply one such *"wink in the Eye of Self-Existence"* emerging from and dissolving back through zero point centers rooted into an underlying Ceaseless Breath within a Parent Space!

The two primary root principles of creation are the higher dimensional seven-skinned *Eternal Parent Space* and the *Eternal Ceaseless Breath*. The *Stanzas of Dzyan* begin before the big bang when the world was empty

---

[150] A. Bailey (and Tibetan Master Djwhal Khul) provides a detailed study of the Stanzas in — *A Treatise on Comic Fire*.

[151] *Ibid.*, xliii.

and void during the *Nights of Brahma*, and the Spirit (Breath) moves across the face of the Waters (of Space). The Stanzas then depict the dynamic emergence of a cosmos, the dropping of a world egg, the emergence of the seven divine intelligences or Luminous Sons, and the unfurling of varied cosmic processes through different hierarchies of creation. These abstract causes and root principles *"phenomenalise in the form of the material Universe, by a process of conversion of metaphysics into physics, analogous to that by which steam can be condensed into water, and the water frozen into ice."* Blavatsky states, *"metaphysical abstractions ... are the only conceivable cause of physical concretions."* [152]

In modern terminology, the *Eternal Parent Space* is the seven-dimensional hyperspace of the *quantum vacuum* — the quantum ether with its zero point fields as postulated within models of physics (including Superstring and M-theory — the supposed "Mother" of all theories). A modern physicist declares: *"All of physics is in the vacuum"* and this is quite consistent with the viewpoint elaborated by Blavatsky. Blavatsky's seemingly bizarre descriptions of metaphysical processes have anticipated essential concepts of modern physics: including vacuum genesis, creation from a singularity condition, 11 dimensional string theory and M-theory, quantum information theory and the holographic principle. Further, they shed a wholly different light on the enigmas of the "uncertainty principle" and the 'baffling holism' of quantum physics. Blavatsky's perspectives on the mysteries of creation are ever more intelligible in light of the theories and findings of modern science. [153]

Monads can similarly be regarded as 'winks in the Eye of Self-Existence.' Of course, since a human embodies the Universe, as a microcosm of the macrocosm, then the same abstract numerical and symbolic formulas applied to understanding the zero point dynamics underlying the creation of the Universe can also be applied to understanding the emergence of the Monad. A *Stanzas of Dzyan* states:

> "THE SONS EXPAND AND CONTRACT THROUGH
> THEIR OWN SELVES AND HEARTS; THEY EMBRACE
> INFINITUDE." (III, 11)

---

[152] *Ibid.*, 45.

[153] These parallels are spelt out in detail in *God, Science & The Secret Doctrine* (Holmes, C., Zero Point Publications, Canada). 2010.

The nature of the 'I AM,' the Monads, the individual living beings, the 'winks in the Eye of Self-Existence' can be considered according to the same formula of the Stanzas for Cosmic Evolution. A Monadic essence existent within a seven dimensional hyperspace, by some hidden inner magic, becomes *"clothed in different bodies"* based upon zero point *laya centres*. Blavatsky offers a higher dimensional model of human existence within holographic Space, in comparison with which 20th century psychology looks meagre indeed.

ZERO POINT FOUNDATIONS & THE ROLE OF FOHAT

> The seven *Layu* centres are the seven Zero points, using the term Zero in the same sense that Chemists do, to indicate a point at which, in Esotericism, the scale of reckoning of differentiation begins.[154]

The Secret Doctrine maintains that the universe is founded upon an original zero point laya centre which further differentiates into *seven zero point centres*. Seven minute *'holes dug in space'* are the means by which higher dimensional forces sculpt the void through the processes of creation. Blavatsky offers this explanation of the *"Forces of Nature:"*

> ... all the so-called Forces of Nature, Electricity, Magnetism, Light, Heat, etc., etc., far from being modes of motion of material particles, are *in esse*, i.e., in their ultimate constitution, the differentiated aspects of that Universal Motion. ... When Fohat is said to produce "Seven Laya Centres," it means that for formative or creative purposes, the GREAT LAW (Theists may call it God) stops, or rather modifies its perpetual motion on seven invisible points within the area of the manifested Universe. *"The great Breath digs through Space seven holes into Laya to cause them to circumgyrate during Manvantara."* (Occult Catechism). We have said that Laya is what Science may call the Zero-point or line; the realm of absolute negativeness, or

---

[154] *Ibid.*, 138-9.

> the one real absolute Force ... the neutral axis, not one of the many aspects, but its centre. ... "Seven Neutral Centres," then are produced by Fohat ....[155]

The Ceaseless Breath or Universal Motion *"digs holes in Space"* to channel intelligence and influences into the material realm. Any Cosmos, Universe, Monad, atom or quantum is thus *"worked and guided from within outwards"* through the dynamics of such zero point centres. Life within a living being thus originates within/without, out of higher space dimensions through the dynamics of a multidimensional heart.

Within *The Secret Doctrine*, understanding the role and significance of *Fohat* is a key to the mysteries of cosmogenesis and the relationship of the laws of physics to ancient metaphysics:

> But just as the opposite poles of subject and object, spirit and matter, are but aspects of the One Unity in which they are synthesized, so, in the manifested Universe, there is "that" which links spirit to matter, subject to object.
>
> This something, at present unknown to Western speculation, is called by the occultists Fohat. It is the "bridge' by which the "Ideas" existing in the "Divine Thought" are impressed on Cosmic Substance as the "Laws of nature." Fohat is thus the dynamic energy of Cosmic Ideation; or, regarded from the other side, it is the intelligent medium, the guiding power of all manifestation, the "Thought Divine" transmitted and made manifest through the Dhyan Chohans, the Architects of the visible World. ... Fohat, in its various manifestations, is the mysterious link between Mind and Matter, the animating principle electrifying every atom into life.[156]

Just as a human has a body, soul and spirit, so also does the Cosmos. Fohat is that agent of spirit which ensouls the material body of the cosmos; *"the animating principle electrifying every atom into life."* Fohat is the *"dynamic*

---

[155] *Ibid.*, 147-8.

[156] *Ibid.*, 16.

energy of Cosmic Ideation" and embodies the intelligence of the spiritual builders or the Seven Luminous Sons.

> THE PRIMORIAL SEVEN, THE FIRST SEVEN BREATHS OF THE DRAGON OF WISDOM, PRODUCE IN THEIR TURN FROM THEIR HOLY CIRCUMGYRATING BREATHS THE FIERY WHIRLWIND. V. 1

The PRIMORDIAL SEVEN entail modifications of the fundamental Ceaseless Breath. These are the first born from the Darkness and Matrix of Non-Being. The Seven Breaths are *"circumgyrating,"* indicating vortices spinning around a center. These in turn produce "the Fiery Whirlwind," which is FOHAT. Fohat links the seven primary realms of spiritual creation above to the seven realms of material nature below. The Stanzas declare: *"SEVEN INSIDE; SEVEN OUTSIDE."*

Fohat is the energetic principle, the fundamental cosmic electromagnetism and it conveys the influence of divine and spiritual intelligences to impress upon matter.

> It is through Fohat that the ideas of the Universal Mind are impressed upon matter. Some faint idea of the nature of Fohat may be gathered from the appellation "Cosmic Electricity" sometimes applied to it; but to the commonly known properties of electricity must, in this case, be added others, including intelligence. [157]

According to Blavatsky, Fohat is the Messenger of the Primordial Sons of Light and Life, the Dhyan-Chohans, running their errands and impressing their divine thoughts and intelligence into the seven realms of material creation below. Further, just as there are seven Luminous Sons or seven circumgyrating Breaths and seven primordial matters latent in the Eternal Parent Space, Fohat is also sevenfold having seven sons:

> Fohat ... is One and Seven, and on the Cosmic plane is behind all such manifestations as light, heat, sound, adhesion,

---

[157] *Ibid.*, 85.

etc., etc., and is the "spirit" of ELECTRICITY, which is the Life of the Universe. ... Thus, while science speaks of its evolution through brute matter, blind force and senseless motion, the Occultists point to *intelligent* LAW and *sentient* LIFE, and add that Fohat is the guiding Spirit of all this. ... the "Messenger of the primordial Sons of Life and Light." [158]

Fohat is Cosmic Electricity, the energetic and vivifying principle linking Cosmic Spirit (Intelligence) to Cosmic Matter. Fohat is *"metaphysically"* the *"objectified thought of the gods"* and *"the transcendental binding Unity of all Cosmic Energies."*

Fohat is also a source of gravitational influence established within higher dimensional Space of one's heart, holding it all together. Fohat binds living cosmoses together and conveys the influences of higher dimensional dynamics into the manifest realm below. The Hearts of living beings are their LIFE centers, wherein we might find Deity, as within *"every point of the universe."* Fohat is also the *"vital electric force that leaves the body at death,"* [159] whether a Kosmos or Son.

The *Stanza of Dzyan* depict the formation of the Laya Centres which serve as the foundations for the universe:

> VI: 2. THE SWIFT AND RADIANT ONE PRODUCES THE SEVEN LAYA CENTRES ... AND SEATS THE UNIVERSE ON THESE ETERNAL FOUNDATIONS .... 3. ... SEVEN SMALL WHEELS REVOLVING; ONE GIVING BIRTH TO THE OTHER. 4. ... FOHAT ... MAKES BALLS OF FIRE, RUNS THROUGH THEM, AND ROUND THEM, INFUSING LIFE THEREINTO, THEN SETS THEM INTO MOTION; SOME ONE WAY, SOME THE OTHER WAY.

The laya centres, the eternal foundations for the Universe, are 'revolving' and 'set in motion' in different directions. They differentiate through

---

[158] *Ibid.*, 139.

[159] *Ibid.*, 673.

sequential symmetry breaking, ONE GIVING BIRTH TO THE OTHER.[160] Imagine such wheels within wheels, through different generations of causes and effects originating from a dynamic zero point center established within the transcendental hyperspace of the Eternal Parent Space!

The Eternal Ceaseless Breath, which is infinitely energetic, manifests as the Primordial Seven -the Seven HOLY CIRCUMGYRATING BREATHS which produce THE FIERY WHIRLWIND, the "MESSENGER OF THEIR WILL," Fohat and his seven Sons, the *Lipika*. Fohat RUNS CIRCULAR ERRANDS and forms seven WHEELS in the six directions of space and one in the middle—depicted in figure 1 by the *flower of life* symbol of ancient Egypt with a central seventh point. A certain *"spinergy"* or 'spin energy' is thus inherent to the zero point foundations of a cosmos.

Figure 15

The Seven Sons of Fohat link Spirit above to Matter below and spin their magic through *seven holes dug in space*, invisible centres within the Eternal Parent Space. Any living Cosmos is set upon such a foundation. These 'holes dug in space' might be regarded as seven mini white or black holes, according to whether we are speaking of the emergence or dissipation of a Cosmos. The seven holes 'dug in space' are 'whirlwinds' of activity—modifications of the Ceaseless Breath—which just like black holes, may have mass, rotational and spin properties. These metaphysical processes in a higher dimensional space are rendered

---

[160] Before creation occurs and the universe is absorbed in Non-Being, there is a state of 'perfect symmetry.' The initiation of creation with the emergence of a first point is the first act of symmetry breaking, which leads to the sequential symmetry breaking within higher dimensional space and the differentiation of the laws of nature and the precipitation of varied quanta or matter/energetic elements on different vibratory levels, all out of the seeming void. The modern concept of symmetry breaking in physics is aptly depicted by the descent of the Line of Light through the *Tree of Life* of the Kabbalist. As symmetries are broken, different worlds are made manifest. In the Vedas, before creation occurs, the three modes of nature, *sattva, rajas and tamas* representing intelligence, energy and matter are in a state of perfect symmetry, hence are unmanifest and described as 'signless.' When the Light of Brahma penetrates the void and breaks the symmetry, each of the three modes of nature manifests at three levels of vibratory existence; just as in physics, each class of particles (hadrons, leptons and gluons) is described as having three generations.

equivalent to outward worlds of seemingly separate energies and material particles manifesting within external four-dimensional spacetime. The central point is thus 'clothed' in different bodies.

In Blavatsky's view, there are varied external four-dimensional spacetime realms — physical, astral and mental worlds on a lower level, and corresponding Atmic, Buddhic and Manas planes on higher levels. Each of these is a projection of dynamics founded upon holographic boundaries or shells surrounding the central holes dug in space. Living beings have such LIFE Centres, as Monads existing within the Eternal Parent Space, and the outward physics of life is created as a great Chain of Being surrounding the higher dimensional metaphysics of a Monad in Hyperspace.

It is from such mysterious zero point conditions that the differentiation of a Cosmos, a quantum or Monad begins; and such dynamics are reiterated through interior dimensions. Modern scientist, Paul Davis described such a model of 11 dimensional theory in modern physics where seven *'compacted dimensions'* are rolled up into elements at zero point levels. Davis explained, *"think of the extra dimensions as somehow inside the atom."* [161] Remarkably, Blavatsky explained exactly this type of peculiar inner dimensionality to 'atoms,' quanta, Monads and cosmoses over a century ago. Accordingly, Blavatsky's model suggests that there is a complex metaphysics to reality at zero point levels.

Madame Blavatsky offers modern science profound gems of insight into the possible mechanisms of Divine and Spiritual Intelligences in creating, maintaining and dissolving any finite holographic Cosmos. Instead of a bearded patriarch sitting on a throne, the Divine Workmen carry out the Will of the Dhyan Chohans and spin their magic through the seven dynamic vortex action centres established within higher dimensional Space. The Gods *"micro-intervene"* within the laws of nature with such holes dug in Space functioning as information micro-processors!

---

[161] P. Davis, *Superforce: The Search for a Grand Unified Theory of Nature* (Touchstone Book, New York, 1984), 160.

THE UNIVERSE AS A HOLOGRAM

In 2003, *Scientific American* published an issue posing the question *"ARE YOU A HOLOGRAM? Quantum physics says the entire universe might be."* In a fascinating article, *Information in the Holographic Universe*, J. Bekenstein discussed some of the unusual features of modern information and holographic theory and the physics of black holes. The holographic principle is being proposed as the possible Holy Grail of physics as it unifies the quantum field theories of physics with an account of gravity.

Bekenstein regards "information" as a third force underlying the manifestations of matter and energy within time and space. This is similar to Bohm's 'pilot waves' and the 'quantum potential' permeating space, as information fields of the implicate orders that inform transformations of matter and energy. [162]

> "Ask anybody what the physical world is made of, and you are likely to be told "matter and energy." Yet if we have learned anything from engineering, biology and physics, information is just as crucial an ingredient. ... a century of developments in physics has taught us that information is a crucial player in physical systems and processes. Indeed, a current trend, initiated by John A. Wheeler of Princeton University, is to regard the physical world as made of information, with energy and matter as incidentals. [163]

In *Black Hole Computers*, Lloyd and Ng similarly emphasize 'information' as third force in the new physics:

> ... to a physicist, all physical systems are computers. Rocks, atomic bombs and galaxies may not run Linux, but they, too, register and process information. Every electron, photon and other elementary particle stores bits of data, and every time two such particles interact, those bits are transformed. Physi-

---

[162] This is explained in Part Three of this series, (Esoteric Journal, Spring 2011) 56-58.

[163] Bekenstein, Information in the Holographic Universe, (*Scientific American*. Aug. 2003), 59.

cal existence and information content are inextricably linked. As physicist John Wheeler of Princeton University says, "It from bit." [164]

The statement *"it from bit,"* suggests that 'it,' meaning a material and energetic system, comes from 'bit,' meaning bits of information. Some modern physicists now regard information as a primary element in nature. From this perspective, everything is a computer, as everything processes bits of information—whether an electron, a black hole, a cell or a human heart. Thus, a trinity of intelligence, energy and matter is basic to the new science—as it is to mystical orientations and *The Secret Doctrine*. According to Lloyd and Ng, the universe itself is a giant computer and not only that, but a quantum computer. They quote physicist Zizzi, *"It from qubit,"* -or quantum bit, as a variation on Wheeler's *"It from bit."*

Bekenstein explains aspects of information theory as apply to black holes and the emerging holographic theory and suggests that: *"Theoretical results about black holes suggest that the universe could be like a gigantic hologram."* The reasoning that leads to such a concept concerns modern views of the laws of entropy and how this relates to the entropy of information. The *law of entropy* traditionally applied to material and thermal processes can also be applied to information processes. In 1877, physicist Ludwig Boltzmann defined *thermodynamic entropy* as the number of distinct microscopic states that particles in a body of matter could be in: For example, consider all the possible arrangements of the gas molecules in the room around you and their possible positions and momentum. It was in 1948, that Claude Shannon defined entropy in terms of information theory. The *Shannon entropy* is the number of binary bits needed to decode the information content within a message. The two measures and concepts of entropy are *"conceptually equivalent"* (under higher degrees of freedom), although they are expressed in different units—either 'units of energy divided by temperature' for thermal entropy, or as 'bits' which are *"essentially dimensionless"* for information entropy. The conservation of information is also demanded within quantum mechanics.

According to the *Generalized Second Law of Thermodynamics*, the loss or gain of entropy in a material/energetic system must be compensated for by

---

[164] S. Lloyd, Y. NG, Y., Black Hole Computers (*Scientific American*, Nov. 2004). Seth Lloyd is a professor at MIT and Y. Jack Ng a physics and astronomy professor at the University of North Carolina at Chapel Hill.

changes in the entropy of information as one balances the other in order to maintain an overall GSL Bekenstein explains a consequence of this principle as applied to the physics of black holes:

> ... when matter falls into a black hole, the increase in black hole entropy always compensates or overcompensates for the "lost" entropy of the matter. More generally, the sum of black hole entropies and the ordinary entropy outside the black holes cannot decrease. This is the generalized second law – GSL for short. [165]

Figure 16 [166]

This implies that when the matter and energy of a quantum system are absorbed into a black hole, huge amounts of information should spew out. *Scientific America* (November 2004) featured an article on *Black Hole Computers*, which suggests: *"Stephen Hawking was Wrong. Matter goes in. Answers come out."* The loss of entropy which occurs as matter and energy are absorbed into a black hole is compensated for by an increase of the entropy of the information – thus, answers come out – like the 0 and 1 sequences illustrated in Figure 16 as emerging from a mini black hole processor.

In *Black Hole Computers*, Lloyd and Ng explain that in the 1970s, Hawking proposed that when matter fell into a black hole, the radiation produced was simply random. However, the newer view now endorsed by Hawking is that the outgoing radiation is not simply random but *"a processed form of the matter that falls in."* The authors thus declare: *"Black holes,*

---

[165] J. Bekenstein, *Ibid.*, 62.

[166] Illustrations 16, through 21 were created by graphic designer Željka Županić of Croatia, based upon similar illustrations from the *Scientific American* articles referenced.

too compute." [167] Furthermore, the authors note: *"... a black hole is nothing more or less than a computer compressed to its smallest possible size."* Thus, when matter falls into a black hole past the event horizon, it cannot leave but the *"information content can."*

The total storage capacity of a black hole is proportional to its surface area. Susskind (2008) states this principle: *"The entropy of a black hole, measured in bits, is proportional to the area of its horizon, measured in Planck units."* [168] Figure 3 depicts a black hole as having its surface or horizon divided into bits, triangular sections containing 0's or 1's. This is counter-intuitive, as one might have expected that the information content of the black hole would be related to its interior volume. However, this is not so and instead the information is encoded on the surface of the black hole – on a two dimensional surface instead of in the 3-dimensional interior volume.

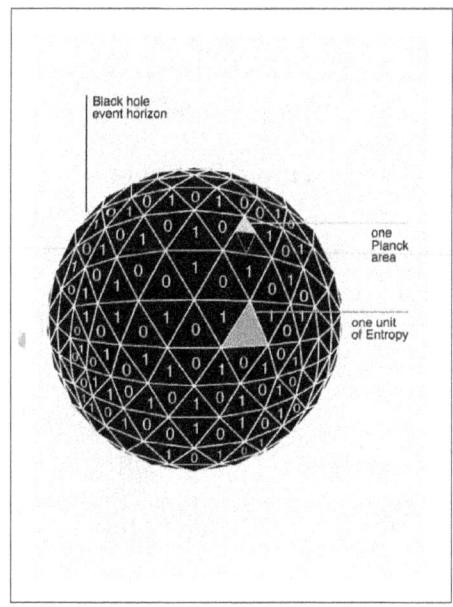

Figure 17

Paradoxically, the physics of black holes suggests that as a physical system of matter and energy collapses down to the level of Planck units at 10^{-33} cm and beyond, the amount of information potentially contained within a volume of space becomes huge. Bekenstein considers the amount of information contained within *'a Planck area'* which is the square of two Planck lengths of 10^{-33} cm – or 10^{-66} cm². At Planck's level, at zero point levels in the quantum vacuum or aether, the information content and capacity is potentially huge. Bekenstein states: *"The entropy of a black hole one centimetre in diameter would be about 10^{66} bits, roughly equal to the thermodynamic entropy of a cube of water 10 billion kilometres on a side."* [169]

---

[167] Lloyd and Ng, *Ibid.*, 54.

[168] L. Susskind, *The Black Hole War: My battle with Stephen Hawking to make the world safe for quantum mechanics* (Little, Brown &Co., New York, 2008) 155.

[169] Bekenstein, *Ibid.*, 62-3.

Bekenstein argues that there seems *"to be no limits to how densely information can be packed-and that our universe might be like a giant hologram."* In Bekenstein's model, the more we penetrate into the heart of being, vast amounts of information might be contained within the seeming emptiness and there might be such complex inner worlds and black hole dynamics. Furthermore, black holes have both mass and rotational or spin properties and could function as the ultimate mini-computers, processing immense amounts of information at Planckian levels. Everything computes in the new science of information theory, including mini-black holes.

Diverse new views of black holes suggest also that they are not such simple structures as once conceived. In string theory, they are regarded as composite bodies made of multidimensional structures called branes. Information falling into the black hole is stored in waves in the branes and can eventually leak out. Black holes have also been described as "a giant tangle of strings," a "fuzzyball" which can act as a repository of the information carried by things that fall into the black hole. Information has another "escape hatch" out of a black hole through 'entanglement,' whereby the properties of two systems inside and outside of the black hole remain correlated across spacetime. Entanglement is thought to possibly enable teleportation, in which information is transferred from one particle to another with such fidelity that the particle has effectively been beamed from one location to another. The annihilation of an infalling photon acts as a measurement, transferring the information contained in the matter to the outgoing Hawking radiation. Scientists are arriving at complex views of reality at zero point levels, looking at the information processor capacities of black holes and other structures at Planck's levels.

Physicist L. Smolin describes the world according to the holographic model:

> The world must be a network of holograms, each of which contains coded within it information about the relationships between the others. In short, the holographic principle is the ultimate realization of the notion that the world is a network of relationships. Those relationships are revealed by this new principle to involve nothing but information. Any element in this network is nothing but a partial realization of the relationships between the other elements. In the end, perhaps,

the history of a universe is nothing but the flow of information. [170]

Smolin describes the atomic or quantized structure of space in terms of spin networks, information and relationships. Certainly, these are profoundly alternative models of deep reality at zero point level! Bekenstein comments on the direction of modern physics towards finding deeper and deeper levels of structure at zero point levels: *"There could be more levels of structure in our universe than are dreamt of in today's physics. ... the deepest level of structure I shall refer to as level X. ... "* [171]

BLACK HOLES & ALTERNATE SPACE DIMENSIONS

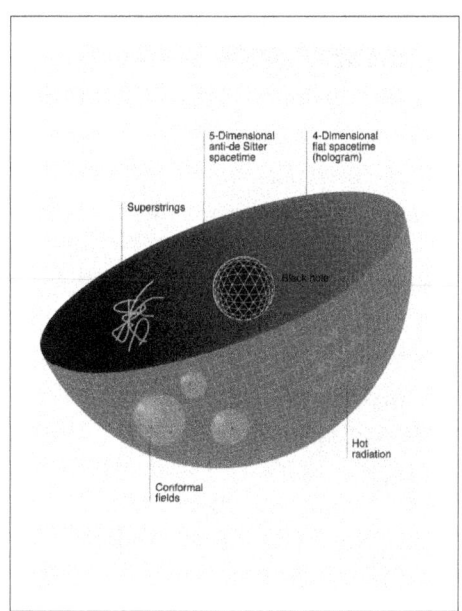

Figure 18

Figure 18 depicts one of the most unusual ideas of the holographic model in physics. The interior of this sphere represents a *"5 dimensional anti-de Sitter spacetime"* and the circumference of the sphere, the shell, represents the *"four dimensional flat spacetime (hologram)."* Bekenstein explains that if the physics of the universe is holographic, then different sets of physical laws that apply in the de-Sitter spacetime (the shell surrounding the black hole) and the anti-de Sitter spacetime (within the sphere) are rendered equivalent. Thus, the *"conformal field theory of point particles"* applies on the two dimensional surface of the sphere (the holographic boundary or shell) and it is rendered equivalent to a physics of superstrings elements and black holes within the *"5 dimensional anti-de Sitter spacetime"* (within the interior of the sphere). Thus, what manifests in the physical realm is rendered equivalent to metaphysical

---

[170] L. Smolin, *Three Roads to Quantum Gravity* (Basic Books, Perseus, Great Britian, 2001) 178.

[171] Bekenstein, *Ibid.*, 60.

processes in an alternative higher Space dimension. Figure 19 depicts how the activities of a black hole in the interior of the anti-de Sitter space is rendered equivalent to swarms of particles on the boundary surface of the spacetime sphere.

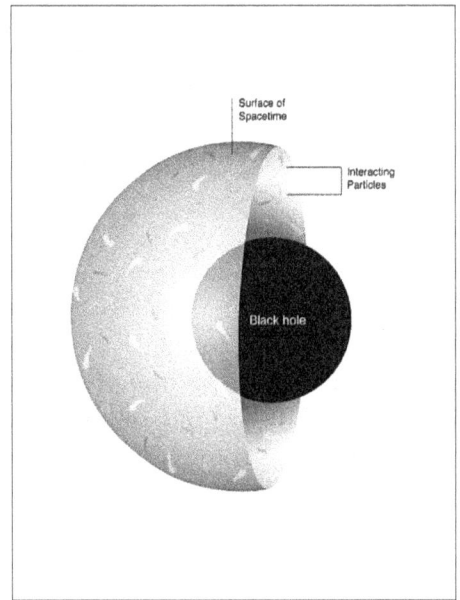

Figure 19

Thus, quantum field theories and point particle interactions might apply on the outer shell, but inside, we have the physics of superstrings and black holes. The holographic principle renders these two theories equivalent. The outer shell or surface of the sphere is compared to a two dimensional holographic plate which records or embodies processes occurring within the interior space. Bekenstein writes: *"Creatures living in one of these universes would be incapable of determining if they inhabited a 5-D universe described by string theory or a 4-D one described by a quantum field theory of point particles."* Bekenstein suggests that in this case, the three dimensional physical world is projected from a flat boundary or screen, the shell of the sphere, just like a holographic image is projected into space from a flat two dimensional holographic plate. In Figure 20, clouds of quarks and gluons on the boundary surface describe related complex objects such as an apple within the interior of the sphere. The object in the interior is subject to gravity even though such a gravitational attraction does not exist on the surface. It turns out that the mathematics of particle physics are almost the same as the mathematics of string theory. What is so startling about this is the fact that these phenomena are on such divergent orders of scale. The protons and neutrons can be 10^{20} times larger than the fundamental strings and they vibrate 10^{20} times more slowly.

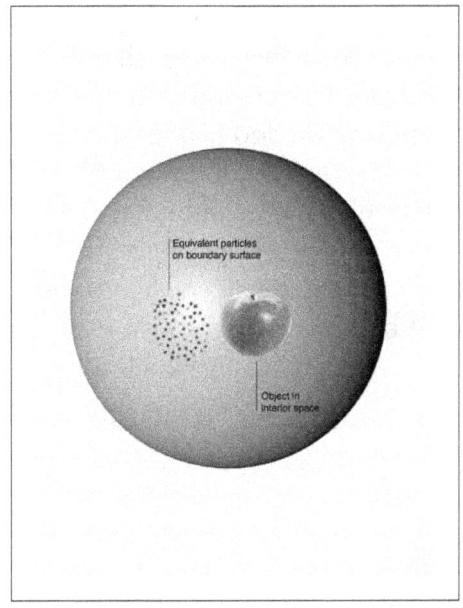

Figure 20

Scientist L. Susskind similarly concludes:

... the three-dimensional world of ordinary experience — the universe filled with galaxies, stars, planets, houses, boulders, and people — is a hologram, an image of reality coded on a distant two-dimensional surface. This new law of physics, known as the Holographic Principle, asserts that everything inside a region of space can be described by bits of information restricted to the boundary. ... everything inside this giant shell is an image of microscopic bits spread over the shell. ... everything taking place in the interior of the region is a holographic image of the pixelated boundary. ... the world ... is pixelated, and all information is stored on the boundary of space. [172]

Susskind notes that of this most peculiar holographic principle: *"Getting our collective head around the Holographic Principle is probably the biggest challenge that we physicists have had since the discovery of Quantum Mechanics."*

On the surface of the sphere, quantum theories and point particle analysis applies, but these reflect a deeper metaphysics of membranes and strings, matrices and spin networks in higher dimensional space. Finally, at the centre of the holographic system is a black hole information processor in this alternate space dimension. This is quite analogous to how Blavatsky depicts material/energetic processes as based upon zero point foundations — *'holes dug in Space'* — established within an underlying seven skinned Eternal Parent Space. Further, from the perspective of Blavatsky, we would consider there to be seven such shells instead of simply one, as related to the sevenfoldness of the Eternal Parent Space, the Akasha or Aether.

---

[172] Susskind, *Ibid.*, 298-299.

Of course, Bekenstein and Susskind do not consider that a holographic model might be applicable to human beings—as their focus is on the black holes, information theory and the holographic principle within physics. It is not immediately evident how one might jump from the levels of Planckian units and elementary quanta in physics to the dimensions of human existence. However, the mystical idea—that the microcosm embodies the nature of the macrocosm based on seven holes dug in space—suggests the rationale for applying these concepts to the inner cosmos of consciousness. These concepts are all particularly significant in light of Blavatsky's description of seven such *"holes dug in space"* as the means by which the Gods and other invisible powers *"clothe themselves in bodies."*

THE ILLUSION OF GRAVITY [173]

A holographic view of physics offers an alternative perspective on the nature of 'gravity.' In *The Illusion of Gravity*, theoretical physicist Juan Martin Maldacena explains:

> ... the theories predict that the number of dimensions in reality could be a matter of perspective: physicists could choose to describe reality as obeying one set of laws (including grav-

---

[173] Blavatsky denies the existence of gravity as commonly understood, regarding it as a variant of the electromagnetic force with its seven variants conveyed by Fohat and due to the electromagnetic influences of the sun, earth, moon and planets as propagated through the Aether of Space:

Thus the Occultists are not alone in their beliefs. Nor are they so foolish, after all, in rejecting even the "gravity" of modern Science along with other *physical* laws, and in accepting instead *attraction* and *repulsion*. They see, moreover, in these two opposite Forces only the two *aspects* of the universal unit, called "MANIFESTING MIND"; in which aspects, Occultism, through its great Seers, perceives an innumerable Host of operative Beings; Cosmic Dhyan-Chohans, Entities, whose essence, in its dual nature, is the Cause of all terrestrial phenomena. For that essence is co-substantial with the universal Electric Ocean, which is LIFE .... (*S.D., I*, p. 604)

These explanations suggest that it is the presence of the "Manifesting Mind" conveyed through Fohat and operative at zero point levels within a universal Electric Ocean, which accounts for the phenomena attributed to the mysterious force of gravity. Blavatsky states: *"Occultists ... see in gravity only sympathy and antipathy, or attraction and repulsion, caused by physical polarity on our terrestrial plane, and by spiritual causes outside of its influence ...."* (p. 513) Similar views are also emerging within physics, regarding gravitational effects as due to electromagnetic fluxes within ethers of space.

> ity) in three dimensions or, equivalently, as obeying a different set of laws that operates in two dimensions (in the absence of gravity). ... A hologram is a two-dimensional object, but when viewed under the correct lighting conditions it produces a fully three-dimensional image. ... Gravity ... would be part of the illusion: a force that is not present in the two-dimensional world but that materializes along with the emergence of the illusory third dimension. [174] [175]

Maldacena describes a quantum theory of gravity as the *"holy grail for a certain breed of physicist"* and explains that string theorists have developed such a *"complete, logically consistent, quantum description of gravity in what are called negatively curved spacetimes—the first such description ever developed. For these spacetimes, holographic theories appear to be true."* [176]

The anti-de Sitter space is the simplest of such negatively curved spaces. They neither expand nor contract, but look the same at all times. Maldacena explains the equivalency of the physics of these alternative dimensions in the interior of the sphere to those upon its boundary:

> ... the boundary of four-dimensional anti-de Sitter space at any moment in time is a sphere. This boundary is where the hologram of the holographic theory lies. Simply stated, the idea is as follows: a quantum gravity theory in the interior of an anti-de Sitter spacetime is completely equivalent to an ordinary quantum particle theory living on the boundary. If true, this equivalence means that we can use a quantum particle theory (which is relatively well understood) to define a quantum gravity theory (which is not). (2005, p. 61)

Thus, gravity can be accommodated within string/M-theory in the interior of the sphere and be unified with particle theories on the holographic boundary. Maldacena explains:

---

[174] J. Maldacena, *The Illusion of Gravity (Scientific American,* Nov. 2005), 57.

[175] Note that this author is talking of two and three dimensions, whereas the previous quote referenced 3 and 4 dimensions, as time was included.

[176] *Ibid,* 59.

> ... gravity in four dimensions is an emergent phenomena arising from particle interactions in a gravityless, three dimensional world. ... physicists have known since 1974 that string theory always gives rise to quantum gravity. The strings formed by gluons are no exception, but the gravity operates in the higher-dimensional space. [177]

According to this formulation, *"gravity operates in the higher-dimensional space."* This is in accord with H. P. Blavatsky who argued that the underlying causes of gravity lay within the higher seven dimensional Eternal Parent Space and within the ethers of the Solar system—the electromagnetic ocean of life. Gravity is not simply due to non-sentient physical mass but has an underlying metaphysical nature, one of the variants of Fohat, as all things adhere within the Aether of Space.

In physics, the holographic principle is a primary contender for the ultimate theory of everything—incorporating gravity with quantum field theory. Gravity is incorporated within the alternate spacetime within superstring/M-theory (and black holes physics), while quantum theory (involving the triune electro-weak and strong forces) applies on the flat holographic boundary. Although there are many unresolved issues to be faced in understanding this paradigm, it is a rich alternative model of how lower dimensional physics could be an outward manifestation of a higher dimensional metaphysics in alternative Space dimensions. This is the basic premise of *The Secret Doctrine* with its zero point holes dug in space as the foundations for the laws of nature.

The conjunction of an anti-de Sitter spacetime to accommodate string theory and black holes and to produce the phenomena of gravity, and the de Sitter spacetime to accommodate the three other quantum forces of nature—produces a profound model of higher dimensional holographic physics. It certainly seems that it is a strange universe we live in, wherein such vast amounts of information might be available at sub-atomic or zero point levels, which might surround a mini-black hole or spinning *'holes dug in space.'* Further, there exists an alternative higher dimensional Space, whether or a 5-dimensional anti-de Sitter space—or some other formulation, such as a 7 dimensional Eternal Parent Space. This is exactly

---

[177] Ibid., 62.

what Blavatsky was articulating, that the laws of physics evident within the material world are the end products of a higher dimensional metaphysics in an underlying hyperspace and this includes gravity.

The authors of these scientific articles do not really elaborate upon the implications and applications of their theories as they might apply to understanding our familiar reality — although they use human examples to depict the themes. The physics within the interior of this realm of the anti-de Sitter space has other 'strange properties' according to Maldacena, depicted in Figure 21. If you were freely floating anywhere in anti-de Sitter space, you would feel as though you were at the bottom of a gravitational well. Any object that you threw out would come back like a boomerang. Surprisingly, the time required for an object to come back would be independent of how hard you threw it. The difference would just be that the harder you threw it, the farther away it would get on its round-trip back to you. If you sent a flash of light, which consists of photons moving at the speed of light, it would reach infinity and return within a finite time. This can happen because the object experiences a time contraction of ever greater magnitude as it gets farther from you. [178]

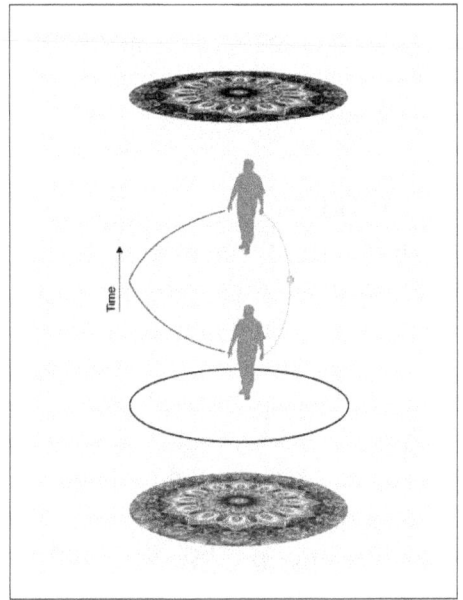

Figure 21

Within the anti-de Sitter space, the person is at the *centre of a gravitational well* and anything thrown out eventually returns to the source within a finite period of time. The negative space-time curvature in the anti-de Sitter space creates a gravitational field that pulls objects to the center, whether or not there is anything there. If a mass is displaced towards the boundary, it is eventually drawn back.

Certainly, since the outward physics on the holographic boundaries reflect that of the hidden inner

---

[178] *Ibid.*, 60-61.

metaphysics, then we would predict that any effects produced in the physical world would similarly return to their source, as occurs within the interior space. As above, so below: This might indeed lead us to hypothesize that the universe similarly will follow this boomerang principle and return to its source or gravitational well. In *The Secret Doctrine*, it is the 'Breath of the Mother' or a movement in hyperspace which ingathers the Kosmos to the Divine Bosom at the end of time. A Stanza of Dzyan notes: "IT EXPANDS WHEN THE BREATH OF FIRE IS UPON IT; IT CONTRACTS WHEN THE BREATH OF THE MOTHER TOUCHES IT." (III, 11) This same logic might actually support another fundamental teaching of *The Secret Doctrine*, the law of Karma. Karma is just such an inevitable cosmic law, whereby the results of actions and inactions come back upon us. It is only a matter of time.

All of these concepts from modern holographic theory are helpful in trying to understand Blavatsky's archaic teachings about invisible zero point centres, circumgyrating holes dug in an Eternal Parent Space, information emerging from zero point levels and the principle of Karma as an intrinsic cosmic law, a metaphysical principle of higher dimensions.

COMPARATIVE COMMENTS

According to Blavatsky, the influx of formative forces manifests from within the higher realms into the lower through *"holes dug in Space"* -*"invisible points"* or *"zero-points."* The Seven Builders or Divine Workmen *"dig holes in Space"* to channel their intelligence/influences into the material realm. Thus, seven invisible zero points holes dug in space are established as a foundation for physical manifestation and the laws of nature.

In terms of the holographic paradigm, a seven-fold white hole--black hole element is established within a seven-dimensional Eternal Parent Space. The whirlwind activities emanating from this center might appear as a radiant sun on the surfaces of the boundary spaces and give rise to energetic and material particles of different densities on different holographic shells. The modern physical concepts of mini-black holes as having mass and spin properties, and spewing out information, are all quite consistent with Blavatsky's archaic teachings. Divine Mind acts through such zero point centres and dynamics, which might manifest as hot radiations and materials on successive holographic shells, the ethers of space. A web of interrelationship is spun of Spirit and Matter through levels of a multi-dimensional holographic universe. Each Star, each Universe, each Son or Monad, embodies such a higher dimensional geometry and metaphysics emerging within-without from zero point centres.

Such zero point centers might be nested one within another and act as portals between worlds established within different levels of the Aether, as illustrated in figure 22. Each of these levels corresponds to a different holographic shell, as surround the seventh element.

Figure 22 [179]

Modern physical concepts actually illustrate such fantastic possibilities and make them more intelligible, rather than discrediting them as invented or exaggerated. In fact, *The Secret Doctrine* postulates a holographic universe with a higher seven dimensional *Eternal Parent Space* underlying familiar reality, instead of the *5 dimensional anti-de Sitter space* postulated within contemporary science. Further, instead of there being a singular black hole processor, there are seven interrelated processors and seven surfaces or shells surrounding the central element—as layers of the Aether. (Actually, we might consider there to be six surrounding surfaces while the seventh layer is the foundation of the central element.) These dynamics are multiplied within without through various levels of higher dimensional space within the hierarchies of creation.

---

[179] Illustrator, Sharon Field.

The newest physical models of seven dimensional Calabi-Yau elements with multiple interior holes, [180] of quantum information theory and the baffling holism of quantum theory, the manner in which *"It"* comes from *"Q-bit"* (a unit of quantum information), the physics of black hole information processors—all of these concepts combined with those of singularities and vacuum genesis, illustrate the profound secret doctrines explained by Blavatsky. While the scientists of her day conceived of solid material particles bouncing around in empty space and influencing each other through only local effects, Blavatsky was elaborating a holographic model of holes dug in higher dimensional Space as the basis for the manifestation of Kosmos, Atoms and Man. In Blavatsky's view, there are no phenomena due simply to 'local effects' because all manifest phenomena are produced by this inner hierarchy of effects reiterated through higher space dimensions.

Remarkably, modern physics is arriving at such zero point levels of creation and now posits just such a new 'metaphysics' to supplement the familiar physics of matter and energy within time and space. Of course, scientists would declare that there is nothing 'mystical' about holographic theory, information theory, black holes in alternative space dimensions, singularities, hyperspace or the quantum ether, or any of their theories and concepts, but that assessment is simply an expression of their assumptions and biases and not based upon any factual evidence and considered argument.

Varied concepts from *The Secret Doctrine* are illustrated by modern physical theories and speculations. Consider for instance how physicists suggest that a string might be expanded from essentially a point size at Planckian levels into any possible size according to the amount of energy added which expands the string structure. L. Susskind notes:

---

[180] Wikipedia : *"A Calabi-Yau space is a mathematical construction used by physicists to describe parts of nature that are too small to see with the human eye. Most people know that there are three space directions and one time direction in the universe - these directions are called dimensions. Physicists use Calabi-Yau spaces in studying high energy physics of which string theory is a part, to add 6 or 7 or other numbers to build up more dimensions to the universe.)"*

The most advanced M-theory posits eleven dimensions, with a seven dimensional hyperspace existing at every point underlying the four large dimensions of space-time. Scientist P. Atkins explains: *"there are seven dimensions compacted ... at each point ... Calabi-Yau spaces ... in seven dimensions ... the strings wind round them and through their holes..."* Part Two of this series, Esoteric Quarterly, Winter 2011, elaborates in more detail on these concepts, pp. 30-31.

Strings that are highly excited are bigger on average than their ground state counterparts; the additional energy whips them around and stretches them to a longer length. If you could bombard a string with enough energy, it would spread out and become as big as a violently jittering, tangled ball of yarn. And there is no limit; with even more energy, the string could be excited to any size. ... black holes—even those giants at the centres of galaxies—are enormously large, tangled "monster strings." [181]

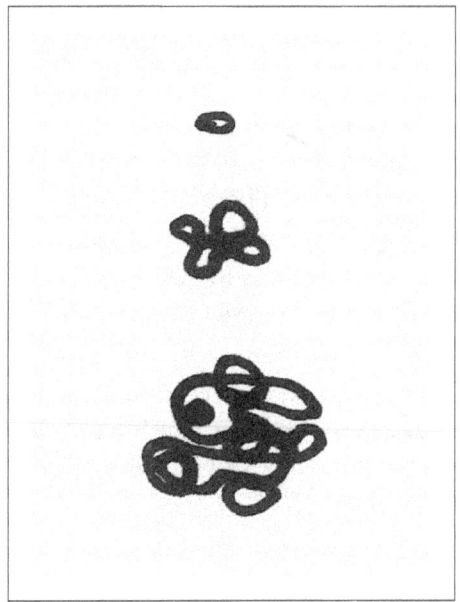

Figure 23

Might similar dynamics occurring through zero point centres lead to expanding structures within both hyperspace and then physical space dimensions within human beings as well as within a Kosmos? Multidimensional holes dug in space could be the basis of expanding structures through dimensions of hyperspace and these dynamics could produce an expanding Kosmos with different materialized dimensions of existence—upon varied holographic shells or boundaries, the veils of nature. As theosophist L. Maurer maintains:

"... the essentially circular spin momentum of the zero-point ... contains the holographic information for the evolutionary construction of the entire Universe ...." [182]

An equivalence is established between *the spinergy of a Monad in hyperspace* with various levels of the physics of M-theory, (Matrix or Membrane), string theory and quantum field theory, on increasingly material dimensions of existence. The holographic boundaries are the seven-fold ethers of

---

[181] Susskind, *Ibid.*, 337-8.

[182] L. Maurer's work has been available through Internet discussion groups at *theos-talk@yahoogroups.com*, *MindBrain@yahoogroups.com* and *www.blavatsky.net*

an expanding or contracting spherical spacetime. On these boundary conditions, the electro-weak-strong forces are unified and can account for the material-energetic processes but 'without gravity.' Gravity, in this case, involves the interior dynamics of the zero point centres within the Eternal Parent Space, through which the inner influences and Fohat serve to bind it all together. The cosmos contracts when the Breath of the Mother, a modification of the Ceaseless Breath, touches it. This suggests that a movement within hyperspace will bring about the eventual dissolution of the Cosmos and not simply gravity acting upon blind matter. Through generations of causes and effects, the Breath of the Mother, adheres in all things. It is as if the love of the Divine Mother holds everything in Creation together as gravity and at the end of time, ingathers the Sons or Kosmos to her Bosom.

A human being in the material body is a quantum system based primarily upon the electrodynamics of a multidimensional heart. The heart functions essentially as a quantum computer and exists within invisible quantized information and zero point fields. Ultimately, there is an underlying Unified Intelligence—or Omniscience which *"thrills throughout every atom and infinitesimal point of the whole finite Cosmos."* [183] Human consciousness emerges through the dimensions of the Heart as the living entity is expanding and withdraws back into the heart at moments of death when it is contracting. The Dalai Lama describes life as entering and withdrawing from the planetary body through the *"indestructible drop within the heart."* From the Heart, according to Tibetan and yogic teachings, the vital and consciousness principles circulate through a system of three channels and seven centers or chakras--each with zero-point centers and dynamics. According to the Dalai Lama, as consciousness and the vital principle withdraw into the heart at death, this induces memories of all of the events of one's life, as if one's life is a unified quantum field at some lower level of articulation within the zero point fields of the heart.

The process of life review which can occur at death follows the same dynamic as that conceived in black-hole computer physics—wherein immense amounts of quantum field information is available within inconceivably small spaces -at zero point or Planckian levels. The multidimensional heart essentially functions as a white hole computer in its role in life generation and a mini-black hole computer at death. The

---

[183] *S.D.*, 277.

withdrawal of human consciousness into the mini black hole computer of the Heart at death is followed by the reawakening within further virtual realities, as the living entity is already clothed in other bodies within other projected virtual realms involving other holographic shells and shifts in the angle of the light. Alternatively, an individual might pass through a seeming tunnel and emerge into a super-symmetrical realm of being—a spiritual world within higher dimensions of space related to the Sun, the central quantum computer within the Solar system, or beyond.

Similarly, might the ingathering of the light of consciousness and vitality to the heart at death serve to illuminate the complex patterns and webs, plots and tales of one's life adventures, all maintaining some wholeness through the superstring and membrane structures of higher dimensional space? Perhaps all the details of one's life still adhere together within the vast zero point information realms of this holographic quantum system, and so can be reviewed and re-experienced through death and afterlife states by such a Mind of Clear Light—illuminating such a gravitational well at the Heart of being with its seven hole mini-processor within the Parent Space!

Complex virtual realities are spun around a central I creating varied planes of being and life dramas that the I might experience as the Web or matrix of life. The Monad is more and more seemingly removed and obscured as consciousness is stepped down through interior dimensions of being and conditioned within varied subtle and material bodies. The metaphysical dynamics of the Monadic essence within hyperspace underlie the electrodynamics of the heart and the influx of the breath and oxygenation which ensoul the living being. There is a body, soul and spirit and ultimately a divine element within higher dimensional Space.

CONCLUDING REMARKS

Esoteric elements within *The Secret Doctrine* provide a way of interpreting modern scientific theories and applying them to develop a physics and metaphysics of consciousness and the heart. Certainly, such a model of higher dimensions, Monads and such, provides an intriguing alternative view of the origins and nature of human existence and it raises many questions and issues which might be explored. The vast evidences for psychical and spiritual phenomena, life after death and such, all suggest a need to consider what higher dimensional processes could enable and account for such phenomena. The aim of this concluding article has merely been to offer some speculative concepts of how such things might work.

This perspective is not intended to suggest that the Monad with its interior holes dug in space actually causes the formation of the physical body. The chakra system involves a sevenfold zero-point dynamic as Blavatsky describes and this organization underlies or interpenetrates the physical and subtle bodies. However, Blavatsky regards the 'lunar pritis' or intelligences as fashioning the material body, while the 'solar pritis' participate in the formation of the inner man. The inner living entity 'inhabits' the material body but can also exist independently of it.

When physicists arrive at the holographic paradigm, higher dimensions, mini-black hole processors and holographic boundaries, they do not provide a philosophy or perspective on what such concepts might mean to us in regards to the phenomena of life and our own existence. In contrast, a mystical perspective allows us to understand that such ideas of higher dimensional metaphysics might not simply be a matter of interest for the physicists but also for us as beings living within a multidimensional universe. Science has yet to begin to explain the many states of afterlife existence, the mechanisms of coincidences, the vast evidences for paranormal phenomena, reincarnation, other worlds and the like. Modern science has few if any models to allow us to understand the mysteries of such things.

Blavatsky's doctrines provide a legitimate scientific model and theory as regards to the existence of such LIFE centres and the mechanisms by which Universes might expand and contract through such zero point dynamics. She provides an alternative model of the fate of the universe, the mechanism of cosmic dissolution and a valuable perspective on the illusions of gravity, space and location. Certainly this comparative study does not allow us to prove or document such peculiar claims of esotericism, but we have simply tried to draw these analogies in a speculative manner.

These teachings provide an esoteric holographic model of the Microcosm and Macrocosm. Perhaps human beings have such higher dimensional origins emerging within/without from point sources, to eventually withdraw at the end of time without/within into other dimensions supported by hyperspace dynamics and zero point metaphysics. Human beings could have white hole origins and black hole disappearances through varied realms of existence. The monadic essence spins another tale and the heart functions as a black hole computer remembering everything that happens since an 'I' emerged out of the nothingness at the Heart of Being.

Zero Point Publications
Box 700, Kemptville, Ontario, Canada K0G-1J0

PSYCHOLOGICAL ILLUSIONS
Explorations of the Gurdjieff Fourth Way Teaching

Christopher P. Holmes

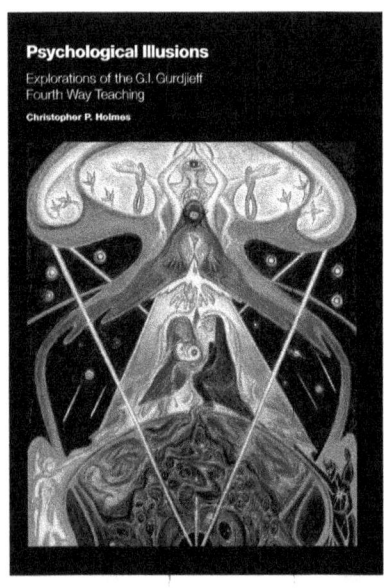

The central illusion of humankind is that we *"know self."* The components of this illusion concern the different powers or capabilities which men and women think that they possess but which in reality they do not. Four primary illusions or misunderstandings concern the faculties of consciousness, the unity of I, the possession of will (or the capacity to do) and the existence of the soul. The fourth way psychology begins with a study of humans as they are under the conditions of mechanical life and then describes the psychology of man's *possible evolution*. Humans can awaken and experience new states of consciousness, achieve a unity of "I" and real will, and thus attain the soul. Unfortunately, wrong ideas and convictions about the nature of consciousness, unity and will, are major obstacles to self knowledge. If we can begin to understand these illusions, then there is a chance of escape, of awakening and evolution.

According to Beelzebub, the central character in Gurdjieff's *Tales*, the three-brained beings on planet Earth are microcosmoses or *"similitudes of the Whole."* As such, they have the possibility of not only serving local cosmic purposes, feeding the earth and moon as part of organic life on earth, but also of experiencing sacred being-impulses, attaining varied levels of objective reason and individuality and even of *"blending again with the infinite."* (1950) As a microcosm of the macrocosm, a human being can potentially coat higher being-bodies for the life of the soul, instinctually sense cosmic truths and phenomena, and maintain existence within the subtle realms of being after death–achieving different levels of immortality. Unfortunately, humankind came to exist only in waking sleep states of automated consciousness, perceiving reality topsy-turvy, conditioned by pleasure and self love, and wasteful of their sacred sexual substances. Human beings no longer realize their deeper cosmic purposes and possibilities, or attain real "I."

Psychological Illusions explores the psychology, metaphysics and cosmology of the fourth way teaching. This includes material on the *Ray of Creation*, the fundamental cosmic laws, the alchemical crystallization of *higher being-bodies* for the life of the soul, and the miraculous possibilities existing for the evolution of the individual human being. The Gurdjieff fourth way teaching is a profound and coherent system of esoteric teaching about the horror of the situation for humanity asleep, living under their psychological illusions.

ISBN 978-0-9689435-2-6

www.zeropoint.ca

$24.95 Cdn

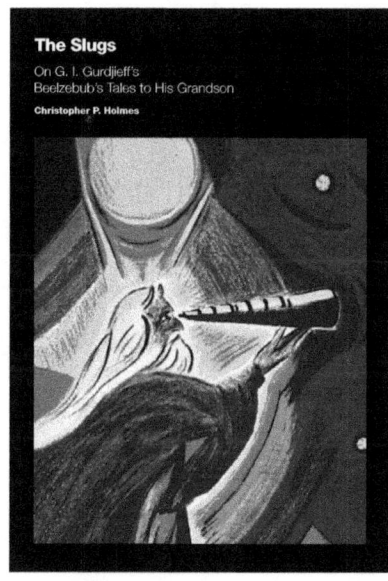

"THE SLUG"
On G. I. Gurdjieff's Beelzebub's Tales to his Grandson

Christopher P. Holmes

The Slugs provides an overview, explanation and interpretation of G. I. Gurdjieff's masterpiece Beelzebub's Tales to His Grandson, undoubtedly one of the most profound and mysterious books of the sacred literature in the modern world. The framework of ideas, claims and objective science offers a fundamentally alternative view of the nature of life, the origins and history of the Solar System and humankind, the nature of the human psyche and psychopathology, and a science of the soul. In the light of The Tales, most of modern thought and philosophy is so much 'pouring-from-the-empty-into-the-void.' The 'sorry scientists' of 'new format' have no conception of the great inscrutable mysteries of Nature and the subtle inner dimensions and alchemy of human beings. Beelzebub's Tales is a work not only of myth, allegory, history and fantasy, but about the secrets of 'objective science' and the psychology of the soul.

Gurdjieff's masterful Tales also provides a shocking portrait of the "strangeness of the human psyche" and explains how humans' essential consciousness and the divine impulses of faith, hope and love, passed into the 'subconsciousness,' while a 'false consciousness system' replaced it, crystallized around their egoism and associated unbecoming being-impulses. Beelzebub as a cosmic figure of higher reason observes the horrific "processes of reciprocal destruction," or war as periodically occurs on Earth, and asks how such phenomenal depravities come about and why humans cannot eradicate such an arch-criminal particularity in their psyche. The strange three-brained beings perceive reality "topsy-turvy," are mechanized to "see nothing real" and squander their sacred sexual substances solely for pleasure and their multiform vices. Beelzebub's portrayal of the "Hasnamusses," individuals who lack the Divine being-impulse of 'conscience,' the 'intelligentsia' and the 'crats,' provides vivid images of the psychopathology of the world's so-called 'elites' with their special societies or "criminal gangs," their "international five o'clocks" and "Hasnamussian sciences." The future of humanity is bleak indeed without the guidance of a being of such a higher intelligence as Beelzebub himself. The Slugs, like Gurdjieff's Tales, provides searing and illuminating insights into human psychopathology, the cause of war and the horror of it all.

The Author: Christopher P. Holmes is a mystic scientist and consciousness researcher, a clinical and forensic psychologist, and truth activist. He has studied the Gurdjieff work for over thirty five years and pursued broad investigations of human consciousness, the physics and metaphysics of creation, the mysteries of love and esoteric mystical teachings.

ISBN 978-0-9689435-4-0

www.zeropoint.ca

$21.95 Cdn 2nd Edition

WITHIN-WITHOUT from ZERO POINTS I

THE HEART DOCTRINE
Mystical Views of the Origin and Nature of Human Consciousness

Christopher P. Holmes

" ... "material points without extension" are Leibnitz's monads, and at the same time the materials out of which the 'Gods' and other invisible powers clothe themselves in bodies…. the entire universe concentrating itself, as it were, in a single point."

H. P. Blavatsky, The Secret Doctrine, I. Cosmogenesis, 1888

Modern psychology and science have been dominated by "the head doctrine"–the assumption that the material brain produces consciousness. In contrast, mystics claim that the origins of consciousness and Self are related to the mystical dimensions of the Heart. We are individual "eyes" or "I"s of "THAT," the divine unity within which we live, move and have our being. Mystical experiences involve penetrating various veils of nature which allow for the awakening of consciousness and the Heart, the realization of higher Space dimensions, and experiences of the unity of things within the inner life. Most importantly, human beings have a zero point centre and this is the means by which higher dimensional influences bring life and consciousness into the living being. These are the deep mysteries explored by the fool at the zero point.

Within-Without from Zero Points is an extremely unusual and provocative series which juxtaposes the most advanced concepts in modern science with mystical and spiritual teachings. It provides a sweeping scope of inquiry into the ultimate mysteries of consciousness, life, creation and God.

"My mission is to help uncover the forgotten, deep heart teachings of Jesus. ... The information you have gathered on the zero point has been a powerful validation of my own inner meditation practice and intuitions. Hence it has greatly enhanced my faith and the effectiveness of my meditation. Thank you so very much for your labors." **John Francis, *The Mystic Way of Radiant Love: Alchemy for a New Creation.***

"... if Christopher Holmes' articulation of 'the heart doctrine' had been restricted to citing and commenting upon those awe-inspiring teachings, he would have accomplished a great deal by establishing the foundation of an alternative paradigm to that which dominates contemporary approaches to the study of consciousness. However, when he introduces the mysterious concept of "the zero point," his arguments take on a level of significance which is, in my opinion, unparalleled in modern consciousness research. ..."
James A. Moffatt

ISBN 978-0-9689435-0-2
www.zeropoint.ca

$24.95 Cdn

UPCOMING

WITHIN-WITHOUT FROM ZERO POINTS II

MICROCOSM-MACROCOSM
Scientific and Mystical Views on the Origin of the Universe, the Nature of Matter & Human Consciousness

Christopher P. Holmes

" ... "material points without extension" are Leibnitz's monads, and at the same time the materials out of which the 'Gods' and other invisible powers clothe themselves in bodies.... the entire universe concentrating itself, as it were, in a single point." H. P. Blavatsky, The Secret Doctrine, I. Cosmogenesis, 1888

"... all the so-called Forces of Nature, Electricity, Magnetism, light, heat, etc., are in esse, i.e., in their ultimate constitution, the differentiated aspects of that Universal Motion. ... for formative or creative purposes, the Great Law modifies its perpetual motion on seven invisible points within the area of the manifest Universe." Madame H. P. Blavatsky, The Secret Doctrine, 1888

"It is necessary to notice that in the Great Universe all phenomena in general, without exception wherever they arise and manifest, are simply successively law-conformable 'Fractions' of some whole phenomenon which has its prime arising on the Most Holy Sun Absolute." G. I. Gurdjieff, 1950

Mystical accounts of states of Union, or unity with the world or universe on varied levels, attest to the fact that there is some kind of inner magic and alchemy going on within the inner cosmos of human consciousness—a metaphysics and physics to consciousness and the human heart.

Microcosm-Macrocosm explores the newest theories in physics and creation science–including materials on superstrings, higher dimensions, singularities, the quantum vacuum and the holographic principle. It also draws from ancient metaphysics–particularly The Secret Doctrine of H. P. Blavatsky (1888), esoteric Judaism and Kabbalah, and the cosmology and metaphysics of G. I. Gurdjieff. This is a challenging and provocative work with deep insights into the Divine Mystery teachings and a unique critique of modern science philosophy. It provides a shocking alternative view of the zero point origins of human consciousness and cosmos.

UPCOMING

WITHIN-WITHOUT from ZERO POINTS III

TRIUNE MONADS IN SEVEN DIMENSIONAL HYPERSPACE
Scientific and Mystical Studies of the Multi-Dimensional Nature of Human Existence

Christopher P. Holmes

Monads draws from the teachings of Madame Blavatsky, Kabbalah and Judaism, Gurdjieff, and a wide range of mystical doctrine about the multidimensional nature of human existence. Esoteric teachings identify the abode of the 'I' as within the human heart, where a triune Monad element is established within a Seven Dimensional Eternal Parent Space which underlies and sustains our normal physical four-dimensional space-time complex. Such ideas from mystical sources bear profound relationships to theories in advanced physics as to the nature of Space itself, quantum interconnectedness and higher dimensional superstring elements at zero point levels. A triune and sevenfold Monadic Essence spins a Web of Spirit, Soul and Matter within a Seven Dimensional Virual Reality out of the Aethers of the void and plenum, the quantum vacuum. In order to illustrate the necessity for such an alternative understanding of reality, this work examines evidences for out-of-body experiences, Sheldrake's fields of extended mind, enigmas posed by heart transplant patients and twin studies, and an interpretation of other paranormal investigations.

UPCOMING

WITHIN-WITHOUT FROM ZERO POINTS IV

A FOOL AT THE ZERO POINT
An Autobiographic Tale about the Strange Case of Professor Z, the Mysteries of Love and Ecstasies of the Heart & the Horror of It All

Christopher P. Holmes

Christopher, by the grace of God, will provide an autobiographical account of his life experiences, his psychical and mystical experiences, his life struggles and relationships, and an account of awakening to the horror of it all. This work includes materials on Christopher's struggles for academic freedom at York University, his twelve years of work in correctional centres as a forensic psychologist, his life and loves, and his awakening to psychopathology of the world elites with their plans for committing genocide against the human race.

GOD, SCIENCE & THE SECRET DOCTRINE
The Zero Point Metaphysics and Holographic Space of H. P. Blavatsky

Christopher P. Holmes, Ph.D. (Psych)

"... the Secret teachings ... must be contrasted with the speculations of modern science. ... To make of Science an integral whole necessitates, indeed, the study of spiritual and psychic, as well as physical Nature. ... Without metaphysics ... real science is inadmissible."
. P. Blavatsky, 1888

H. P. Blavatsky's *The Secret Doctrine* was published in 1888 and is relatively unknown in modern times. As it happens in this strange universe, Madame Blavatsky over a century ago anticipated numerous modern concepts concerning the creation of the Universe and the mechanisms of the laws of nature, including the holographic paradigm in psychology and physics. Blavatsky articulated the concept of the zero point or singularity origin of the Cosmos and of Sons, and a profoundly alternative view of the nature of the Aether and higher Space dimensions.

Blavatsky states: "... 'material points without extension' (zero-points) are ... the materials out of which the 'Gods' and other invisible powers clothe themselves in bodies ... the entire universe concentrating itself, as it were, in a single point." Dr. Holmes has grasped the profound meanings of this claim and related these ancient mystical teachings to the newest ideas in physics and science, and to explorations of human consciousness, spirit and soul, and the mysteries of the Heart. *God, Science & The Secret Doctrine* raises the ultimate question of the existence or non-existence of God—and what we mean by this term.

"While portions of this book are not easy going, Holmes plunges the reader into the deep places of the occult and the new frontiers of science to come up with a lucid and provocative book. It unseals many of the Secret Doctrines mysteries as it weaves the seeming opposites of spirit and science into a new synthesis. It is a must read for those wishing to understand the complex and seemingly impenetrable world of Helena Blavatsky alongside the newest ideas of quantum theory. Holmes has created something of his own tour de force in God, Science and the Secret Doctrine. His book is destined to serve as a guidebook for all those that follow." **Donna Brown,** The Esoteric Quarterly, Spring 2009, www.esotericstudies.net

ISBN 978-0-9689435-6-4

www.zeropoint.ca

$24.95 Cdn

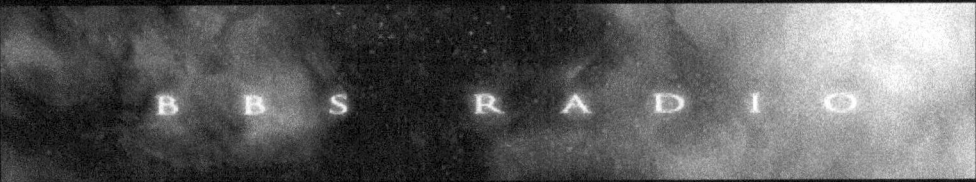

ZERO POINT RADIO
Live two hour Internet Radio Broadcasts

every second Saturday 4 pm Eastern Time
www.bbsradio.com.

In North America- 4 to 6 pm Eastern Time, 1 to 3 pm Pacific, 10-12 pm GMT Dr Christopher P. Holmes hosts an online internet Radio Broadcast through **www.bbsradio.com.** Previous broadcasts are available for online listening at the Zero Point archive service. These include shows on the zero point hypotheses, the magical formula of 137, on consciousness and the heart doctrine, the metaphysics of H. P. Blavatsky's The Secret Doctrine, the insanity of humankind and the criminality of the elites. James A Moffatt serves as commentator and interviewer, with invited guests. Shows archived at **www.bbsradio.com.**

ZERO POINT TEACHING
With Dr. Christopher P. Holmes

A two DVD set for computer use with assorted sound files, videos and power point presentations / DVD includes a complete set of BBSRADIO Zero Point Radio Shows, 2006-2011

Additional features include Christopher's New Zealand seminar; a four part three hour lecture series on zero points, consciousness & the heart; varied radio interviews of Christopher and two Power Point Presentations on "God, Science & The Secret Doctrine" and "The Heart Doctrine."

$35
North America,

$40
to Europe,

www.ingramcontent.com/pod-product-compliance
Lightning Source LLC
Chambersburg PA
CBHW080534170426
43195CB00016B/2562